Robert Holland, MD PhD

BLOWN AWAY

BLOWN AWAY

HERB PAYSON

Sail Books, Inc.
BOSTON

Distributed to bookstores by W. W. Norton and Company, Inc.
500 Fifth Avenue, New York, New York 10036.

Library of Congress Cataloging in Publication Data:

Payson, Herb.
  Blown Away.

   1. Sea Foam (Ketch)   2. Payson, Herb.   3. Voyages
and travels—1951–   4. Travelers—United States—
Biography. I. Title.
G477.P39   910.4′5   80-214
ISBN 0-914814-24-9

to Nancy

"The greatest sin is despair."

—Trevanian, *The Main*

As I sit here in front of the typewriter wondering whatever made me undertake the seemingly endless project of writing a book, I think back to the period when Nancy and I first chose to go to sea. At age 44, I had been working as a nightclub pianist five hours a night, six nights a week, 50 weeks a year for 12 years. Nancy, not yet 40, worked as a cocktail waitress. We dreamed of a different kind of life, a life of bluewater cruising.

One book was especially influential in persuading us to take the leap before the dream dissolved in the breaker of irresoluteness. *The New Way of Life*, by John and Pat Samson, named what we were looking for. Its text, a series of vignettes about the humorous struggles of novice sailors, encouraged us to do the same; its conclusions gave specific ways to cut middle-class ties.

Turning your life around—changing it completely—is a thought which is attractive to many, but which most people reject as too risky. For some, the armchair is enough. Others will be satisfied only by doing it themselves, and perhaps this book will help keep the dream alive until the moment of decision has been reached.

Carved in the deck beam in the forepeak of a friend's yacht are these words: BETWEEN THE DREAM AND THE DEED LIE THE DOLDRUMS. To me this says much. The dangers we might encounter in a strange new life-style never threatened us the way lethargy did. It is so easy to let time slip by, to drift down the river of routine, each day losing a micro-erg of youthful energy and adaptability, until finally it is too late. Decision by default. We felt this happening to us, and it was a bad feeling.

So we invite you to join us and our teen-aged—for the most part, grown—children as we cram ourselves into a sailboat and bob nervously through the South Pacific, encountering the troubles and rewards of our initiative. Our purpose: to entertain, and to paint a realistic picture of one family's cruising experiences. If this helps a reader or two through the doldrums, the struggle to get our story on paper will have been worth it.

H. P.
JANUARY 1980

ACKNOWLEDGMENTS

Many people have been helpful to me as a writer. However, I would especially like to single out the following, whose timely assistance and encouragement were particularly crucial: Marvin Myers; Bob and Jackie Nyquist; Conni Myers and Kim Weston; Patience Wales; Marjorie Hlava; John and Pat Samson; and Doug Stewart, whose urgings and proddings kept me from getting hopelessly off course.

BLOWN AWAY

I T WAS A DULL, RAINY SUNDAY. My wife, Nancy, was juggling figures in the credit-card version of the old shell game. I was doing some creative writing: a letter to a finance company explaining why we were going to be late again this month. The TV was giving equal time to an old movie and a car salesman, the latter trying to persuade us to drive a hundred miles to get ripped off instead of having it done locally.

The scene suddenly struck us as a nightmare. Our feelings were in total sync, a mutual mood of rebellion, of recklessness, of daring, of flight. Prudence would quickly bring me back down to earth, but not before it was too late. Unwittingly, I rubbed the magic lamp.

"Why don't we give up all this nonsense, buy a boat, and sail around the world?"

"Yes, let's!" said Nancy, brightening for the first time that day.

The hair on the back of my neck bristled at the enormity of what I had done. In the short time—two and a half years—that we had been married I had already learned that when my flame-haired and irrepressible companion set her mind to do something there would be no rest for me or anyone else around until it was done. Attesting to that was our dining room, made over now into an aquarium room, the result of my joking remark that, since she loved tropical fish, why didn't we go into the business of leasing aquariums and call the business Rent-a-Fish? Several thousand dollars later I wearily retrieved our aquariums from our four clients. An epidemic of ick had filled the fish morgue to capacity, transferred all our cash to the vendors of miracle fish-cure drugs, and exhausted the patience of our customers.

Nancy, undaunted, still spent countless hours watching, encouraging, nursing, and burying her beloved pisces.

"Do you mean it?" I asked, hoping for a reprieve.

"You better believe it," she replied. "Why not?" The genie was out of the lamp and had taken complete charge.

"How do we finance it?" I asked, bringing up a why-not that was screaming for attention.

"Oh, sell everything," she said, her mind already on more serious problems.

"Lord, love, are you sure? You've had this house for 15 years, raised all your kids in it—"

"Where else is the money going to come from? Do you honestly think a banker might lend it to us?"

I ran it through my mind. Bank manager receives loan request, evaluates it:

1. Applicant's job: *none.*
2. Previous job: *musician.* (Owp!)
3. Wife's job: *none.*
4. Previous job: *cocktail waitress.* (Double-owp!)
5. Collateral: *boat they intend buying with loan.*
6. Prospects: *sail boat into sunset, around world.*
7. Previous sailing experience: ——.

"Okay, we sell the house. But how do you know you'll *like* sailing? You might get seasick, be scared, hate it."

"Maybe," said Nancy. "We'll have to try it. Could we rent a boat?"

"Charter," I said, absent-mindedly beginning the endless campaign for the correct jargon. But the idea appealed to me. As a native of Maine, I had spent all the summers of my youth on the water in Casco Bay. I had learned to sail in my own small boats and on my grandfather's 40-foot cutter. Over the years, friends had intrigued me with tales of their cruising adventures in the South Pacific. The fantasy might not be so far-fetched after all.

A rare happening, two weeks' vacation for Nancy and me at the same time, was due in a couple of months. A trip with the kids would set us back a thousand dollars, unless we camped (and they don't stock enough gin in California to get me to sleep on the ground anymore). I was sure we could charter and provision a boat for less.

I reached toward the foot of the bed into the shambles we'd made of the Sunday paper, looking for the classifieds. (Bed is the place Nancy loves most, and since we'd been together we'd spent a lot of time there, doing the usual, but also doing whatever else we could adapt to bed living, such as eating, reading, writing letters, paying bills, watching TV, telephoning, playing cribbage, plus planning what we would do when, if ever, we got up. Cruising has changed this somewhat, but not, in Nancy's opinion, for the better.) I finally found the classifieds, and turned to "Boats." I reached for the phone, dialed a number.

"Yes, sir, we do happen to have a Mariner 32 available for those two weeks, but we'll need a deposit to hold her. Will you be coming down to look at her today? We close at 5:00."

It was 3:00 P.M. Although we hadn't intended to get up till Monday, I knew that I might be able to bully Nancy into doing a quick enough number on washing, combing, brushing, outfit choosing, earring inserting, up making, patting, adjusting, changing, and finally approving of the result so that we could make it by 4:50.

"We'll be there," I assured him, and hung up.

Until I met Nancy I had always thought of myself as being pretty casual about appointments, but she beat me by light-years. In the beginning I made one or two attempts to change her, but I quickly learned that of all the things I could do to make her furious, this was far and away the most effective. (Today, after years of cruising, she remains unchanged: an early start is 10:00 A.M., maybe; a usual start is noon. If we want a dawn start we simply stay up for it.)

This time, however, she astonished me by bounding out of bed first and calling to *me* to hurry. If I'd had any doubt whatsoever about her determination to follow through on my impulse, this one act blew it away. We were at the broker's dock in an incredible 20 minutes, had made a deposit by 4:00, and by 4:30 Nancy was on the phone inviting kids and relatives to join us.

A Mariner 32 is about the right size for a cruising couple, though some might find it a trifle cramped. On a weekend, four people who really like each other could probably get by. The brochure claimed the Mariner slept five. We were six.

"Kids are rugged," said Nancy. "They can sleep on deck."

"What if it rains?" I asked.

But it didn't. We had a marvelous time, pushing each other out of the way and saying "excuse me" for two weeks. Nancy Great-Provider made the tiny galley hum, turning out a stream of feasts. Nancy Naturalist strolled the hills on the Todos Santos Islands, exploring, startling tiny gulls, watching seals at play. Nancy Party-Girl enjoyed the restaurants and cabarets of nearby Ensenada.

"I *love* cruising," she said as we emerged from our third nightclub at 3:00 in the morning. It is on such slender threads that the cruiser's future hangs.

TWO

W E SCHOOLED OURSELVES in the art of boat-buying by going to every boat show within 100 miles, and by strolling, misty-eyed, through countless fiberglass-boat lots which abound in Southern California. This was about as intelligent as training for a heavyweight boxing match with three geisha girls and a water pipe. All those shiny, plastic, apartment-sized, shag-rugged, lushly equipped, low-down-payment-and-your-ass-a-month price leaders had done irreparable damage to our thinking. Naturally, we reasoned, we could shop around and find a second-hand boat which was just as nice but infinitely cheaper. The reality—that a "sail-away" boat required thousands of additional dollars to become "*really* sail-away," and thousands more to become "cruise-away"—was beyond our initial comprehension. And, of course, having eaten from the tree of knowledge, we now lusted for showers, pressure water systems, freezers, stereo, radiotelephone, radar, RDF, diesel auxiliary, Onan, Omega, Loran, autopilot, carpets and drapes—the works. To say the least, we had not yet reached an elemental state of mind.

Three or four times a week the *Golden Bullet*, my 300-horsepower Chevy convertible, would launch us on a trajectory toward San Diego, Santa Barbara, Marina Del Rey, or wherever the ads indicated good hunting. Top down, hair (Nancy's) streaming in the wind, we would make an excursion out of each foray. We would summon hopeful owners to the docks from their homes or offices only to shake our heads sadly at their vessels' hopeless inadequacies. Then we would seek out an attractive restaurant with a bar and, over a business lunch, discuss what we had seen.

Because even though we had burned so many bridges that we

could no longer turn back, even though the blast-off button had been pushed and we were beyond aborting—we still did not know it. If this strikes you as too fantastic to be believed, join the club. I lived it and can hardly believe it myself. But the fact re-Fantasyland. We had no idea of the enormity of the deed we viewing the passing parade of buyable boats like spectators in mains: Nancy and I were *playing* at being boat-buyers. We were were contemplating. We were about to give someone everything we had in the world (or an amount so close to it that the difference was academic) for a *boat*, a commodity about which we essentially knew nothing.

But the game was such fun. We drank less desperately each night, awoke more clear-eyed each morning. There was always a love-tussle over the classifieds. Time spent soaking up the regurgitations of television was reduced to nearly nothing. The days all had a purpose. We were pushing joyfully toward an absolutely unrealizable goal: the perfect boat at a price we could afford. And the cost of admission to this marvelous game was only gas for the *Bullet* and drinks and a meal in a good restaurant, a pittance compared to what we'd been wont to spend to ward off existential drear.

But He works in wondrous ways. Through the haze of our mindless dilettantism seeped scraps of information. Recurring experiences took the form of statistics, some of which pierced our euphoric cocoon. Six months, $1500, 6000 miles, and 1,000,000 words later, the scales fell from our eyes.

"You know, love—," I said, looking at her thoughtfully over the rim of a frosty martini glass. It was our sixth lunch in this particular restaurant, our twentieth expedition to this marina. "I don't think we're going to *find* a 40′ fg dsl ktch, slps 6, Brstl, for 15M."

"You know, love—," she said, looking at me thoughtfully over the rim of a frosty gimlet glass. She had probably come to the same conclusion, but in matters of decision she usually lets me go first. "I don't think so either."

And with this admission came eviction from Eden. Cast out

into the world of truth and compromise, the real search began. No longer was our guideline "what do you want in a boat?" Now it was "what do you refuse to do without?" The list of our requirements shrank to one-third its former length, and even those items were shuffled, reconsidered, and modified. Boats we would not even have looked at before were now seriously considered. But the sunset we were going to float off into had lost none of its allure. Only the floater had changed. . . .

During the incubation period of the cruising bug the thought of building our own boat occurred to us several times. Each time we rejected the idea as not for us, not at that stage in our lives. One, I am not all that great at building things. Two, I am not all that great at sticking to long-term projects I'm not all that great at. Three, it would take years to finish the job because I would have to continue to work for our daily bread; and my work, though it may seem to the uninitiated to be frivolous, was not undemanding.

Still, we might have been sucked in by the do-it-yourself dementia of the times had all our children not been free to come with us if they wished. Another two to five years and the oldest ones might well have been married, involved in careers or raising families. If we wanted them to share our adventure, and we did, we would have to act right away.

Since then we have met many people cruising who did build their own boats. Most boats are well made, finished off with care and skill. Maybe 20 percent went to sea sailable but by no means, completed. A very small percentage were abortions. But I noticed that by far the largest category of boat owners who long for something smaller, bigger, roomier, or faster are those who are presently sailing boats they have built themselves. The sad part is that so many of the home-builts are the owners' first boats— recipients of all that time, energy, and creative concentration— conceived before they had acquired the experience to know what they really wanted. Sadder still are the countless hulls which are rotting, rusting, or crumbling in some back yard, representing the terminal illness of a man's dream.

Noah, one of our neighbors, was a dreamer. He had a house and yard which we often passed. We called him Noah because he was building a 50-foot fiberglass boat in his front yard and because he started when Bill Cosby's "Noah" recording was at the height of its popularity. People used to note Noah's progress and discuss it with amusement over self-satisfied cocktails. The most exciting event was when the hull, built upside down, was righted. No one gave him any help; he asked for none. Single-handed, he turned it with block, tackle, and a carefully thought-out plan. When it was finally righted, lots of money changed from the pockets of the "bet he can't's" to those of the "bet he can's." Noah was doing what he set out to do, but people were still amused.

I knew Noah, but not well. He was the cousin of a good friend, and I had met him once long before. He had worked on my runabout in his capacity as mechanic for a boatyard. I knew him to be a fellow musician. I knew that his job at the boatyard was a six-day eight-to-fiver, that his dance-band job was a five-night eight-to-twoer in a town 30 miles from home, and that whenever he could find a spare minute (and he managed to find quite a few) he worked on his boat. I knew that he had been doing this for five years, without respite. I began to feel sorry for the people who understood so little as to be amused, but I felt sorry for Noah, too.

I stopped by his house one evening just before we left on our own trip. Two televisions were going, one for the sound and one for the picture. Tired chairs furnished the bare-walled, bare-floored room. It wasn't hard to guess where all the cash was going. And the boat was months from launching, years from departure.

Noah was still enthusiastic, but in his single-mindedness he had left everyone else behind. His family was bone-tired of the whole project, and from what I could gather, not one of them was planning to sail with him. Maybe he had already figured the personal cost and had come to terms with paying it. If I were in his boots, I would long ago have deemed the price too high.

Sea Foam, the boat we finally bought, has a similar story. She was built by a master shipwright in his own back yard, for him-

self. When she was completed after five years, he packed provisions and a wife aboard and sailed to Hawaii. The wife hated
it. She got off the boat in Honolulu and delivered herself of an
age-old ultimatum:

"It's me or the boat, and it better be me!"

He took personal inventory, decided that he had more equity
in the boat than he had in her, and chose the boat. She, wife
spurned for buoyant mistress, managed to spirit all the sails off the
boat. Before the couple could work out a compromise, he had
died. She got the boat, paid to have it delivered back to the
mainland, and promptly sold it. A generation after this apparent
injustice, *Sea Foam* is finally doing what she was built to do.

We met other cruising folk who were buying their boats on
installments—a pay-as-you-sail arrangement—but after a lifetime
of living on credit, we craved an unmortgaged future. We were
looking for a new life-style, a new set of values, a whole new bag.
We weren't sure what shape it would be, but we knew that the
bag we sought didn't have monthly payments in it. Besides, at
that time the cost of a blue-water insurance policy to satisfy a
lender equalled the cost of six months' provisions. For us, the
loan route would have been a final desperate measure after all
else had failed. We chose to pay for the boat, and as a result we
later suffered a lack of ready cash, but it was the right choice
for us. We could always spot the installment buyers. They had a
haunted look, a low serenity quotient. In a way, they had never
left home.

After six and a half years of pulling into South Pacific ports
and getting to know scores of cruising people, I have decided
that it doesn't make any difference what kind of boat you buy as
long as it is well found and has been maintained in, or can be
brought back to, good condition. I have seen the most amazing
variety of floating vehicles. The only conclusion I've reached is
that small boaters seem to enjoy themselves ashore more than
big boaters do.

But in general, almost any well-found boat, properly equipped
and properly handled, will take you where you want to go. This

being the case, why can't you just phone your broker and put in an order for a cruising boat for six, somewhere around 18 thou, to be ready for world cruising in three months? You would just arrive at the dock with your suitcase, step aboard, and cast off.

You almost could, but because of the unique relationship that exists between ship and crew, such a union would be too much like a mail-order marriage. Most of us these days insist on choosing our own mates, and the similarity between committing yourself to a mate and committing yourself to a boat is a lot stronger than one might think.

So what are we to conclude? That you should go out and buy the first boat you fall in love with? No. The first one you fall in love with that you can afford? Still no. The first one you fall in love with that you can afford and that offers features that months and months of looking at boats have taught you are important to you?

Well, now we're getting close.

"I suppose you want to buy a boat," said Chuck, eyeing us speculatively. At our nod, his head disappeared back down into the forward hatch of an ancient 40-foot sloop docked outside his office.

"Anyone crazy enough to buy a boat deserves all the headaches he gets. A man has to be half nuts to want to own a boat in the first place." The voice was muffled, but the message was unmistakable.

"But," he continued, gray-maned head reappearing, "if you've got the bug there's no cure. You just have to go ahead and find out for yourself. This one is mine," he said proudly, "as beautiful-sailing an assemblage of dry-rot, corrosion, and electrolysis as you'll ever want to see. What kind of boat are you looking for?"

"Oh, something about 35 feet. We're going to sail around the world."

He laid a glance on my flabby form, mod shoes, sharply creased trousers, horn-rimmed shades, then on Nancy's hot pants and makeup, her expensive hairdo. How he could see through our camouflage I'll never know. Perhaps he always treated everyone alike till he cut the potential buyers out of the herd of dreamers. Whatever, I had the conviction that Chuck believed us from square one.

"You poor kids," he said sympathetically. He wasn't that much older than we were, but he recognized our naïveté as we entered the jungle known as the used-boat market. "Come on up to the office and we'll take a look at what we have. Not too much in the way of cruising boats at the moment, I'm afraid."

From this point on, our education began in earnest. Chuck and his star salesman, Fred, took turns at showing us available boats in Newport Beach, and demonstrated what I now recognize to be limitless patience as Nancy and I discussed the cost and feasibility of various sorts of modifications. We were still remarkably unrealistic, but with the understanding of born teachers, Chuck and Fred guided us from the impractical to the practical.

Besides Chuck and Fred, we made friends with Dennis in Marina Del Rey and with Betty in San Diego. They, too, spent hours with us looking at and talking about cruising boats, becoming both friends and instructors. They were unique among the dozens of brokers who discounted us as dreamers or unqualified buyers.

Our main difficulty was that our needs kept changing as, one by one, Nancy's three children and my three decided we were really going to follow through with our scheme. It finally looked as though four of them would leave with us, and the other two would join us for short cruises along the way. Assuming that we could shuffle personnel so that we were never more than six at one time, we still needed a far bigger boat than we'd originally intended to buy.

As our space requirements increased, the ages of the boats for sale within our price range also increased. We soon became Southern California's leading authorities on the location, history, and price of derelicts, near-wrecks, and other leaking monuments to poverty and neglect. Something had to give.

What gave, of course, was the ceiling we had put on the amount we could pay for a boat. Our very top was upped to $20,000, so that we were now shown boats in the $20,000 to $30,000 range. Once more we were looking at arks which appeared to have a floating future, but our hopes of finding the ideal boat were inversely proportional to our prospects of paying for it.

During the course of our search we became certain of wanting several features, and in the end we got all but one of them.

1. Most important for a protracted cruise was a private stateroom for Nancy and me. This was an intuitive home run. Subsequent observation showed that without privacy a couple cruising with children, and particularly grown children, *always* developed marital problems. Physical affection seems to atrophy when it's reduced to the furtive midnighter or the apprehensive quickie.

2. Diesel auxiliary. Add the worry of a gasoline explosion to all the others you have at sea, and it's just one worry too many.

3. Fiberglass hull. This was the one we didn't get. (We've probably paid for this by hauling three times as often as glass hulls at an average cost of $250, also by being subject to dry-rot dementia, toredo terrors, and fastening phobias.)

4. Large fuel and water capacity. The extra fuel is a help on boats which are poor to windward. Plenty of water is for peace of mind, and also because of the increasing availability of dehydrated foods.

5. Wheel steering. If you stand steering watches, and we did for 20,000 miles, a wheel is far less fatiguing. If you have a good rugged windvane, however, tiller or wheel makes no difference.

6. Three- or four-burner stove, with oven. As I pointed out, Nancy thrives on playing Great Provider in the galley.

Fourteen months had passed since we'd made the decision to go cruising, exactly one year since we'd chartered the Mariner. *This* Fourth of July we weren't going to go *anywhere*. Just lie around the house all day, go to work at night, but leave the highways, traffic, heat, smog, and actuarial statistics to others. We made one mistake. We forgot to take the phone off the hook.

"Man, have I found the boat for you!" It was Fred calling

from Long Beach, 20 miles up the coast. "This is the one you've been waiting for."

"Hell, Fred, won't it keep till tomorrow? We have to be at work in three hours. Traffic's horrible."

"You'll kick yourself from here to Tahiti if you miss this one," he said. He wouldn't let me hang up till I'd agreed to come.

Logistics demanded that we go in our work clothes: Nancy in the briefest of uniforms, with a top that tended to make male customers dislocate their eyeballs; myself in a gold-thread tux complete with ruffled shirt and patent-leather boots. As we pulled up in the *Bullet* we were greeted by the sounds of hammering, sawing, sanding; it seemed as if everyone in Long Beach was down working on his boat. But by the time we were halfway across the yard there wasn't a sound. We had never made a more successful entrance.

Our embarrassment was forgotten the minute we set eyes on *Sea Foam*. She was a 36-foot ketch. Her white topsides were emblazoned with a happy red stripe just below her bulwarks. Her masts were cockily raked, giving the impression of motion even when she was at rest. Deadeyes and lanyards reeked of tradition. She had a bowsprit which pointed jauntily up and away to far-off shores. She exuded competence and eagerness for the sea.

Gathered round her were the owners, a friend, and Fred. Everyone was somber except Fred, who was bubbling. I guessed immediately that we were the rabbits he had pulled out of the hat to save the day, but our arrival hadn't cheered anybody up much. I admit we didn't look much like saviors.

"What's the story?" I asked, having gotten Fred off to one side.

"She's a steal," he whispered. "The owners have already bought another boat, and now they just want out. So why don't you climb that ladder and take a look at your new boat."

Fred knew his business. He let us go alone. We sat in the cockpit in a dreamlike state. I ran my hand over the varnished wheel. Nancy stroked the burnished teak deck. Together we went forward and stood in the pulpit. Then we went below.

The salon was huge for the size of the boat, a result of the nearly 14-foot beam. Rich in dark mahogany, it felt like home. Nancy stood in the galley, mentally preparing feasts. The survey lay on the salon table. "Two-inch Douglas fir planking . . . Everdur fastened . . . masts of Sitka spruce . . . 150 gallons water . . . 100 gallons diesel . . . 55 hp Ford Osco . . ." From time to time one of us murmured, as much to himself as to the other, "This is it. This is the one."

Tossing our absolute upper limit into the litterbag of best-laid plans, we floated down the ladder and offered a thousand dollars less than the already-bargain price. During the interval between offer and acceptance we learned that (1) a person can virtually hold his breath for 24 hours, (2) he can make love and remember to keep his fingers crossed for luck, and (3) when he graduates from boat-shopper to boat-owner, he is likely to explode with a reckless, raucous joy.

THREE

I REMEMBER THE EXCITEMENT I felt when I was given my first brand-new bicycle, my first electric train, my first trip up the Empire State Building, pride at my Yale graduation, the satisfaction of seeing my first story in print, the elation while listening to my first arrangement played by an excellent band, the thrill of my first new car, the day I broke 100 in golf, hitting the jackpot on a one-armed bandit, getting up on one ski. All these experiences together add up to a fraction of what I felt as we watched *Sea Foam* slide gracefully into our slip.

"She's all yours now, my friend," said Fred, handing us the keys, "and what a sweet sailboat she is."

I could hardly speak. *Sea Foam* had just come from the yard and was Bristol, gleaming. Her caprail and taffrail were freshly varnished. Bright red trailboards and nameboards were lettered and decorated in gold leaf. Fred walked me through and showed me where everything was. I remember none of it. My mind, incapable of registering details, was a medley of impressions.

"Let's call up the kids and invite them for a ride in the bay this evening," said Nancy. I knew how her mind would work. First the kids. Then every friend we had, ever. Then a "boat-warming" party ("they bring *us* things"). Then an "open-boat" party, followed by a "family" party. (Nancy is related to every single citizen of Long Beach, California.) Going sailing, if it occurred to her at all, was somewhere far down the list.

Newport Harbor, purported to have the highest density of boats in the U.S., is one of the toughest boat-handling classrooms around. In addition to the hundreds of skilled skippers who take to the water each weekend, there are the drunks, the neophytes, and the millionaire yachtsmen with the might-makes-right philosophy of right-of-way. A plethora of Lasers, Sabots, Hobie Cats,

Sunfish, Lido 14s, Finns, and countless other class and classless sailboats compete with single-mindedness, swarming into the bay from hidden hives and enclaves. Trailerable runabouts arrive from all over Southern California, buzzing about like trapped bottle flies. In this environment we made our first tentative efforts to get to know our new boat. Near-misses were legion, but Fate was kind, our egos became calloused to "get out of our race, you big clunk," and somehow we survived.

Nancy and I reached a meeting of minds. I learned to enjoy the partying, and Nancy learned to love the sailing. We found to our amazement that many of our night-people friends—musicians, bartenders, restaurant managers, waitresses, entertainers, all unlikely sailors, we assumed—took to day-sailing with grateful enthusiasm. We derived sadistic pleasure from fertilizing the kernels of their discontent. Little by little we indoctrinated skilled crews and grew used to *Sea Foam*. Eventually, we were bringing her back to her slip under sail, tacking our way around moorings and weaving our way through the mob.

Because Nancy and I rarely had a weekend off together, and because our children could leave no other time, it was several months before we managed to get away overnight. But one November Friday, seven of us took off for Catalina Island. It was a bright day. The ocean was a deep blue, the wind fresh from the southwest. We were creaming along on a close reach about a half-hour out of the harbor when Nancy ran up the companionway.

"We're sinking!"

I rushed below. The carpet on the lee side was soaked. I took up the floorboard to find half the ocean in the bilge, and leaped for the pump switch. It seemed to take forever, but eventually I noticed the water level receding.

"It's okay," I informed everyone. "We're gaining."

"Hadn't we better turn back?" asked Nancy.

"Maybe so."

We tacked around while I stayed below to watch the bilges. When they were dry I shut off the pump and waited. Nothing. Dry they were and dry they stayed.

"I don't understand it," I said, after taking up more floorboards and checking all the through-hull fittings. "Everything seems okay, though, so let's come about and keep going."

I put the floorboards back, and by the time I went topsides we were once more on the port tack, lee rail dipping to the swells. Then minutes later when I went to check, the bilge was nearly full.

What the hell's going on, I thought, starting the bilge pump again. By the time I had all the floorboards removed and stacked on the bunks, the bilge was dry. I turned off the pump.

"Water's coming back in again," said Nancy, "right through the pump."

I groaned, electrons finally shunting through the right circuits. I opened the hanging locker and took out the tools, marline, tape, flares, spares, shackles, blocks, flashlights, horns, bells, and other gear and added them to the pile of floorboards on the bunks. Then I removed a board in the floor of the locker and turned off a gate-valve. The water stopped coming in immediately.

The bilge pump was acting as a syphon. Normally the outlet was above the waterline, but when we were heeling on the port tack it was underwater.

"Quite an arrangement," I muttered, viewing the chaos I'd made of the cabin. "I wonder who thought it up."

We reached White's Cove with plenty of remaining light and picked up a mooring. We had our choice of all of them, as we were the only boat there. As Nancy and I sipped drinks in the cockpit in the balmy twilight, Sarah waltzed up and down the rail in her bikini, staring into the water and worrying at great length about sharks and other bitey things. Chris and Craig were below indulging in their favorite pastime, arguing at great length about nothing. Conni and a friend had taken the dinghy ashore to have a word with a few buffalo that had wandered down to the water's edge.

"I wonder how come nobody comes here in November," I said. "It's perfect weather, no other boats and all." Both Nancy and Fate were listening, but Fate was taking notes.

"I don't understand it either, but I'm glad," said Nancy.

"Should I jump in or dive in?" asked Sarah of nobody in particular.

"This is really the life," I said, lolling luxuriously on a cushion.

Nancy sat up, looked around at the blue velvet shadows of rugged Catalina in the late afternoon light. She sighed a mighty sigh, sipped a mighty sip.

"I think I'll jump," said Sarah, not jumping.

"Maybe we could come back sometime after Christmas vacation," Nancy mused.

"Why not?" I replied. "I'm sure we can finagle a couple of days off during the week."

There was a splash, three high-pitched squeaks, and Sarah shot back aboard via the ladder, dripping and ice-blue.

That night we barbecued steaks on a grill on the afterdeck. All of us ate hugely, appetites whetted by salt air and sun. After listening to everyone's grandiose plans for the next day, which included hiking across the island, beachcombing, picnicking, and having a fishfry using fish Chris and Craig were going to catch, we went to bed anticipating an early start.

We awakened to rain and a raw, cold wind. By 9:00 we had eaten all the blueberry pancakes we could hold, cleared away the debris, and were sitting around the salon staring moodily at each other through the chilly gloom.

"Let's have a fire," said Nancy.

"Are you referring to the fireplace," I asked her, "or did you have something more destructive in mind?"

"We have plenty of wood and charcoal," she said, ignoring me.

The wood was wet, but lots of kerosene fixed that. In no time at all we had a roaring fire which, after briefly but violently blistering the paint on both sides of the bulkhead by the chimney, moderated somewhat. The cabin was toasty warm in minutes—and filled from overhead to sole with thick smoke. Soon we were all standing out in the rain, cold, soaked, and miserable.

With everything open, the cabin was soon free of smoke and any trace of warmth, and I went down to fool with the fire. I believe all males consider themselves authorities on fire-building and fireplace management. Although I had once managed to turn the three-story metal chimney of an A-frame house into a roaring blowtorch simply because I tried to burn up our Christmas tree, with the ensuing fountain of sparks bringing the fire truck to our tindery lot in something under three minutes, I still considered myself an expert, and on retirement from the music business I fully intended to become a consultant to less gifted men. But all my talented flue-fiddling, blowing, poking, and swearing did nothing, and I was accused, among other things, of being a fugitive from an orange-grove smudge match. I finally admitted defeat, threw a bucket of water into the fireplace, and endured the family's observations that, to the cold dampness of our confining prison, I had added a stinking mess.

We suffered through the day with hot tea, scalding soup, and finally hot toddies, wanting only for night to arrive so we could crawl into a warm bunk. Sunday dawned dull and dreary, and right after breakfast we cast off and started powering toward the mainland. But before long the sun came out bright and warm, the wind freshened, we raised sail and experienced that amazing sleight-of-mind that happens when a beautiful day on the water blots out all thoughts of previous discomfort. By the time we reached the slip we were raving with perfectly straight faces about what a marvelous time we'd had.

When I offered the stove on consignment to Sarah's Dock Box, one of the local second-hand chandleries, Sarah, the proprietress, said, "Oh, I know that stove. Don't sell it. It'll work fine if you just seal off the top third of the opening."

Later, during New Zealand's winter when day after raw day reminded us of our Catalina Saturday, we remained cozy and warm in *Sea Foam*'s smoke-free cabin. And every time I recall that Sarah could easily have bought our $300 fireplace for a cash offer of $19.95, I mentally doff my hat and kiss her hand.

FOUR

WHEN IT CAME TIME to move out of Nancy's large, four-bedroom house and into temporary quarters in a one-bedroom apartment right next to *Sea Foam*'s slip, we were stuck with a new problem: what to do with all of our excess junk accumulated over the years.

We finally managed to relocate most of it in the attics of friends and relatives. We had the good sense to choose only those whom we judged to be stable maritally, financially, residentially, and vocationally. Since then, one family has left the state, another has moved ten times and filed and unfiled for divorce twice, and the last couple, married for 39 years, finally got a divorce because *she* wanted to keep a neat yard and *he* would never clean it up. It takes some people a while to make up their minds.

Having moved into our attractive and convenient new pad, we found we had another stroke of luck. Into the slip next to us hove a 40-foot Newporter, and on board was a family that had just returned from cruising for three years in the South Pacific. We were able to buy much of their gear—charts, sextant, radio—which saved us hundreds of dollars. But best of all, our new friends were a living library of information about what we'd need for equipment and provisions. Viola actually took Nancy by the hand and led her through the supermarket saying, "Get a lot of toilet paper, and any other paper products you use. They're either unavailable or expensive down there. Packaged mixes, or anything in cardboard, must be removed and put into plastic containers (cardboard absorbs moisture and the contents will spoil). Buy square, plastic freezing containers. They tend to be cheaper than other kinds, and they stow well. Get no fewer than a dozen funnels of all sizes. Get everything you can in plastic or stainless steel—all else rusts. Get rolls and rolls of plastic bags. Margarine will keep, but in Tahiti you can buy canned butter from New Zealand." And on and on.

Scooping up another pearl of wisdom, we made at least three trips in the *Bullet* up to the Used Food Store in East Los Angeles. The name was ours for a store which sold, at tremendous reductions, canned goods that had been dented in shipment. If one carefully examined the seams, one could soon learn to tell if the can was still sound. It was at the Used Food Store that we picked up such essentials as mushrooms in butter sauce, cranberry jelly, hollandaise, canned sour cream, artichoke hearts, cartons and cartons of ordinary foods, and 100 (unused) rolls of toilet paper.

Most of us try to stretch each dollar as far as possible, but this can lead a person into the error of cutting corners where he shouldn't. We answered an ad for a used Avon inflatable dinghy. When we arrived at the address, there it was on the lawn, inflated and looking in great shape. It was black. (Avon hadn't made black ones for years, but we didn't know that.) We paid $100 for it, and in addition bought several other odds and ends of doubtful use but attractive price. Bargains are addictive, after all.

The dinghy was to become known as Black Benny, and was a thorn in our sides for three years. (Benny was short for Benzedrine, as any journey in it was bound to produce excess adrenalin.) No matter how often we pumped Benny full of air, he refused to stay fully inflated. He was mysteriously porous. With each stroke of the oars, Benny would fold up in a mass of wrinkles, and progress was limited to meager gains on a watery treadmill. He would conform with fluid grace to the shape of whatever waves were under him, and our sense of participating in an absurd charade was often heightened by the hoots and guffaws of our friends.

Much later, after sailing thousands of miles, we sent Benny to the sick-rubber-dinghy clinic run by the New Zealand Air Force, who sent him back with 47 new patches, a bill for $64, and a kindly worded note advising us not to spend any more money trying to fight a lost cause.

Determined to paddle the last penny's worth of use out of old Benny, I patched and fought with him for another few months until, one day, searching for a pinhole with a moist forefinger, I put my whole hand through the airchamber wall. After swimming back to *Sea Foam* and changing to dry clothes, I hauled the dinghy aboard, bent on trying to cure even this catastrophic breakdown. I crumbled away the rot until I had enlarged the hole to the size of my fist. The remaining rubber was relatively sound, so I applied a huge patch made from an old inner tube. Somehow the patch stayed absolutely airtight, but because it was weaker and more flexible than the impregnated fabric of the dinghy, it swelled to a large bubble that threatened to burst. Benny looked like a huge, black doughnut with a goiter. I wasn't above trying to flog the last mile out of a geriatric Avon, but to coerce one with such an obvious thyroid problem was beneath me. Although Benny remained on board for several more months, I never had the heart to blow him up again.

In mid-February 1973, we sailed *Sea Foam* to San Diego. But it wasn't until March 13 that we moved on board for good. The intervening weeks we spent ferrying by car those things we would take from Newport, storing the last of our leave-behinds, and wrapping up our earth-bound affairs. It is hard to believe how many strands bind one to a complicated life ashore.

The crew assembled. Ten-year-old Craig, the youngest, had been the first of the children to believe us. An authority on dinosaurs at the age of five, he needed just one look at photos of the Galapagos to decide that there would be boobies, tortoises, albatross, and iguanas in his future. He sold the rosy boa, freed the king snake, gave away the guinea pigs, traded the hamsters. Having assembled a sleeping bag, notebooks, pencils, and an

Instamatic, he was shining-eyed ready 13 months before we cast off."

Chris, 18, was convinced that Nancy and I were incompetent. He came along to keep us from making fools of ourselves.

Philip, 19, was between school and college and had no immediate commitments. He came along as an experienced sailor, navigator, and first-line defense against the elements.

Conni, also 19, had been a rebel since she was 14. Buffeted by a broken romance and wanting to escape the fate of a peer group involved in the drug scene, she made the decision to look at new horizons.

Lee was 20 and had college to finish. That done, she would join us in Tahiti for several months.

Sarah, 15, was in high school, but would spend her summer vacation with us cruising Costa Rica.

As soon as we moved aboard, we hauled *Sea Foam* to do a last-minute bottom job, raise the waterline, and paint the topsides. It was then that I discovered some softness in the deadwood of the stem, right around the bobstay fitting. I would have been wise to scarf in some new wood and design a stronger fitting, but I listened to some bad advice and merely treated the weakened part with a patent rot remedy. In a few months a near-disaster would remind me of this poor decision.

Back at the marina we busied ourselves with a final check list that, like Zeno's Paradox, was continually halved but never eradicated. I tripled our bookshelf space, worked on the engine, and designed and built a varnished mahogany toilet-paper holder which we still point out when we're giving the tour. Philip, Craig, and Chris made ratlines, rigged our twin spinnaker poles, and made baggywrinkles. Conni and Nancy stowed food.

"Hon?" said Nancy. Her smile was sweet, her voice silky. "I need $300."

"Sure thing," I said, just as if we had an unlimited bankroll. "What for?"

"Provisions," she said briskly, and within minutes she departed, taking Conni as co-advisor, and stealing Philip, Chris, and Craig as bearers.

We'd already spent several hundred dollars on provisions, but we *had* raised the waterline three inches, after all, and I wasn't really worried. Beamy *Sea Foam*, I was sure, could hold tons.

That evening the $300 was gone, and deckhouse, decks, and cockpit were buried under cartons of food. For several days we varnished cans, made lists, and discovered nooks and crannies under bunks and behind bulkheads, spaces heretofore unused. I was told to build a spice rack two feet wide and three shelves high. It turned out to be too small. Then came phase two.

"Hon?" said Nancy. Her smile was tentative, her voice pleading. "I need $200."

"Oh?" I said in a tone which I hoped implied affluence tempered with prudence. "What for?"

"Provisions," she said, her chin quivering.

"There's no more room," said Philip.

"There's absolutely no room at all," said Chris.

"Where are you going to put them?" asked Craig.

Nancy and Conni had it all figured out. There was a large lazarette in the cockpit which wasn't completely full. I could build some bins in the ample, empty bilge. Please?

Minutes later Nancy left. The grumpy bearers went with her. A few hours later they were back. There weren't quite as many cans as before, but there seemed to be a lot. We made more lists, repacked several places which proved to have been not quite full after all, and, one way or another, all the food disappeared. The waterline, however, was only visible at low tide. A couple of days later came phase three.

"Hon?" said Nancy. Her mouth was grim, her voice steely. "I want $100."

"What the hell for?" I shouted in a controlled attempt to communicate impending bankruptcy.

"A few last-minute things," she grated, her eyes drilling mine like lasers.

"We have enough," Chris stated flatly.

"We have too damn much," said Philip, shaking his head.

"Don't we have enough, Mom?" asked Craig.

One hundred dollars and three hours later, *Sea Foam*'s crew was busy varnishing cans, revising lists, and repacking every single storage area on the boat. Miraculously, all the food found a place, but *Sea Foam*'s waterline was only a memory.

I found it hard to believe that so much money could go for provisions. Nancy explained later that she'd never be frightened of going to sea if there was plenty of food on board, and that meant filling every available space. We suffered early to profit late. Six months out we were still enjoying canned sour cream on our tacos. One year later we were still eating canned bacon bought in San Diego. Our menu remained varied and offered such goodies as blueberries, artichoke hearts, and cranberry sauce. With minimal reprovisioning ($100 in Acapulco, $200 in Costa Rica), the six of us ate like kings for better than nine months. The only real wonder is where we managed to stow it all.

We would probably be in San Diego yet, building and buying, shuffling and stowing, turning *Sea Foam* into the most efficiently organized seagoing pantry in the marina, had not some of our friends arrived with farewell champagne (two bottles) and a backup of sparkling red wine (six bottles). We jovially ho-hoed in the cockpit until the bottles were empty, at which point our visitors clambered off the boat and stood on the dock expectantly.

"Well?" said one of them.

"My turn to buy?" I asked. I was in the mood for a whole weekend of camaraderie.

"Not that," he said.

"What, then?"

Our friend looked embarrassed about coming to the point. Suddenly his wife emerged from her private, glowing world like the dormouse coming out of the teapot.

"We thought you were leaving today," she said, working up to a tear or two. "We came all the way down to wave goodbye as you sail off into the sunset. Aren't you going to leave?"

"Damn," I said to the crew. "I think we've *got* to leave."

"There's absolutely no question about it," said Nancy, getting to her feet.

Which is how and why *Sea Foam*, plimsoll line two feet under, wallowed out of San Diego Channel into the stunning Saturday afternoon sunset. It was an inauspicious April Fool's Day Eve.

FIVE

A s WE STEAMED out the channel under power, we were still filled with a buoyant *joie de vivre* and blissfully unaware of the import of the step we had taken. We had said goodbye many times, at farewell parties, or last suppers in cozy restaurants, but this time we had said goodbye and *cast off*. More than selling the house, the chattels, more than buying the boat, the charts and provisions, more than boasting of our intentions to bored friends, more than any previous act, this last was the most decisive. We had now cut the cord, bought ourselves a piece of adventure, travel, and romance, changed our lives in dramatic fashion. We were, as the producer said to the starlet, on our way.

We were bound for the Todos Santos Islands, just off Ensenada, Mexico, and roughly 50 miles south of San Diego. We planned to cruise the Central American coast, but our greatest anticipation was for the Galapagos. From there we would go to French Polynesia and take stock of our finances, our options. We had charts all the way to New Zealand, beyond which we had a rather pre-Columbian concept of geography. Once there we had some undefined notion of getting jobs, immigrating maybe, we didn't know. New Zealand was as far as our already-stretched imaginations would take us.

By the time we'd all eaten a good dinner we were sober and serious, and Nancy, Chris, and Philip were sick. There wasn't much wind, and the combination of wine, the excitement of leaving, the inexorable swells, and the fumes of the diesel were enough. But from day one, when it came time for someone to stand his watch, sick or not he was there.

Sea Foam's crew, after several months aboard, complained at not having a self-steering vane. We have a friend who, when his children point wistfully at the windvane on other boats, informs them sternly that standing watch is character-building. In our case it was sailor-building. Chris, Phil, and I had a modicum of experience. Craig, Conni, and Nancy had none. By the time we had steered *Sea Foam* all the way to Tahiti, everyone aboard had learned the rudiments of sailing. Each had learned how to steer by the compass, how to spot threatening squalls, at what point to reduce sail, and how to assume responsibility for the boat and her crew. And each had experienced the impressive loneliness of night-watches when one is a pinpoint on an empty ocean, a microdot in an eternity of stars.

Much later, Nancy, Craig, and I delivered a boat, equipped with an excellent self-steering vane, from Tahiti to Los Angeles. It was a totally different experience. Even though we maintained a watch schedule at night, the person on duty only had to go topsides three or four times per hour to check course, weather, running lights, and the horizon for other ships. We called it a responsibility watch.

During the day, with the vane, there was no formal watch, and only very casual supervision was maintained by whoever felt like maintaining it. The vane steered the boat faultlessly to the apparent wind. Sometimes I had to force myself to leave my cozy bunk to go topsides for ten minutes in the morning, ten in the afternoon. I would stand in the companionway, breathe deeply of the pure air, scan the horizon for survivors to rescue (not too many, please), and then return below to book, chart, or typewriter. Whereas without a vane, man retains his close relationship to vessel and sea, much like the symbiosis of rider and steed, with a vane the relationship degenerates to that of a passenger to his seat on the bus. The purist in me says "steer," but whenever our ship's company dwindles to its hard-core complement of three, the realist in me says "vane."

At the start of *Sea Foam*'s voyage, we scheduled four-hour watches to be stood in pairs, an "experienced" sailor with a tyro. This way the experienced could lead the novice gently by the hand through the problems and perils of helmsmanship and command; more importantly, I thought, we all could have companionship and conversation to cheer the long, lonely vigil.

"Yeah, yeah," said everyone, happy with my arrangement. They made just one alteration on their own: why stay awake for four hours, when with a private agreement between you and your co-watcher, you need only stay awake for two? Thus, though they went topsides in pairs, one would sack out on deck while the other took half the watch. The main purpose of the plan was defeated.

But the one who really got gypped was Philip, who drew Craig for a partner. Craig, at age ten, never really woke up between 8:00 at night and 8:00 in the morning. He would *seem* to wake up, and would allow himself to be gently eased to the helm, where he would appear to grasp the situation firmly and responsibly. Look away for an instant, however, and his head would fall to his chest, his breathing would slow, and *Sea Foam* would be free to wander wheresoever she would. During the day, Craig would agree emphatically with my lectures on sharing the load, the necessity for group effort, and how he must do his part. But during the night, Nature proving stronger than Determined Resolve, he would be somnolent. We finally changed the watch schedule, giving Craig the late afternoon and early morning watches, and from then on things went better. However, until the change was made, Philip would spend two hours steering and the other two hours standing in the companionway saying, "Wake up, Craig. Don't fall asleep, Craig. God *damn* it, Craig, wake up!" It was decidedly unnerving to everyone aboard, except, of course, Craiger, who slept through it all.

The morning after our departure I was chagrined to discover the familiar profile of the Todos Santos Islands 12 miles to port instead of two miles to starboard. April Fool, Mr. Navigator, sir.

There's an old story about the farmer who ordered a mail-order wife, picked her up at the station, and was driving her home in the buggy when the horse shied for no apparent reason.

"That's one," said the farmer.

They continued on for a little way, when the horse stumbled for no apparent reason.

"That's two," said the farmer.

They proceeded, but before they had gone much further the horse shied again.

"That's three," said the farmer. He stopped the horse, took a large timber out of the back of the buggy, and smashed the horse on the head, killing him instantly.

"Why in the world did you do that?" asked his horrified hitherto-silent bride.

The farmer looked her right in the eye. "That's one," he said.

Which is why I understood what the guru who lives in my brain meant when he looked me right in my mind's eye and said, "That's two." Because two years before, in a chartered boat, I had made the very same tenderfoot mistake—I had confused true and magnetic headings when plotting our course, a 14-degree error. The next time might be more than funny, more than embarrassing. It might be fatal. I took the crew's kidding stoically, severely chastened by my error.

We stayed overnight at the Todos Santos before checking into Mexico at nearby Ensenada. Chris and Phil caught fish and abalone for dinner, and we dined by kerosene lamp and candlelight. After dinner, everyone wrote entry number one in his journal. Later, as our cruising personalities took shape, I would have given anything to read six different versions of the same event. But logs were sacrosanct, and it was agreed that anyone caught reading another's log would have to walk the plank.

I understand that the process of checking into Mexico has been improved, but at that time it was a trying experience. We had prepared ourselves as best we could by going to the consulate in San Diego and paying their special secretary to type up all the necessary papers, but in Ensenada I was subjected to the promenade. The Ensenadans had it worked out so that in order to have all copies of the crew list stamped by the proper authorities in the proper sequence, you must spend half a day walking between two offices a half-mile apart. As we had stopped in Ensenada only to complete formalities, I was annoyed to learn that I would also have to check *out* of Ensenada before leaving. For some reason this required five more crew lists to be typed by a Mexican secretary, and they could not be stamped until I had completed checking in. By the time I'd finished my sixth hot, dusty round trip, I'd become the local brewery's greatest hope for a smashing fiscal '73.

While in Ensenada Harbor, we met a couple on a Sea Sprite who were headed for a life of cruising. A Sea Sprite is exactly like a Sea Witch (*Sea Foam*'s design), but four feet shorter. Naturally this boat caught our eye.

She turned out to be the most completely equipped cruising boat I had ever seen. There were five anchors on deck, each with its own chain and rode, each ready to be dropped right away. She had VHF and SSB radios. In fact, the boat was so well equipped, so fully thought-out to meet any emergency, that by comparison I felt like we were going to sea on a raft with a long pole.

We later heard that they had turned back. I often wondered why. If it wasn't for personal or non-cruising reasons, my guess is that the couple on board had overtrained. They were so well prepared that maybe when the first emergency came along that required improvisation—a solution not in their book—it destroyed their confidence. To be sure, preparation is the most important part of safe cruising, the best insurance you can get. But after a certain point a person must be confident enough to ad lib.

The day we were to leave for Isla de San Martin, 80 miles to the south, we had our plans changed by the weather. A santana (a condition in which desert air suddenly decides it must go west at breakneck speed) hit the harbor and reshuffled boats, anchors, and even moorings at an alarming rate. Gusts of 70 knots came down off the mountains, picked up clouds of dust, mixed them with spume, and threw the concoction in our faces as we were in the throes of anchor drill. Chris, Philip, and I re-anchored *Sea Foam* five times. It was after the fourth time that we decided to try something different.

The problem was not that the wind was all that strong, or that everyone's tackle was too light. The trouble was the bottom of the harbor, a mixture of grunge, mud, and silt that resembled quicksand. In fact, Ensenada Harbor had good claim to being the worst holding ground in the world. I have watched careful, prudent yachtsmen drag anchor in near calms, scratching their heads and cursing all the way across the bay. Most who regularly cruise there rent moorings.

But this day, even the moorings were sliding off to leeward, and I was anxious to try something I'd read about: put down two anchors on the same chain, one about 30 feet outboard of the other. I made sure they were laid out carefully so that one anchor didn't fall on top of the other, spoiling the whole scheme. We rigged a 35-pound yachtsman inboard of a 30-pound Danforth, then put out normal scope for conditions—in this case, ten-to-one.

We had been standing anchor watches, wearing diving masks to protect our faces from the blowing sand. Now our problem was not dragging our own anchor, but guarding against other boats dragging down on us. We have since anchored this way in other severe blows, and as long as the wind blew from the same direction, we were locked to the substrata.

(Footnote: in 1979, one of the most competent skippers I know put out this arrangement during a moderate blow in the Australs. Both the anchors dragged, and my friend, unable to get all that gear back aboard his pitching, 38-foot sloop in the inky darkness, had to buoy the whole mess and spend a nervous, all-night vigil riding to a light lunch hook, the last anchor on board. Not knowing what went wrong, I can only insist that throughout our cruise the system never failed for us, but that nothing's infallible, and each of us must choose his own antidote to the real fears and dangers of dragging.)

We left the next day, heading down the coast of Baja California. From now on, we would be poking about in strange waters, seeking shelter in strange harbors. Our knowledge of where we were going would all be second-hand, from charts, books, and the indispensable Sailing Directions. It was a whole new ball game, and, with the bliss that is born of ignorance, we could hardly wait to get into it.

San Martin, a volcanic island with a protected cove, rose up out of the water several miles east of where I'd expected it. All the way down the coast we continued to arrive west of our destinations, a phenomenon I finally attributed to the fact that I'd warned everyone about the currents that were supposed to set shorewards, which we evidently never experienced. The terrible tales and visible evidence of the wrecks of boats that had been swept ashore fed my nightmares, and I repeatedly cautioned everyone to steer high. Long before we reached the tip of Baja, the crew was fed up with always making landfalls several miles abeam. I wondered about the accuracy of the compass and a possible *offshore* current and finally decided that I had simply infected everyone with my nervous caution. Understandably, it was discouraging to spend two or three unnecessary hours sailing straight for the coast. On the other hand, *Sea Foam* did stay off the beach.

We spent the weekend at San Martin enjoying the solitude, gorging on the abalone that we caught by wading among the rocks at low tide, and tramping along the shore to watch the antics of pelicans and seals. In the evening, Mexican fishermen arrived to spend the night in shacks on the beach. Otherwise, we had the place to ourselves.

Monday, April 9, we headed south along the coast toward Turtle Bay. There was no wind, so we powered in a flat calm past Sacramento Reef, a fabled hazard that was allegedly the downfall of *Goodwill*, among others. We were accompanied by a pod of gray whales. Totally unconcerned by us (though this attitude was not reciprocal), they put on a performance of swimming, blowing, and sounding for our benefit.

I spent much of the afternoon trying to get a meaningful line of position from the sun. To this day I don't know what I was doing wrong. Three of us—Nancy, Philip, and myself—had taken navigation lessons from a tutor in Newport Beach. We had learned the rote without the theory, and though I've since met many sailors who navigate successfully knowing only what's needed on the work forms, this has never satisfied me. Lack of understanding causes me to make stupid errors both in procedure and arithmetic. If you throw in the additional handicap of clumsiness with the sextant itself, the likelihood of error soars. By the time we set sail from Costa Rica for the Galapagos, I had developed enough skill to feel confident of finding *something* in that extensive, towering archipelago, but it was months before I developed what could be called, even generously, consistent accuracy.

So we piloted down the coast, taking bearings on landmarks, and planned to raise the larger San Benedito Island at dawn the next day. The strongest light on the coast—400,000 candlepower and visible for 28 miles—sat atop a hill on the north end of the island.

As a New Englander, I was taught to admire the heroic lighthouse keeper who would give his life to keep his light burning, a constant beacon on which sailors could depend. The Mexicans, we had been warned, hadn't nursed at the same teat. Whether or not any navigational aid was lit was a matter of chance. Forewarned is forearmed; nevertheless, after the blackest night I have ever seen, it was a shock to have the first light of dawn silhouette the towering island no more than four miles ahead! Whether we would have seen it in time is something that haunts me to this day. As it was the second most important light on the whole coast (the other was on the tip of Baja and *was* lit), I had thought it might be dependable. From that moment, however, we always assumed there would be no light, and were pleased when there was.

After a beautiful day, we creamed into Turtle Bay under full sail. A fresh, fat bonita, our first catch on the trolling line, lay on the deck in a damp burlap sack. (We had been advised that we must have a fishing license, a $56 expense we need never have made. By the time we left Mexico, the bounty of the sea had cost us $14 per fish.) The anchorage was completely sheltered. There was a small fishing village and a cannery that processed mostly abalone. Although there were tons of fresh abalone each day, due to a mysterious company rule no one was permitted to buy any. Nor was any liquor available. A company town, the inhabitants were poor, hard-working, and Catholic. Virtually the only communication with the outside world was by boat or, for the hardy, by jeep. Truly an outback of an outback.

Marie, a tiny sloop anchored by the village, was one of the lowest-budget cruising boats we met. Two young men, with only a cuddy for shelter, planned to sail their little boat to Acapulco and ship her overland to Florida. We last saw them in Mazatlán. Among others, one of their money-saving ideas struck me as ingenious. For a taffrail log they used a bicycle odometer connected by braided wire to a home-made rotor. Calibrated against a measured mile, they claimed accuracy within ten per-cent. Though not as precise as a Walker log, it cost virtually nothing and was far more effective than guessing.

"Hey Dad, the head's not working." This from Philip, and before my coffee, already. "The flapper valve isn't closing."

The head, a Grocco, was to become my Sisyphus stone, a thing of duty that annoyed forever. Six people cruising will use a head more in a week than weekend sailors will in a year. Even so, the inadequacy of this design, rather than frequency of use, was the main reason I had dismantled it, at sea and in port, a total of 26 times by the time we'd reached Tahiti. Turtle Bay was the first time, and I approached the task with virginal innocence.

The weak link, the flapper valve, was a weighted, neoprene flapper at the bottom of the bowl. The flapper was kept closed by a small, fragile copper spring. It was this spring that failed with persistent regularity, pushing my patience and endurance past their limits.

As you pumped the head, the upstroke sucked waste down

past the flapper into a lower chamber. The flapper was then supposed to close, and the downstroke, a compression stroke, would force the waste through the outflow. Discovery that the valve wasn't working was often the result of a mighty downstroke which, because the flapper valve was open, forced a monumental geyser of sewage all over the walls and floor. In the course of our cruises, Craig had grown fond of saying, "Eat a live toad first thing in the morning and you know nothing worse can happen to you all day." I would like to submit an exception.

Rarely would the spring break when the toilet was full of mere urine. At first, I would dutifully bail appalling mixtures out of the bowl into a bucket prior to dismantling. Soon the rule was, "You did it, you bail it." Finally we got smart and attached a tennis ball to the end of a stick. This device, if you were coordinated enough, could be jammed into the bottom of the bowl to block it for the downstroke and removed to open it for the upstroke. Once the head was pumped clean and flushed repeatedly with clear water, the job became significantly less vile. (The tennis ball on the stick was a refined version of Chris's prototype, a Sunkist orange and a rubber glove.)

Even at best, not only was the job a smelly, dirty one, but it required the talents of a contortionist midget. I can only guess, but where there was now a fireplace in the saloon, there might once have been a locker, as on the starboard side. If so, access to the outflow loop, while inconvenient, would have been at least possible. When the fireplace was added (if this was the case) two things happened: (1) because of limited space, the outflow hose now had to bend in such a way as to buckle it, thus creating a site for blockage, and (2) the whole loop became virtually inaccessible. To battle with a frozen through-hull valve, to remove hose clamps, and to wrestle calcified hoses from copper fittings, there was an access hole big enough for one small arm.

That first time in Turtle Bay I did most of the toilet rehab myself. It took me eight hours. By the time we reached the Marquesas I had a team trained to the speed and skill of an Indianapolis pit crew. Disassembly, cleaning, replacing damaged parts, and reassembling: 90 minutes. Flapper valve only: 15. But getting there was *not* half the fun.

Later, in Tahiti, we stumbled on a near-new Wilcox Crittenden with two sets of spare parts for a paltry $40. One of the speediest jobs I've ever done was to tear out the Grocco and install the Wilcox. I didn't want anyone to change his mind.

"What'll we do with our old head?" I asked Nancy.

"Sell it," she said.

"It would be worth it to me to take it outside, perform a small ceremony, smash it, and drop it piece by piece into the sea."

"Don't be childish. When we tie up at the quay for the fête in Papeete, we can put it out with a sign on it. Someone'll buy it."

All during the Bastille Day festivities, *Sea Foam*, moored in one of the more prominent slots, played host to friends and acquaintances. During the harbor races of canoes, sailing outriggers, and hydroplanes, as many as 30 guests would troop aboard past our throne, regally ensconced on the sidewalk with a FOR SALE sign on it. Not one person mentioned it. Even the French authorities were too polite or too understanding to complain.

After 14 days with no response, I was beginning to lose hope when, coming back from a beer run, I saw Nancy hurrying toward me.

"The guy off *Vela* offered us $12. He wants it for spare parts."

There was a repair kit, $9 retail, that went with the head. We had been asking $20.

"No sale," I said. "I'd rather deep-six it than *give* it away."

Nancy seldom gets angry with me, but this enraged her. She shops and compares, bakes and preserves, scrimps and schemes to save pennies wherever she can. When I indicated I'd happily give up $12 for symbolic revenge, she was furious.

"I—think—we—should—take—it," she gritted. "Now."

She is usually right about these things, but I can be stubborn, too. "If we haven't sold it by the end of the week, he can have it," I declared. Nothing she said would change my mind.

When the end of the week came with no further action, it fell to me to approach our one customer. Recognizing a buyer's market when he saw one, he dropped his offer to ten dollars. Remembering Nancy's temper, I sold it to him, holding back the kit of spares which I was positive I could sell down the line.

Shortly thereafter, *Vela* unfortunately went up on the reef in Fiji, and the unlucky skipper posted notices at the Royal Suva Yacht Club advertising provisions, tools, and gear of all kinds for sale. When he came by to try to sell the Grocco back to me, I commiserated with him over his bad luck and pointed out that I now owned a different kind of head and had no use for the Grocco. As he walked away, shoulders drooping with the weight of his misfortune, I could only sigh and think, "Jesus, if I'd known how bad the karma of that stinking head really was, I'd have scuttled it no matter *what* Nancy said." I still have the repair kit.

SIX

W E LEFT TURTLE BAY in the late afternoon of April 14 in about 25 knots of wind from the northwest. To our left was the rolling, arid emptiness of Baja, a mountained wilderness, a science-fiction landscape in a foreign, hostile world. The eerie loneliness was accentuated by memories of the Southern California anthill we had just left, and by the semitropical wind, the unexpected chill of which cut through parkas, mittens, scarfs, and ski hats. I was getting a lot of pressure from the crew to head straight for the tropics, but I had bought all the charts for Baja and I was damned if we weren't going to cruise some of it. Thus our destination was Punta Abreojos, another overnight sail.

It was Chris's watch. He had spotted a coastal freighter, but lacked the experience to judge her course and distance from the position of her lights. By the time he decided we were on a collision course, we were in an emergency.

"Herb, you'd better come up, quick. There's a ship coming straight at us!"

The touch of panic in his voice cut through the fog of sleep, and I was on deck in seconds. The freighter was a little over a mile away. The low, white light on her bow and the higher white light on her superstructure were nearly in line, and I could see both the red and the green running lights. She had us zeroed in.

"Check our running lights," I told Chris. "On deck, on deck!" I yelled below.

"They aren't working!" called Chris from the foredeck.

"Ready about!" I shouted. "Nancy, get the searchlight."

She grabbed the searchlight, a handheld job, and shone it on the sails.

"Shine it right at the freighter," I said, "right at the bridge."

We were on a broad reach. I spun the helm hard to starboard. *Sea Foam* rounded up, losing way until she came to a dead stop. Now we were locked in irons, and I needed the engine to push her through the wind. I turned the key and pressed the starter. Nothing.

"It's the searchlight," I said. "It's drawing too much current. Turn it off till I get the engine going."

The second the light went off I pushed the starter again. The diesel burst into life. I grabbed the gear shift. It was frozen, immovable. By this time the freighter was so near that even were we to back the staysail and fall off into a jibe, it would have been too late.

As soon as the engine started, Nancy had turned on the searchlight again and was flashing it on the bridge of the little coastal ship. Just when I figured we'd had it, the freighter veered off course, passing us at a distance of about 100 yards. Three or four hundred yards beyond she came to a stop and shone her lights on us. We must have looked as if we were in distress, hove-to, mizzen and staysail flogging in the wind. She watched us until finally, staysail backed, we fell off and resumed course.

Chris and I had a terse discussion about how to identify a freighter's course from her running lights, and when to call me if there was the smallest doubt, after which I hit the sack and fell into a fitful sleep. But it was not till the next day, at anchor, that I was able to make sense out of the chain of failures that had left us helpless in the face of near-disaster:

1. Chris had called me too late. Discussion with the whole crew now obviated a repeat of that.

2. The engine hadn't started immediately. We had solved that on the spot.

3. The running lights had shorted out. This was partly my fault. The running lights were traditional-style kerosene lamps

to which had been added electric bulbs. I had thought this a great idea, and had filled the kerosene reservoirs as a back-up if the electric lights should fail. How I thought I'd ever be able to light the damn things in half a gale I can't imagine. Because of the wires, which had no removable connectors, the lamps couldn't be removed and taken below. The rolling of the boat had caused the kerosene in the lamps to spill, shorting out the electric circuits. I removed the kerosene and relied for the future on keeping the electric circuit in order.

4. The gear shift had frozen up. Unbeknownst to me, the drain from the galley sink, located right over the engine, had developed a leak, and saltwater (which we were using for dishes) had been dripping on the transmission and the linkage. It had chosen just the wrong moment to seize up.

5. I had wanted to come about, using the engine to bring us around. Now, sailing off the wind in a similar emergency, we would effect a controlled jibe.

The one thing we did right was to have the searchlight rigged and ready, and to flash it from the freighter's bridge to the sails and back to the bridge. Flashing the bridge is eye-catching. Flashing the sails shows the other helmsman what he's up against.

We were lucky. Had the freighter been larger and less maneuverable, our cruise would have ended there. It wasn't and we escaped. To depend on luck is to court disaster; to sail without it is to do the same. From this delicate balance is a sailor's superstition born.

Disasters are supposed to come in threes. Our second occurred the night we left Abreojos. Our jib halyard was originally rigged with a one-to-one purchase and a snap shackle with a swivel to clip to the head of the jib. I had thought it advantageous to add a block, doubling the purchase, but had failed to replace the swivel snap shackle.

We were broad-reaching to a west wind, having left Abreojos about noon. In the late afternoon the wind rose to 30 knots, and we decided to douse the jib. Nothing we could do would bring it down. The swivel shackle had allowed the now-doubled halyard to twist into a tight, immovable lay. We were lying hove-to, the jib flapping like a panicked bird.

"I'll go up, Dad," offered Philip. Unable to think of an alternative, we rigged the bosun's chair and hauled him up the mast. The motion on deck was wild enough. As he was pulled higher, Philip experienced motion of increasing violence. It took every ounce of his strength to cling to the mast. His task was made even more difficult at the top, where, with the motion amplified to its maximum, he had to hang on with one hand and fight the shackle with the other. He succeeded, and we lowered him safely to a hero's welcome.

We've since heard numerous stories about others who have gone up the rigging at sea, lost control, and been battered senseless by the mast. Later, with time to brood over a life risked, I spotlighted my two errors.

Our mistake was to use a swivel shackle with a double purchase. Rope under stress tends to untwist. Thus the swivel allowed the two lines of the taut halyard to twist around and around each other. Once more our inexperience was to blame, and the lesson almost too costly. As soon as possible we replaced the swivel with an ordinary shackle.

This problem was compounded by my own inflexible thinking. On a rising wind, our habit had been to douse the jib first. I failed to realize that we could have lowered everything *but* the jib and postponed retrieving it until we reached the shelter of our next anchorage. We have since sailed *Sea Foam* free in winds as strong or stronger under jib alone. Had Philip been injured, the fault would have been due to my poor judgment.

Why didn't I go up the mast myself? I offered, but youth, lighter weight, and better physical condition made Philip the logical choice.

As my mother told me when I was a child, life is a series of lessons with no chance to practice. Second only to foresight, a sailor's best insurance is his ability to improvise. It's an ability that depends upon attitude, an art that can improve with experience. Once again, it was good fortune that gave us the time to learn.

The third crisis came at dinner time. We had hardly recovered from the trauma of retrieving the jib when there was a burst of flame from the galley.

"Jesus," yelled Nancy. "Fire!"

Before I could get there she had already thrown one glass of water on the flame and was pumping a second one. The water had killed the fire momentarily, but right away it blazed up with renewed vigor.

"Get a bucket of water!" I called to Chris, who was on watch. At the same time I reached for the main shut-off valve. The flames were now licking the overhead and the ceiling. I was having trouble with the alcohol-feed valve, but the smell of hair burning off my forearm spurred me to greater effort. By the time I had the valve closed, I felt as though I'd been reaching into Hell.

Chris arrived in the companionway, a full bucket of saltwater in his hands. Without a moment's reflection he threw the water from where he stood. Thank God it was an alcohol fire. The first bucket smothered most of it, and a quickly brought second put it out. The galley, however, was a mess, the stove was dripping saltwater, and our incipient dinner was history.

"What happened?" I gasped.

"I'm not sure," said Nancy, hands clasped to her chest to keep her heart from beating its way to freedom. "I was priming it, and the boat took a sudden lurch. The alcohol spilled out of the cup into the pan underneath—it's done that before, lots of times—and I was just getting a glass of water to pour on it when the whole stove kind of exploded."

The stove itself was a gimballed three-burner with oven. Under the top burners was a tray of metal (actually the top of the oven) so that if alcohol spilled out of the priming cup it should have been harmless even if allowed to burn itself out. The problem was that, because the stove was gimballed, it was connected to the remote tank by a flexible, clear plastic hose. Notoriously susceptible to heat, the hose would melt when the flaming alcohol flowed anywhere near it. Once melted, fuel under pressure squirted out the hole, and a voracious tongue of flame, unquenchable until the main valve could be turned shut, shot out to engulf the galley.

It was several weeks before I was able to acquire a piece of fire-resistant refrigeration hose to replace the clear plastic one, and in the interim we had two more fires, both in rough weather. With practice, however, we learned to shut the valve quickly and quench the fire with minimum devastation. We've since learned a trick which would have been helpful. Take a short piece of asbestos rope and make a coil filling the priming cup. The asbestos wick soaks up enough alcohol for an effective prime, and prevents the liquid from sloshing out. Not knowing this at the time, however, we lived tenuously, as if on the lip of a rumbling volcano.

Until recently, I was always against propane stoves on boats because (a) I have watched gassers lug their empty propane bottles for miles to get them refilled; (b) I've seen them struggle with incompatible foreign fittings; and (c) propane brings, with its admitted convenience, the possibility of explosion. This is because propane is heavier than air and can accumulate in the bilge, where you may be unaware of its presence until a random spark ignites it.

There are many excellent fail-safe devices in propane installations, such as solenoid valves and warning lights, but for personal reasons I distrusted them. I have seen Nancy lock herself out of a fail-safe car by the simple expedient of sliding out the curb side after hiding her keys under the front seat. Mornings, I myself would frequently stagger into the galley and patiently perk six cups of clear water for seven minutes, having neglected to put in any coffee. And Craig and I have watched, with cruel glee, while

Nancy sleepily put a pinch of instant coffee into my cup, a heaping spoonful of tea leaves into hers, and then proceeded to fill the sugar bowl with boiling water. Given the human material that engineering would have had to cope with in our case, I was of little faith, and took the only precaution I knew against the hazard of propane, which was to refuse to have it aboard.

But by the time we reached Tahiti our old alcohol stove was a porous pile of rust, and Nancy had been on enough other yachts to know exactly what she wanted to replace it with. Had there been an inexpensive propane stove available I would have had to acquiesce. There wasn't, and when I came back to the boat with a brand new two-burner kerosene stove for only $50, Nancy accepted the inevitable with good grace.

Most kerosene stoves work on the same principle as the alcohol stove, or as the old-fashioned kerosene blowtorch. A priming cup under the burner is filled with alcohol and lighted. When the burner reaches a high enough temperature, kerosene under pressure is vaporized and burns with a hot blue flame. That's the theory.

On our boat, losing the prime was a sin. There were many ways to lose it. One was to walk away and forget it, as I often did in the morning before mental gears had meshed. Another was to underestimate the amount of alcohol necessary to get the burner hot enough. A third was to leave the hatch in the galley open so that the breeze blew on the burner, cooling it enough that it wouldn't light.

When you've lost the prime, the proper procedure is to let the burner cool, as repriming too soon has a risk similar to throwing lighter fluid on a smoldering charcoal fire. But we were impatient and sometimes reprimed immediately. Often we were successful and just a little alcohol would finish the job. Sometimes the burner, though not hot enough to vaporize the kerosene, was hot enough to make the alcohol burst spontaneously into flame, leaving my hairy hand balder but wiser.

After many years of cruising, Nancy finally became fed up with the constant battle. The animosity she bore the stove was only exceeded by the latent animosity she bore me for having saddled her with it in the first place. A typical bad morning went like this:

1. Little plastic priming bottle is empty. A search that terminates in the very back of the locker reveals that the large bottle of alcohol is also empty, and a grumpy exchange between Nancy and Craig as to who is to get dressed to go on deck and fill the bottle from the jerry-can finally ends with Craig's stomping topsides. (I am hiding in my typewriter.)

2. Prime wasn't hot enough, and burner ignites with raw kerosene in a yellow, smoking, overhead-high flame.

3. Nancy reprimes too soon with accompanying flare-up, provoking unmotherly swearing.

4. Burner lights but burns weakly. Nancy turns knob to clean jet, and the needle, which is pushed up into the jet, breaks off in the hole. Burner goes out.

5. I emerge from my cocoon of concentration long enough to point out to Nancy that the needle broke because she treated it too roughly.

6. Nancy primes other burner successfully. Burner lights but promptly goes out. Stove is out of kerosene. Result of ensuing debate is foreordained, as the person who is already dressed is the logical one to go topsides and get the kerosene.

7. Irritation causes slapdash pouring, and Craig returns below smelling badly.

8. Nancy fills stove tank through a funnel filter, spilling enough on her hands that whatever she eats for breakfast will now smell like kerosene.

9. Nancy reprimes burner, after being reminded by me not to prime (for Chrissakes) the plugged-up one.

10. Burner fails to light—Nancy has forgotten to pump up the pressure after refueling. She pumps furiously, applies a second match. Burner has cooled, burns yellow, smoky, and out of control.

11. Nancy, showing childish impatience, reprimes too soon with too much, burns arm.

12. Burner lights. After a short time we get our eye-opening

teas and coffees, but Nancy doesn't recover her normal cheerfulness until well into mid-morning.

I suggested several times that when she felt tension building up, she would feel better if she'd scream at the stove, call it names, castigate its inventor, manufacturer, distributor, retailer, and anyone else who for crass, commercial reasons perpetrated such a diabolical device. The few times I was able to persuade her to try it she stood in the galley with fists clenched, eyes closed, but the only thing she could come up with to yell was "WHY CAN'T WE HAVE PROPANE?"

Domestic rumor to the contrary, I am not totally heartless. We finally installed a propane stove. The gas bottle sat safely outside on deck, encased in its box of rich-grained Fijian wood. There was a solenoid which turned off the gas at the bottle when the stove was not in use, and a wall-mounted panel boasted a controlling switch and a light that glowed red when the gas was on. The stove was new, the procedures were new, and everyone aboard helped whoever was cooking to remember to hit the switch when they were done. I decided the risks of propane were minimal and well worth taking. One morning I was sitting gloomily in front of my typewriter, glaring angrily at a page that had remained blank for hours. Nancy was grousing about arthritic pain in her right elbow. Her sewing machine was acting up, and she was bogged down in mid-project. The air in the salon was charged with repressed snarls. Suddenly Nancy got up and stumped into the galley. She switched the switch. The red light glowed. She lit the grill and browned a perfect piece of toast. As she buttered the toast, a hint of a grin grew to a broad smile, and I wondered at the fact that after so many years of cruising together her pleasure could still brighten my gloomiest day.

SEVEN

MAGDALENA BAY, 120 miles north of the tip of Baja, is a long finger of water hiding behind a row of low mountains divided by the entrance from the sea. After a lovely downwind sail we reached into the bay and tacked north toward Puerta Magdalena, where there was good anchorage. The mountains cast a shadow from the setting sun, and beating to windward in the shade gave us a whole new perspective on what we earlier had thought was a pleasant, cool breeze. Now an icy blast, it kept everyone huddled below except the unlucky helmsman, who was relieved every half-hour. It was hard to believe that it was April 19, and that we were over 800 miles south of Los Angeles.

At anchor that evening, just as I was about to drop off, I heard a violent thrashing in the water. As I groped my way topsides, it sounded as if our mooring had been magically transplanted into the middle of an Olympic swimming meet. I shone the spotlight on the water and saw thousands upon thousands of smelt churning the surface to spume. The light drove them wild, and whole schools would leap out of the water, so densely packed they seemed a solid platform, darting and zigzagging in a blur of speed. The miracle of their coordination made me wonder if schools of fish had a collective brain. It was inconceivable in *my* cosmos that individuals could react in concert so quickly. Furthermore, if my three-day observation was any indication, the locals could set their watches by the roiling of the smelt.

The next day we motored up the winding, 15-mile channel to San Carlos in hopes of buying fresh vegetables, treating ourselves to fresh meat, and replenishing the liquor locker. Behind the "L"-shaped pier was a 40-foot power palace from Marina del

Rey. The pale man sitting in the cockpit with a glass in his hand looked to be a storehouse of the kind of information we sought.

"Where can we buy fresh stuff and booze in this town?" I asked.

"Fresh stuff in the village," he replied. "For booze, you have to take a cab to the hotel. Two bucks."

Thanking him, I unshipped my oars.

"But not today," he added. "It's a holiday."

"What Mexican holiday is it?"

"Easter," he said. "Today's Good Friday. Nothing will be open till Monday."

Which illustrates an aspect of cruising life that we'd been unaware of. Without newspapers, advertising, and other pre-holiday hooplah, one loses track of dates. Our insulated existence was as far from the civilization we'd left as if we'd gone to the moon.

Furthermore, each country has its own holidays. Time and again we would arrive in a tiny port, eager to take on fresh supplies, only to find everything closed. New Zealand, for instance, has 17 legal holidays, only three of which match ours. We learned eventually to roll with such minor inconveniences, but initially we criticized our guardian angel for being asleep at the switch. Chagrined, we retraced our way back down the channel to Puerta Magdalena.

What had been a sleepy little fishing village on Thursday had turned into Party Beach by Friday evening. As we dropped anchor, one from a group of celebrants who were sitting in a semicircle performing certain rites over five cases of beer, stood up and beckoned to us to come ashore. Chris, Philip, and I piled into the dinghy, and Nancy handed me my wallet.

"See if you can get some lobsters for tonight," she said.

We rowed ashore. The Group Leader, a young man of 20-odd years, handed us each a beer. Things were looking up.

"Iee speek Eenglees, a leetle," he ee'd.

"So do we," I said. "Speak a little Spanish, I mean."

"We weel speek Eenglees," he ordered.

The beer was cold and good. But short.

"Beer?" asked the Group Leader, handing me another.

"Sí," I said, gratefully.

"Eenglees, pleese," he said, wagging his finger.

Three beers later he got round to what had been on his mind all along.

"You have a girl on board, yes?"

"Yes."

"Your daughter?"

I never bother going into the intricacies of step-relationships anymore except with immigration officials.

"Yes."

"She like to dance?"

"Sometimes," I said.

"We have party tonight." He showed me the two houses where the party would be. "You come? She come?"

"Maybe," I said, and he was satisfied. "We'd like some lobsters."

"Langusta? Okay, I find you some." He whistled, called a name. A small boy, eight or nine years old, came running up from a nearby shack.

"—— —— —— —— ——!" snapped the G.L.

I can understand Spanish when it is spoken very slowly and the nouns are near enough to be pointed to. This was gibberish. The eight-year-old, obviously precocious, seemed to get every word. He turned and ran down the beach to the first of a row of houses. Soon he was back.

"—— —— —— —— —— ——, —— ——," he said in a clear, small voice.

"—— —— —— —— ——! ——! ——!" said G.L., his machismo bearing authoritative. The little boy took off like a streak and went to the second house in the same row. Soon he was back, once more with a negative answer.

"—— —— ——! —— ——! ——! ——!" commanded G.L.

The small runner took off for the third house like a somewhat slower streak. When he got back he was decidedly pooped.

"—— (breath) —— (breath) ——."

G.L. dismissed him and called another name. A new small boy, maybe a year older, reported for duty. G.L. sent him to the fourth house, and the fifth.

"Might I make a suggestion?" Philip asked me as the kid started for number six.

"Let him do it his way," I said, setting an example of tolerance for other peoples, other customs, "as long as the beer holds out. What you are watching is a spectacle, an art form. More important than efficiency is ceremony, hierarchy." I could have droned on, but the runner returned.

"—— ——! —— —— ——!! ——!!!"

"——," said G.L. Turning to me, he said, "Manuel has lobster. He wants four dollars for six lobsters."

"Bueno—I mean good," I said.

"You go to Manuel's house," said G.L. "The boy will take you."

Manuel, a large man for a Mexican, was sitting on the front porch of house number six. We stood in front of him, a line of supplicants.

"Four dollars, five lobsters, okay?"

"Group Leader said it was four dollars, six lobsters," I said.

"Big. Four dollars, five lobsters."

"Sí," I said after a slight hesitation. What the hell, it was the only game in town.

Manuel got up. There was a pair of heavy, hip boots by his chair, but he ignored them. There was a line with a weight on the end of it hanging coiled up by the door, but he ignored that also. We walked in a procession to the water's edge.

"Pedro!" he barked. "—— —— —— ——!"

A brand new member of the little-boy class ran down from the house, sand flying from flashing feet.

"—— —— ——!" ordered Manuel.

The little boy ran back to the house, picked up two boots, changed his mind, and staggered down with them one at a time.

"Roberto!" Roberto appeared, listened, then steadied Manuel while he struggled into the boots.

"Fernando!" Manuel seemed to have an unlimited supply of small boys. This one brought him the coiled line and the weight.

Manuel waded out till the water was nearly at the top of his boots. He tossed the weight at the lobster car, a wooden crate with chicken-wire sides where lobsters are kept in the water, alive. The idea was to hook the weight over the edge of the car and pull it in to shore, there supposedly being enough anchor line on the car to allow this. On the first throw Manuel missed the car completely. With infinite patience he coiled the line to throw again. On the second throw the weight hit the box, slipped off. Third throw: miss. Fourth: just beyond box, seemed to catch, box came in about two feet, weight slipped off. Fifth: miss. Sixth: weight seemed to catch, slipped off immediately, no progress. Seventh: weight hit wood, bounced off. Twenty-first: weight caught, two feet of progress made before it slipped off. Half the distance had been won. I figured we had 30 minutes more of daylight.

I'd started counting at what I guessed was throw 10. We were at number 48 when Manuel finally coiled up the line, turned, and waded back to dry land.

"Paco!" he yelled. Only the extra decibels betrayed his irritation. A tiny fellow ran to the water's edge and, with only a moment's hesitation, swam out to the car and towed it in. He was only in the water for one minute, but when he came out he was shivering. Because not a word passed between Manuel and Paco, it dawned on me that the two of them had played out this scene many times.

Manuel selected five lobsters, one of which was huge, and put them in a burlap sack.

"Five dollars," he said, putting the sack down on the porch floor.

"You said four dollars," I answered, my bargain unsweetening before my very eyes.

"One is very big, no? And I work hard to get them in. Five dollars."

I had seen the lobsters, could almost taste them. Manuel had me and knew it. I reached for my wallet, laid a fin on him, and picked up the sack.

On the way out to *Sea Foam*, Chris and Philip got on my case.

"You sure drive a hard bargain," said Chris.

"One tough hombre," said Philip.

"I did all right," I replied. "As far as I'm concerned he only got a dollar for his lobsters. The rest was for entertainment." And by the time I'd finished telling an only slightly embroidered version to Nancy and Conni, I'd convinced myself I'd made a really sharp deal.

Cabo San Lucas is the southern tip of the Baja peninsula. The town, on the shore of a bay on the inland side, was our destination. From Magdalena Bay to the Cape, current helped us average nearly eight knots over the bottom. Reaching across the tip, we were on our best point of sail. As we cut through the water in the lee of the cape, the temperature warmed perceptibly until, as we rounded the inner point and saw the town, we were in bathing suits. The temperature had warmed 20 degrees, and we had a fat little tuna on our boatline. It was too small a fish to feed all of us, but while Nancy and I went to town to check in, the boys dropped a line over the side and caught three barracuda. It was a day when everything went right.

We spent six days at Cabo. Protected from the open ocean by the Baja peninsula and from the south by a chain of granite hills, it was the most beautiful bay we had yet seen. We anchored in 20 feet of water so clear and calm that the white sand bottom seemed close enough to touch. Only when we saw a school of fish swim under the boat with plenty of fin room did we finally believe our depthmeter. The prevailing winds were from the west and were gentled and warmed by their journey over the land. By contrast with the raw chill and the barren ruggedness of the coast we had left, we felt we had sailed through the looking glass.

The change of climate from hostile chill to embracing warmth also changed the crew's attitudes from sullen discontent to smiling camaraderie. We had finally reached the tropics. Chris and Craig declared a temporary truce. Philip climbed out of his foxhole of silence. Conni became more sociable. Nancy and I relaxed, found more time for each other. We took long walks, picnicked on a secluded beach, swam nude, caught our dinner on handlines, watched gay mantas do their dramatic backflips, and sat up late in the cockpit, thinking exotic thoughts. We had sampled adventure, discomfort, real danger, and the anxiety induced by novice navigation. Now we were getting a taste of snug protection and comfort.

We met Dianna, a young mother of two towheaded sons, who lived aboard a 50-foot ferrocement ketch with two dogs. One morning Dianna rowed over for a cup of coffee. We sat in the cockpit under the awning, warm and comfortable in minimal clothing. While we were talking, I suddenly realized there was a dog swimming around *Sea Foam*, eyeing us wistfully.

"Go home," Dianna commanded.

"What's he going to do when he gets there," I asked, "swim around your boat till you get back?"

"Just watch."

After giving us the mournfully accusing stare of the persona non grata, Dog swam back to Dianna's high-sided ship. Without a moment's hesitation, he swarmed up the boarding ladder like a chimp. Dianna said that both he and the other dog jumped over the side and swam ashore for their daily needs, returning when and as they wished.

Ultimately Dog came to a tragic end. Not wanting to take him with them to Tahiti from Ahe in the Tuamotus, Dianna and her husband left him with some Aheans till their return. Dog disappeared. The Aheans claimed he went swimming at the pass and was eaten by sharks. There is some speculation that the eaters might have been the Aheans themselves. Be that as it may, it was all the same to Dog.

As we'd planned to reach Acapulco in early May, we were finally forced to tear ourselves away from Cabo's soothing languor. Through an enduring calm we powered across the Gulf of California and down the Mexican coast, stopping briefly in Mazatlán and San Blas before arriving in Puerto Vallarta. Our transmission had begun to slip badly, and the engine was running as if terminally ill. We limped into the marina, determined to cheer ourselves with dinner at Carlos O'Brien's.

The restaurant was packed with boisterous celebrants of Cinco de Mayo, Mexico's national holiday of independence. We drank, ate, and boistered with the best of them. An astounding bill and a surfeit of synthetic energy persuaded us to walk rather than taxi the three miles back to the boat.

"Fireworks! Oh boy!" said Nancy, pointing ahead of us.

The square in front of the church was packed with Mexicans in clothes of happy colors. A small, cleared area was reserved for setting off the skyrockets, Roman candles, cherry-bombs, and other delights. Naïvely, we wormed our way to the front row.

"My God—look out!" shouted Nancy, pushing me to one side. As she did, a skyrocket shot by, singeing my beard, and ended up in the lap of a hysterically merry Mexican in a wheelchair. Thinking quickly, he tossed the hissing remains into the crowd, while willing ladies subdued the conflagration in his crotch.

There seemed to be no design to the performance. It was a Quaker meeting of arsonists. Individuals, having scrimped for pesos to buy a portion of incendiary bedlam, stepped forward when the mood struck them, beer can in hand, and lit off. Rockets shot sideways, scattering shrieking serapes. Aerial explosives failed to ignite in the air, then changed their minds after falling into the crowd. Skyrockets did loops and barrel rolls, usually about head-level. Craig wanted to set up a stand, UNGUENTINE TO GO, but Nancy declared the surroundings too hazardous. As we left the square, we could hear screams of merriment interspersed with howls of pain, and looked forward to wishing the Mexicans well in our own, conservative way: a tequila *salud* in the calm of *Sea Foam*'s cockpit.

That night I lay awake, long after Nancy had drowsily disentangled herself and curled up for some serious sleeping. Nancy is a true optimist: given fact after depressing fact, she cheerily believes that reprieve is just around the corner. I'm with her until a certain point when the facts mobilize into a vast, invincible army. In this case I was going over our problems and options prior to waving the white flag.

1. We were obviously in need of expensive mechanical repairs.

2. We had only a few hundred dollars left.

3. We could never beat our way back up the coast of Baja with no engine.

4. As the hurricane season was upon us, we did not want to continue south without an engine.

5. We could sail to Hawaii and work, a repulsive thought for one so recently retired.

6. We could win our lawsuit.

7. We absolutely had to win our lawsuit....

The legion of musicians who elect to go into the nightclub business, knowing full well they can do a better job than the dummies they've been working for, makes a tragic roster equalled only by late-comers to a chain letter. The ratio of bankruptcy to survival is 99 to 1. Joe, my music partner, and I started out as the 1, the exception that proved the rule.

After only four months of operating The Painted Pony, a tiny bistro with a maximum capacity of 110, we had piled up scandalous profits. Our little operation was perfect for two morons who wanted to work 18 hours a day, seven days a week, doing everything from entertaining five hours a night to taking care of all the business details. But once we started delegating responsibility and thinking big, profits sifted into the pockets of others, and month after marathon month found us making less.

But to all outward appearances, business was booming. Waiting lines were standard on the weekends. Our club was run like a party. Between us, Joe and I could call over half our customers by name, and without being asked could come up with one of their favorite songs. But nothing dampens a party faster than a bloody fight. We had had a few—about normal for the business. Suddenly the number increased radically. One or two instigators turned up so frequently that we began to wonder if it was harassment planned by the competition.

After arguing the pros and cons, Joe and I decided to go to the police. An ex-musician worked in the plainclothes department, and we knew he'd be sympathetic. His name escapes me for the moment, so I'll call him Jock.

"Who's the worst of these guys?" he asked.

"Franco," I said promptly. "He comes in three times a week, at least." Franco was strong as an ox, gentle and friendly when sober, brutal and belligerent when drunk.

"Yeah, I know Franco. Don't you worry about a thing. That son of a bitch steps outa line one more time and I'll nail him. He won't bother you no more." With talk like that, I figured the Marines had landed and our worries were over. The only thing I didn't know was that everyone in the business knew who Jock was and what he did. He had about as much cover as a bottomless dancer.

About a week later I noticed a weirdo sitting at the end of the bar. He was a stocky, middle-aged number, neatly dressed and wearing sensible shoes. His hair, however, was trimmed Prince-Valiant style. The total effect was of a country sheriff wearing his wife's wig. My God, I thought, it's Jock!

Jock saw that I recognized him and semaphored for secrecy. It was rather a long semaphore, attracting the attention of most of the people in the room. Jock gave up in the middle and sidled over to the piano to whisper in my ear. All eyes followed him as he made his round trip. At the bar a few seats down from Jock sat Franco, drinking quietly and taking everything in.

The evening progressed uneventfully, with Franco behaving himself and Jock keeping him under surveillance. Finally Franco stood up, walked over to Jock.

"You lookin' at me?" Franco's delivery, when he's belligerent, is with his chin stuck out while talking through his nose, and he ends up sounding like Peter Lorre with a harelip.

"Not especially," said Jock, hard as nails.

"You been lookin' at me all night," said Franco, clenching his fist. "I don't like people lookin' at me. You wanna step outside?"

It was obvious Jock would have preferred to drink and spy. To his credit, however, he got up and went outside with Franco right behind him. The minute they reached the parking lot, Jock spun around. In his fist was a gun of sufficient caliber to make portholes.

"See this?" he yelled. "I'm the law, ya hear? You fuck around with me and I'm gonna blow your fucking head off." They stared at each other for a minute, after which Jock turned and, in true undercover style, sneaked off to his unmarked car.

Franco returned to the bar just long enough to punch out the only three customers with whom he could trump up a grievance. Then he left. Although he came back to sip a quiet drink several times during the next six months, he never gave us any more trouble.

If Franco was *my* nemesis, Giovanni was Joe's. Giovanni was a petty crook who liked to play big man around town with stolen credit cards, and his ersatz affluence acquired him a string of hangers-on.

One evening, Giovanni started making a play for Joe's girl. She was a new one, and Joe was feeling possessive. Joe watched Giovanni's campaign from the bandstand. I couldn't understand why Joe was calling all fast tunes. Finally Giovanni started dancing close to Joe's girl even though the music wasn't slow. Joe put up with about three and a half hip-grinds, then stopped the music in mid-measure.

"God damn it," he yelled at Giovanni from the bandstand, "I told you to leave my girl alone. You leave her alone, understand? And as for you," he said to the girl, "you sit down over there right now!"

Not very professional, you might say, but you've got to admit it's Italian. Giovanni played it cool, stayed around just long enough to prove he wasn't afraida nothin'. Then he split. A half-hour before closing he was back, along with 13 godsons. Although it was a hot night, all of them were wearing jackets. They dispersed throughout the club, as inconspicuous as erections in a locker room shower, and sat back to wait for the customers to leave. What few there were got the hint, and within minutes we had the place to ourselves.

"I didn't like that shit you gave me tonight," said Giovanni, wagging his finger under Joe's nose. "You know, if me an' my friends decide to, we can turn this dump into a warehouse." For a creep, he had some pretty descriptive lines.

"You're not supposed to use Saturday Night Specials on weekdays," I said.

"You think I'm kidding?" he asked, turning to me. I assured him I didn't.

What followed was the Old Italian Backdown Game, a game I'd witnessed so many times in my dozen years' association with Joe that I could give you the lines backwards.

Stage 1: You have _____ (insulted, injured, cheated) me. I will _____ (sue you, hit you, kill you, insult you back).

Stage 2: I'm sure you didn't mean to do what you did.

Stage 3: I'll be a big man and forgive you (but only if you play fair and forgive me).

Stage 4: Now that we've gone through this charade, we *respect* each other.

Stage 5: I'll buy you a drink.

Stage 6: You're supposed to buy *me* a drink.

Stage 7: We are now buddies (till next time).

As the months wore on, business dropped off, but Nancy's and my scale of living remained at halcyon height, and little by little we were going into debt. It was time to man the life rafts. We sold out to our only serious buyer. Within a year he was out of business, and as soon as the doors closed his monthly checks became bimonthly, then stopped altogether. He had a few hidden assets which our lawyer was going after. A few thousand dollars wouldn't make a dent on the amount we'd lost, but it was an amount that would determine whether we had a cruising future.

We must win that lawsuit, I thought groggily, my mind finally running down as dawn tinted the sky. We've absolutely *got* to win that lawsuit. . . .

EIGHT

W E LIMPED INTO ACAPULCO HARBOR, our appreciation of its beauty severely compromised by our empty pockets and the prospect of expensive repairs. We had made the 400-odd miles from Puerto Vallarta in four days, having powered most of the windless way. Our transmission had been slipping more and more, until at the last we were barely able to make two and a half knots. We rounded the point and dropped anchor about 400 yards off the yacht club quay and ate dinner, everyone glum and quiet.

After dinner, as I rowed over to the yacht club, I was greeted from the cockpit of a sleek, 50-foot steel ketch named *Scaldis*.

"Stand by for repelling boarders," slurred a cheery male voice.

Had I allowed my black mood to govern my first reaction ("Who are you calling repelling, fella?"), a lifelong friendship might have gotten off to a shaky start.

"Hi," I said, choosing my word carefully.

"Come aboard for a drink? My name's Phil Walker, and this is my wife, Flo."

"No, thanks," I said. "I'll take a raincheck. We just finished dinner."

"Any time. We watched you coming in—you sure have a beautiful little ship. Really pretty. Classic. What can we do for you?"

My ego preened, my heart warmed. Obviously the salt of the earth, this man.

"I'm looking for information," I answered. "Does the yacht club have a mechanic?"

"Yup. Virgilio will fix you up. Pretty reasonably, too, I suspect. You gonna anchor out? I wouldn't."

"Why not?"

"Lots of theft," he explained. "One night last week a guy anchored out, expecting a blow. Next morning he pulled up his stern anchor and found a rock tied to it. No note, nothing. He was happy they didn't take his bow anchor, too. But hell, man, if they'll go to *those* lengths . . ."

He let it hang, and I mused.

"How much does it cost here?" I asked.

"About five bucks a day for you. They've got a pool, showers, an expensive bar, guards with guns at the gate. There's a cheap restaurant across the street, a drive-in with good hamburgers a block away."

I brought the info back to *Sea Foam* and we talked it over. I couldn't believe what won them over. One month aboard, eating gourmet ship's fare, and they get turned on by a hamburger and a malted. I shook my head in wonder, but I was with them in line the next day when the Tastee Freeze window opened for lunch.

Next morning we met Virgilio, honcho; George, assistant honcho; and Emil, grunt. The trio arrived on board armed with nothing but three grins and the hope that I had all the necessary tools. I was a little worried about having to pay triple time, but I needn't have been. Virgilio collected his money, about what I would have expected to pay one good man in the depressed Mexican economy, and divided at least part of it with George and Emil, making each of them happy because, although nobody got very much, they hadn't had to work very hard either.

They spent a couple of days on *Sea Foam*, taking the injectors out and sending them to a lab and fixing the transmission, for which we finally had to order spare parts. When the injectors came back, the engine ran beautifully. By the time we reached Costa Rica, however, I discovered that we were getting diesel fuel in the crankcase, and my diesel lessons began.

Diesel engines are basically simple. There is no carburetor, no electrical ignition system. Fuel, filtered to pristine purity, is pumped under high pressure into the cylinders through injectors, which are essentially atomizers. There the vaporized diesel oil is compressed to such pressure that the temperature rises enough to ignite it. After combustion, the transfer of energy to the drive-shaft is exactly as in a gasoline engine.

In order to insure that enough fuel is pumped through each injector, the pump delivers more fuel than is necessary, and the surplus flows through a return line to be filtered and pumped again. On a Ford, part of the return line is inside the valve cover. It was this, I was convinced, that was leaking, allowing diesel to reach the crankcase through the valve-guides.

"We check the injectors, no?" asked Victor, the mechanic we hired in Punta Arenas, Costa Rica.

"No," I said. "The injectors were just serviced at the lab in Acapulco. It can't be them."

We inspected the return line, but because it was continually sprayed with a film of oil, a small leak would have been almost impossible to see. Victor removed the return line, replaced all seals with new ones, guaranteed his work, and left. One week later I called him back—there was still a leak. Having brain-washed him with my diagnosis, he, too, was convinced that the leak was coming from the return line. Once more he replaced all the seals, and we left confidently for Golfito.

The problem stayed with us. Herb Saxton, chief engineer for the large United Fruit operation in Golfito, loaned us Rocky, his best mechanic.

"We check the injectors, no?" he asked.

"No," I said. "They were just serviced at the lab in Acapulco. It can't be them."

We ran the engine for about an hour. With the valve cover removed, Rocky wiped the return line clean of oil and inspected it with a bright light and a magnifying glass. He did this over and over. Finally he turned to me.

"It does not leak," he said.

We continued to run the engine. Rocky gripped each injector feed line between thumb and forefinger, one after the other. The detection of a rhythmic pulse indicates that the pump is pumping fuel to that cylinder. After he was satisfied that the pump was pumping to all four cylinders, he removed, one at a time, each injector line from its injector. If he could hear a difference in the way the engine ran, we could safely assume that the disconnected cylinder was okay. After repeating these operations several times with the concentration of an internist, he looked at me compassionately.

"Could be the high-pressure pump," he said.

I had begun to fear the same thing. Pumps can cost over $1000. Tolerances are so close that they can only be repaired at great expense by specialists. If it was the pump, we were facing a long wait and a bill that to us would amount to a small fortune. Gloomily, I gave Herb Saxton Rocky's verdict.

"Have you taken out the injectors and tested them?" asked Herb.

"No," I replied. "They were recently completely gone over by a lab in Acapulco."

Herb looked at me, patient with my pathetic ignorance.

"When a diesel engine has a mysterious ailment, you *always* check the injectors. It's simple, costs next to nothing, and nine times out of ten it's the problem."

I slunk out of his office like a third-grader after a bawling out from the principal. We removed the injectors (an unnecessarily difficult task on a Ford, as they are inside the valve cover and pushrods must be removed to get at them) and brought them ashore to the tester. All four atomized perfectly at the specified 2700 pounds per square inch. One, however, produced an additional quarter-teaspoonful of unatomized fuel through a leaking seal. Herb laughed when I showed it to him.

"See?" he said. "The surfaces that make the seal must be of a smoothness so nearly perfect that it can only be measured using reflected light. Some idiot took sandpaper to this one." It had to have been the Mexican lab.

The lesson here was priceless, and applies to all types of diagnosis. Make a list of all possible causes of a particular malfunction, keeping in mind the possibility of multiple causes. List them on a scale from simple-and-cheap to complex-and-expensive. Work them through without making any assumptions or jumping to any conclusions. So elementary. So simple.

Yet it seems I'll never learn. Years later in American Samoa I was faced with the same problem—diesel getting into the crankcase—and without even a cursory look at the return line I confidently removed all the injectors and rowed across the bay to the shipyard to have them tested. None of their fittings fit my injectors. The machine shop took half a day to make some proper fittings. Then we put the injectors on the tester, one at a time. The gauge didn't register, so we had no idea at what pressure they were atomizing.

A day wasted, I replaced the injectors and did what I should have done in the first place: run the engine with the valve cover off. A myopic moron would have seen the leak in the return line. Ten minutes with some silver solder repaired it; my satisfaction at finally fixing something, however, was undercut by knowing that not only had I done it the hard way, but I would no doubt do it the hard way next time, too.

"We won, we won!" I cried, waltzing Nancy around the huge, overstaffed office of the Acapulco Yacht Club. "Ken says we won. I don't have to fly back to California—the lawsuit's settled."

"See?" said Nancy, for whom reprieve is never a surprise.

This meant that we would have plenty of money to get to Tahiti, and maybe even further. Our undercapitalized venture had been given new life. Nancy and I planned a prodigal week in Mexico City to celebrate.

Greyhound has a familiar slogan: "Next time take the bus, and leave the driving to us." I am among the many who can't do this. I drive every mile. The bus driver arrives at our destination fresh and relaxed, whereas I always need a shower and a stiff drink— but I never experienced anything like our bus ride to Mexico City.

Nancy is different. She has no faith in the laws of aerodynamics, so she distrusts planes. It makes no difference to her that pilots are carefully selected and highly trained, whereas Mexican bus drivers are dropouts from demolition derbies and act as if they'd trained on hashish and Superman comics. She has faith in the concept, "buses work." As a result, I drive each blind curve with clenched fist and knotted stomach, while Nancy reads and absent-mindedly pats my hand.

We boarded the bus to find that our reserved seats were right behind the driver, giving me the good visibility so necessary for safe driving, and absolutely guaranteeing my involvement. The bus was air-conditioned (excellent) and besides a driver carried a stewardess (yum), who would subsequently serve coffee and snacks (double yum). Unfortunately, though she gave me a choice of milk or no milk, I was not allowed a choice of sugar or no sugar. Mexicans realize that their coffee is unpalatable without four teaspoons of sugar per cup. I kept asking for my unpalatable coffee unsweetened, but all the way to Mexico City the stewardess stubbornly misunderstood me.

Bus timetables in Mexico are hopelessly optimistic. On an un-crowded, rainless weekday they might be in touch with reality, but we had chosen to travel on a rainy Sunday. Not only was the machismo maniac who was our chauffeur going to try to make it, he was handicapping himself with a start just late enough that we could only arrive on time by flying in the face of immutable kinetic law. I was given a hint of what was in store as we pulled away from the terminal, 22 minutes late, to the scream of tires, the cries of scattering pedestrians, and the mumbled incantations of our crucifix-fingering stewardess.

The two-lane highway climbed tortuously out of Acapulco, and 90 percent of the Sunday traffic was, like us, headed for Mexico City. Our driver's strategy was to play this statistic for all it was worth, counting heavily on the fact that a very low percentage of the few vehicles coming toward us would be as big as we were. The occasional times he was wrong we were lucky to be passing something small enough to force off onto the shoulder in our mad swerve to safety. But by the time we reached the top of the first range of mountains, we had traveled half the distance in the left lane, and I was an emotional mess.

Nancy offered to drive for a while, but we've tried that on

other trips and it's never worked. She finally drew my attention away from the road by informing me that the stomach upset we'd all had for the past week was bothering her again and she felt like throwing up. My memory of the remaining 50 miles to the rest stop is that of riding in a runaway missile while sitting next to a ticking bomb.

We had a ball in Mexico City, spending all the money we had with us on hotel, sightseeing, drinking, and dining. When we got back to Acapulco, we were once again down to our last few dollars. We had sent a letter asking for more, but no one at home believes you when you tell them the only form that is instantly negotiable: a Mexican money order. It always goes the same way.

Friend or relative: "Good morning. I'd like to buy a Mexican money order for $300, please."

Banker: "Why?"

Friend or relative: "I want to send some money to a friend in Acapulco."

Banker: "Oh. Well, then, what you want is one of our _____ (cashier's checks, standard money orders, international money orders)."

Friend or relative (not wanting to hassle around to other banks if he can avoid it, and believing erroneously that bankers know the banking business): "Well, if you think it would be just as good ..."

It isn't. The Mexican banker will look at you compassionately but resolutely.

"I am sorry, Señor, but this is not a *Mexican* money order. You will have to wait for it to clear the American bank. This will take from one to three months."

So we were temporarily broke, but we weren't as badly off as Charlie Gonzales. Charlie was a Chilean. Under Chile's then-Communist government, he was not allowed to take a vacation outside the country with his family; they knew he'd never return to Chile. So he sent his family off to Europe while he remained at his job. Then, one Sunday, he went for a sail in his 30-foot sloop and never turned back.

His first night in Acapulco, he was awakened at 3:00 A.M. by the Mexican police, who held him at gunpoint while they turned his boat inside out looking for dope. It seems they'd had a tip that the couple whom Charlie had taken on as crew in Panama were smuggling. Fortunately for Charlie, the couple had left that afternoon, taking with them all incriminating goods, if in truth there were any. The cops finally certified Charlie clean, but left him badly shaken.

From then on, Charlie spent every day at a table on the patio of the yacht club bar. His companions varied, ranging from garrulous sailor to unattached sailoress, but the invariable item was the never-empty martini glass in hand.

He kept telling everyone he was going to leave, but the next day would find him back at the watering trough. When he had gone through what money he had, he talked kindhearted Phil Walker out of $200, purportedly to provision for leaving. Still he continued with his daily routine, and Phil regretfully watched his money being converted, glass by glass, into gin.

The rest of the *Scaldis* crew decided to take a hand in giving Charlie a sendoff. They had a roisterous farewell party that lasted all one day in the bar, during which Charlie's courage grew by leaps and bounds. He swore adamantly that he would leave the following afternoon.

The next morning, some fellow yachtsmen got Charlie out of bed. It took several rehabilitative martinis to prime Charlie enough to talk to, and several more to shore up his crumbling resolve. They then led him back to his boat and helped him navigate her over to the fuel dock, after which they gave him a thermos of martinis and pointed him out the channel.

At the time I was convinced that I had witnessed a cruel and callous sendoff, but I was wrong on three counts:

1. Charlie made it to Los Angeles, where he sold the boat. He thence made it to New York, where he rejoined his family, and, in time, he repaid Phil's $200.

2. I have since decided that Charlie might never have left Acapulco without such drastic treatment.

3. After many years of cruising I have increased my respect for the sea and my appreciation for shelter to the point that, were it not for the objections of the crew, I would leave every port in exactly the same condition Charlie did.

Not long after Charlie's departure, Nancy and I were having cocktails on *Scaldis* with Cole Weston, the boat's owner, and Phil and Flo Walker. It, too, was a farewell party. Phil and Flo, professional cinematographers, were Cole's partners in a movie-making venture. The film was to be called *Aroha*.

Cole, the son of one of America's greatest black-and-white photographers, Edward Weston, was enjoying a growing reputation for his color photography, but his second love had always been sailing. His grown sons, Ivor and Kim, and his 16-year-old daughter, Cara, made up the crew. Their planned route was the same as ours, the only difference being that we Seafoamers hoped to continue west after Tahiti.

Their plan intrigued me. Cruising needs no purpose. Sufficient unto itself, cruising simply *is*. But it will keep its enchantment far longer if, attached to it, there is a special interest, like shelling or photography, or a project, like a movie.

"I think *Sea Foam* should be in your movie," I said. *Scaldis* was leaving in the morning, and there was no time for beating around the bush.

"That would be nice," said Phil drily, "but unfortunately we have to leave. We're already way behind schedule, and we've only just started."

We were waiting for transmission parts. It was impossible for us to sail when *Scaldis* did.

"I really think we should be in your movie," I said, following my usual habit of ignoring facts. "How are you going to take pictures of *Scaldis* under sail? We could be your camera boat, your comrades at arms."

"Herb is so droll," said Flo. "Isn't Herb droll, Darling?"

"Most amusing," said Phil.

"Have another drink," said Cole, reaching for the shaker.

It was getting late. Nancy and I said our goodbyes. As we walked along the quay in the balmy, tropical evening, heading for *Sea Foam* and supper, I mused that I, having had a taste of notoriety as an entertainer, was probably more susceptible to fame's blandishments than most.

"I don't think they *want* us to be in their movie," I confided wistfully.

"No kidding," said Nancy with a grin. And there, for the time being, the matter rested.

NINE

THE OLDER I GET, the more things there are that tend to make me nervous. I don't see myself as full of cowardice, but as lacking in courage. Given death on the one hand and destruction on the other, I have occasionally behaved in manly fashion, but show me an easy way out and I take it. People say, "Hey, you sold everything—went to sea!" But it was fear of a boring middle age, of missing great portions of life, which forced my decision. Hornblower, Hillary, or Chichester I'm not.

Before setting sail from Acapulco, I was nervous about three things: (1) the local hurricane season had started, and we were heading for the area where most of them formed; (2) the Gulf of Tehuantepec, which we had to cross, had a reputation for sudden, violent storms from the north that were known, irreverently, as Tehuantepeckers (their thunderclouds as Tehuantepeckerheads); and (3) the natives between Mexico and Costa Rica were hostile.

As for the hurricanes, I was already breathing easier. The further south we got, the safer we were. Although we might run into the beginning stages of one, we would soon be out of the area where tropical depressions build up to devastating cyclonic force. In spite of statistics, a rogue can kill. Statistics were all we had, though, and in those days I placed great faith in them.

Furthermore, we had gone round the Gulf of Tehuantepec in a flat calm, running the diesel at least nine-tenths of the time and keeping close to shore as we'd been advised. Our only minor thrill came one night when, sailing to a light breeze, we were struck by an angry squall. We got the sails down without damage, and 45 minutes later we were steaming along under power again, the sea a millpond, the darkness a blindfold, the lightless coast presumably three or four miles to port. Powering is dull at best, but it is a real downer to power a sailboat, constantly aware of how much more pleasant it would be to sail. I had to keep reminding myself that the alternative was to sit still. In my scale of values the order is fair winds, calms, headwinds, storms, so we weren't doing too badly.

What we *were* doing was rapidly using up our diesel. We wanted to spend time cruising northern Costa Rica, and we guessed—correctly—that fuel there would be hard or impossible to come by. I had studied the map. Guatemala: dangerously anti-American. Tiny El Salvador: at war with tiny Honduras on alternate Tuesdays and Thursdays. Nicaragua: perpetually in the throes of revolution. It was even said of nervous Nic that if a boat sailing the coast failed to show a friendly flag to patrol planes, she might very well be strafed. The one bright spot was Acajutla, El Sal, which a friend had recommended as a possible pit stop. We were approaching Acajutla now, and the time was coming when I would be forced into deciding "pass" or "no pass." As usual I was putting it off as long as possible.

"What're we going to do, Dad?" It was son Philip, pushing.

"I don't know," I said. "It's an open roadstead—no protection from waves or weather. It'll be dark by the time we get there. Tomorrow's Sunday, and the officials will be annoyed if they have to process us on a weekend. It could be expensive. I don't know."

"George said we could anchor behind the breakwater. There aren't any hazards, so darkness isn't a problem. And if the officials are nasty we can just leave."

"What if they put an armed guard on the boat?" I asked.

"Oh, come *on*, Dad," said Philip.

I relented, and we motored in. It was a piece of cake. That night we all slept like logs after our five-day passage, our longest so far.

With two other yachts, we planned to sail the rhumb line to Costa Rica rather than hug the coast. We had four reasons for doing so: (1) It would be shorter and, with fair winds, about a half-day quicker. (2) The coast was straight and exposed, offering no chance to duck for shelter. (3) Unless the breeze was offshore, in heavy weather it would be safer at sea than close to land. (4) If disaster struck, it would be comforting to have another boat close by.

The sleeper, sabotaging this arsenal of logic, was in (3): "unless the breeze was offshore." The first night we battled several squalls, one of which was particularly violent. By morning the winds were east-southeast, averaging 25 knots, driving us 15° seaward of our course. At noon it had increased to 30 knots, and either the added force or a slight change in wind direction was pushing us farther off course, farther out to sea. We were power-sailing with staysail and reefed mizzen. By 1400 the winds had increased further, and I decided to head for the lee of land, even though this would mean a 40-mile detour. By dawn we had picked up the coast, the wind and seas having diminished radically. The only damage was the loss of our American ensign, and a small tear in the staysail. And, of course, the discomfort of having everything soaked below.

"God *damn*," I said, coming topsides at dawn. "We've lost our ensign." Paranoia, always ready to leap into the breach if my mind isn't concentrating on something, flashed me vivid scenes illustrating the disadvantages of being a strafee. "We're in Nicaraguan waters and we've got no *flag!*"

"Relax, love," said Nancy. "Maybe one of the other boats has one we can borrow."

One did. The flag was brilliant of color and the size of a double bed. At great risk to bowsprit and standing rigging, it was transferred to *Sea Foam* in the heavy swell. I kept it by the companionway available for quick display, but we never saw even one plane.

Because of the offshore wind, our decision to sail the rhumb line rather than follow the coastline cost us a half-day instead of gaining it. So much for the best-laid plans. But though the percentages gave the edge to offshore wind, even more dangerous would have been to bet the short odds and follow the coast, then run into onshore winds. I no longer make decisions based on saving time, and have adopted, where possible, a bet-hedging philosophy. In my next life I will follow the coast at a distance of five to ten miles, hopefully retaining the options of shelter and sea room.

The approach to Bahia Elenas is striking: rugged green hills with a canyonlike cut for an entrance. Once inside we were virtually landlocked, completely sheltered. One large ranch across the bay purportedly belonged to the president of Nicaragua, but it was quiet, pastoral, unimpinging on our solitude. It was Eden, beautiful enough in and of itself, but enhanced by contrast with the open ocean, and for three days it belonged solely to us, a perfect environment for beachcombing, swimming, puttering, and our first meal of octopus.

People rave about octopus. I can endure the taste if the garlic sauce is strong enough, but the only people for whom it might be a bona fide treat would be marathon bubble-gum chewers. I had good octopus once, in a paella, but the fisherman should have been arrested for infanticide, as the tentacles were so small I mistook them for bean sprouts. *The Joy of Cooking*, encyclopedic as it is, gives instructions on how to make mature tentacles tender, but I can assure you that all the recommended methods are totally ineffectual. I have beaten tentacles with a club for hours, and the only achievements were tenderized hands and spirits. Perhaps someday I'll have the opportunity to order octopus in the Tour d'Argent, albeit with a touch of pessimism.

An added attraction of Bahia Elenas was the sight of *Scaldis* lying quietly at anchor, weeks behind schedule. Our timing couldn't have been better: Phil Walker had decided they would need a camera boat after all. Getting involved in their film project still sounded like something that would add excitement to our cruising. Furthermore, as it turned out, if we hadn't gotten tied up with *Scaldis*, the officials in the Galapagos would never have let us in. So when I offered Phil Walker our services once again, our guardian angel, working overtime, smiled and murmured, "Right on!"

The following day, *Scaldis* and *Sea Foam* sailed across the Gulf

of Papagayo, with Phil Walker's probing lens recording our progress. We arrived in the tiny beach town of Playa del Cocos and
met Sarah, 16, my youngest daughter, who would cruise Costa
Rica with us. By way of a welcome to Sarah and a thank-you to
Sea Foam for acting as camera boat, Phil Walker footed the bill
for a party at the local open-air restaurant. Food and wine fueled
toasts and songs. Somewhere toward the end of the evening, Phil
W. and I had a slightly muddled but still coherent talk.

"Got some great pictures from *Sea Foam*. Great pictures. Really
great."

"Yeah?" I said. "Too bad there wasn't more wind. The pictures of *Scaldis* sailing couldn't be all that exciting."

"No, but that's all right. That's all right. Kind of in the mood
of the thing, you know, the placid tropics, the contentment of
serenely lazing along, nudged and coaxed by friendly, gentle
zephyrs, rocked in the arms of the all-encompassing sea, suspended in a timeless wonderment of—"

"Gotcha, Phil. Gotcha. Gotcha, Babe," I said, reaching for the
wine bottle. Empty. Just as well, except that Phil was probably
lonely up there, and I wanted to join him.

"Great pictures of young Phil, too, boating that sailfish. Great
action, drama of the sea, man battling the raging forces of—"

"Gotcha, Phil. Gotcha, Babe." Stopped him in mid-takeoff.
Where's that hostess, damn it? I'll spring for another bottle myself. Ah, she's coming, finally.

"Great pictures of young Chris, too, landing the mahi-mahi,
Nature giving up Ocean's generous bounty, rich store of suste-
nance from briny depths, nutrient in finny splendor."

Hang on, I thought, filling my glass to blast-off level. I'll be
right with you.

"Great shots of you, too: skipper at the helm, piloting skillfully across the unpredictable Gulf of Papagayo, soldier of fortune, intrepid wanderer seeking adventure and welcoming danger, braving the unknown, hurling your body into the Bessemer
of experience."

I love it, I love it—never mind that we'd been shooting in a flat calm, I love it. And who cared that *Aroha* might never make the drive-in circuit back home? I was already picturing my name in lights.

We chose to retrace our steps across the Gulf of Papagayo for two reasons: the boys had learned of a surfing spot near there, and we wanted to visit the Bat Islands. We had passed these uninhabited islands on our way from Bahia Elenas to Playa del Cocos, unable to stop because of our rendezvous with Sarah. I had looked wistfully at the empty, protected cove, at the sandy beach, and at the rolling hills, just right for climbing, dressed in virgin new growth after a lightning strike had burned off the old underbrush. We had already found that some anchorages are better than others, and that idyllic ones are rare. For each perfect anchorage there are nine with flies, mosquitoes, poor holding ground, insufficient shelter, too many neighbors, a 24-hour cannery, or a sewer outflow. The isolated beauty of the Bat Islands drew us like a magnet.

We spent several days there. Each morning, Chris and Philip would be taken to nearby Ackerman Island and left there to surf. *Sea Foam* would return to the Bat Islands to spend the day, where we would snorkel, sunbathe, or roam the grassy hills. In the evenings we sardined it below or, if it was clear, ate picnic-style topsides. The sleeping arrangements were like a Korean flophouse: Craig and Philip in one double, Conni and Sarah in another, Nancy and I in our stateroom, and Chris on a pipe berth in the fo'c's'le. Most of the time, the cabin looked like a rummage sale in a rat's nest. Topside looked like drying day at summer camp. We were happy as clams.

One day another sailboat came in. She looked as though she had been sailing to weather for 20 years. The old rubber dinghy had once been gray. Now it was a rainbow of patches, the original color almost completely hidden. The skipper was a middle-aged man, slender, who had just completed a voyage around the world. He had built the boat with a partner, and about the time of commissioning, the partner had died. After nearly a year's fruitless search for another partner, his mother volunteered to make the trip with him. She was one of the world's stauncher 70-odds, and crewed every mile. They were an impressive pair, stoic and determined. I often wondered how he handled his odyssean tales:

"Mother and I rounded South Africa during a . . ." "Mother took the helm, while I took a double reef in the . . ." "I said to the bosun, I said, 'Mother!' "

Heroic as their story is, it lacks that epic zing.

The day we were to leave, Nancy, Craig, and I climbed to the top of the highest hill, cameras in hand, to capture *Sea Foam*, isolated and regal in the cove below. We circled the slope, startling gulls and iguanas. Panting and sweating, we finally crested the summit. *Sea Foam* was lazing at anchor, the two girls sunbathing on the foredeck. One boatlength away was a Costa Rican shrimper, all hands on deck.

"I don't believe it," I groaned.

"Oh well," said Nancy, who rarely fails to turn adversity into good fortune. "I'll bet we can trade for some fresh shrimp. Wouldn't that be yummy?"

"And ice," I added, brightening at the thought of cold drinks. "But if you're thinking what I think you're thinking, the girls'll never go for it."

"I'm thinking of gin, dummy. Or .22s. Or *Playboys*."

By the time we reached *Sea Foam*, the girls had gone below. The fishermen were wandering in and out of the pilothouse, eyeing us hopefully.

"Get up on deck in bikinis," I told the girls. "Tactics. We're going to storm the storehouse of the treasure of the seas."

Nancy and I rowed the three strokes over to the shrimp boat and were ushered aboard like visiting royalty. Conni and Sarah puttered around *Sea Foam*'s deck, striking postures.

"Buenos tardes," I said, exhausting 20 percent of my Spanish in one swoop. "Como estas?"

"Bueno," said the captain, easily looking over the top of my head at *Sea Foam*. "You like shrimp?"

"Sí," we chorused. A deckhand appeared immediately with ten pounds of fresh shrimp.

"That's too much," I said. "We have no refrigerator on board."

I hardly had the words out when another deckhand, all smiles, appeared with a 30-pound block of ice in a wooden crate. The shrimp was packed around the ice and put into our dinghy.

"We come see your boat later, okay?" said the captain.

"Sure," I said. "Any time."

Later stretched into hours. What little we could see indicated that the whole crew was bathing and shaving. The time had long passed when we should have left to pick up Philip and Chris at their surfing spot.

"I thought they'd come over right away," I said to Nancy. "What do we do now?"

"Row over with a bottle and some girlie magazines and tell them we'll see them some other time—we have to go."

"You wouldn't like to do it, would you?"

"It's your job, brave captain," said Nancy. "Go get 'em."

The skipper greeted me warmly, and soberly accepted the gin and magazines.

"We come soon, no?"

"I'm sorry," I said. "We have to leave. We have to go pick up our boys."

Shrimper captains in Costa Rica are promoted according to physical size. This one was slated for admiral of the fleet. I watched dark clouds of anger gather round his Olympian brow.

"You come back here?" His voice reminded me of distant thunder.

"No. We go to Huevos Bay. We'll see you some other time."

"Huevos Bay. Okay." His hand enveloped my hand and lower forearm. "We see you later." His tone was one part courtesy, nine parts vendetta. My feelings were one part apology, nine parts compulsion to flee. I fled. As we raised anchor and powered out of the cove, five Costa Ricans watched us, their spruced and shining faces ranging from glum to sullen.

We picked up the boys, and for the third time powered across the ever-fearsome Gulf of Papagayo in a flat calm. At last light we dropped anchor in Huevos Bay. Iced drinks sluiced away twinges of guilt. A shrimp feast banished remnants of remorse. With no thought of what tomorrow might bring, we slept with the innocence of Fate's favored prodigals.

Whenever Conni was aboard, she took over the job of being Craig's teacher. The morning after the shrimp feast, she and Sarah took Craig to the other side of a tiny island where they found a secluded beach, Craig to take his term test, the girls to get away from the boat for a little reading, sunbathing, and swimming in private. They'd been gone maybe an hour when the shrimper barged into the bay and anchored a few hundred yards away. The captain and two crew promptly lowered a huge punt, climbed in, and rowed over.

"Come aboard," I said, my back to the wall. I could have saved my breath—the captain had one huge calf over the bulwarks, and as I said "aboard," *Sea Foam* gave a lurch to starboard. Soon we were sitting around the cockpit, binnacle substituting for campfire, mizzenmast for totem pole, peace pipe conspicuously absent.

"Drink?" I asked. It was 10:00, 10:30 at the latest. Silent nods answered, and I went below to bartend. I poured the shrimper captain a double.

"The girls—they aren't here?" I could tell from the tone of his voice that he'd missed breakfast.

"They've gone on a picnic," said Nancy. "They'll be gone all day."

The captain handed me his glass, empty, and nodded toward the companionway, his meaning obvious. I hadn't seen him suck up the first one, and chalked up sleight-of-mouth as another of Gargantua's talents. After he'd downed his second drink in an eight-ounce swallow, four ounces of which were vodka, he leaned forward and jackhammered my sternum with his forefinger.

"You have bullets? .22s?"

"You bet," I said. "But only a few," I added. Barter as a means of appeasement appealed to me, but I still had courage enough to resist large-scale extortion.

"You give bullets, we kill a deer, have a big party tonight. You bring your girls," he added.

"Okay," I replied, buying time. I dug out a box of 50, and after a final drink he climbed back into his punt. As his men rowed him homeward, he smiled and waved, his first sign of friendliness since the Big Bat Island Rebuff.

"Shall we stay?" asked Nancy.

"It might turn out to be fun," I said. "Sometimes these things are."

"Fun for whom?" she muttered.

We kept an eye on the shrimper. Eventually the whole ship's company appeared on deck and climbed into the punt. Freeboard was only a memory. They sang as they went, a rhythmic, boisterous tune, and once in a while the pop of a rifle would highlight the downbeat. During the afternoon we could hear shouts from afar and an occasional shot. It didn't take much to deduce that all animals not totally deaf had long since split for sanctuary.

About 3:30 the girls returned with Craig. We weighed anchor, raised sail, and ghosted out of Huevos, the shouts and pops of the distant safari coming clearly across the acoustic perfection of the calm bay. It wasn't until we'd rounded the point, putting another peninsula between them and us, that we dared hope we'd get clean away. We anchored in Culebra for the night, spoke more softly than usual, and said our private prayers. From then on, each sighting of a shrimp boat evoked a spate of plans for evasive action, but Gargantua never reappeared. For all I know he is still stomping, shouting, and shooting his way into Papagayan legend.

TEN

S AILING DOWN THE COAST to the Gulf of Nicoya, our biggest hazards were either mating turtles or debris disgorged by swollen rivers. There were so many logs afloat that we hated to sail in the dark. Nancy's and my preference to anchor every night, the girls' desire to press on, and the boys' insistence that we investigate each point for surfable waves, all stretched the strings of our dispositions to a brilliant pitch. As we gunk-holed south mile by mile, *Sea Foam* shrank inch by inch. Thus, when we finally reached Punta Arenas we shot ashore like a hail of bullets. For about a fortnight we indulged in an orgy of shore-side pleasures: a barbecued-pig feast on the beach at Joe Hill's (an American expatriate who offered yachtsmen the hospitality of his cove, and, for a small fee, his modest facilities), number-less treks through the streets of Punta Arenas sampling cheap Chinese food, engorgement of ice cream, and two fantastic meals at Ken Hayes's island restaurant.

Our last port before jumping off for the Galapagos was Puerto Armuelles, an open roadstead at the northern border of Panama. The morning we were to leave on our very first offshore passage, we discovered a huge air bubble in the compass. The compass card floats in liquid so as not to overreact to the boat's motion. There is an airchamber, ingeniously designed to allow the liquid to expand and contract harmlessly with varying temperatures. Eventually, in the Galapagos, I removed the compass from the binnacle, turned it upside down and shook it, gently. The bubble magically disappeared, but at Puerto Armuelles, I knew from nothing.

I'd already struggled for three profane hours that morning with the stopped-up head, and the meteorology of my psyche was by now storm warnings and gales. I set out in the dinghy for town in order to post a frantic request for advice from the compass company, and to buy a "plumber's friend" with which I planned either to fix or to destroy the head. On my way ashore, I was hailed from the cockpit of another yacht, a sleek Offshore 40 named *Black Duke*.

"Come on aboard, neighbor." He was fit, pleasant, and appeared to be in his late fifties.

"Another time," I said, trying to keep my burning hatred of all things mechanical from making me sound too brusque. "We're trying to get away today, and I have to get into town before the stores close for lunch."

"Aw, you've plenty of time. It's only ten o'clock. Besides, you look like you could use a drink."

What the hell, I thought to myself. This is one of those days.

The minute I climbed aboard, a full glass was placed in my hand, and during the next hour of conviviality it was never allowed to become empty. His name, Ed; his wife's, Opal. They gave me a tour of the yacht, pointing out items of interest between, beside, and above countless cases of Panamanian rum.

"It's hard to get enough booze for long passages on a boat this small," Ed confided, "so we stick pretty close to the coast."

I barely made it to town before the stores closed, but the euphoric abandon with which I attacked the head brought success in only 20 minutes. We had a quick lunch and were just about battened down for sea when Ed and Opal rowed over from *Black Duke* and climbed aboard, bottle in hand.

"Just a little sendoff party," said Ed, filling glasses all around.

Ed, over six feet tall and with holding tanks in both legs, seemed, except for ebullience, to have felt no effect from the liquor he'd been consuming since before 10:00 that morning. After an hour of lie-swapping, Ed poured Opal into his dinghy. *Sea Foam* weighed anchor and set sail, surfing a pipeline of synthetic optimism.

During the next two years I published several cruising articles. In two of them I referred to portions of our encounter with Ed and Opal, as I thought it was an amusing bit. Not wanting to make capital out of the foibles of friends, I was careful to identify neither them nor their boat; I knew for sure, however, that if they read the stories they would recognize themselves.

Exactly three years later, in a harbor in the Marquesas, we again encountered *Black Duke*. As we rowed past, I wondered aloud if Ed and Opal would remember us. I needn't have worried.

We were about 50 yards away when I saw a tiny figure in the cockpit, glass in hand, rise unsteadily to her feet. With a sinking feeling of *déjà vu*, I knew that one of my bad dreams was actually about to take place.

"You're that writer fella, ain'tcha?" It was good ol' Opie, and there was certainly nothing wrong with her vision *or* her vocal cords.

"Hi, Opal," I said. "Hi, Ed." It's hard to make a full shout sound warm and friendly, but I was trying.

"It's you! It's you! You *bas*tard! You *bas*tard!"

Oh shit, I thought to myself. She read the stories, took offense, and now I'm really gonna get it.

"You bastard," she shrieked again, having tumbled on a good line and now reluctant to give it up. "You wrote that story about us and you didn't even mention our *names.*"

We finally raised anchor and set sail for the Galapagos. The wind was fair, the day was sunny, and we were revelling in the stereo rhythms of Santana, Chicago, and the Grateful Dead. We were a Norman Rockwell painting of yachting bliss, off on our first blue-water crossing, well supplied and excitedly optimistic. The boys spotted a flock of birds to windward. Fish—maybe mahi-mahi! I pushed the starter button. No response. I switched to the reserve battery. Zero. Both banks together only produced a weak click. With no way to charge the batteries, we were suddenly without an engine.

We knew it would probably be a windward trip. We'd also heard about sailboats with no engines getting caught in the Humboldt Current and being swept helplessly past the Galapagos, unable to make it back. We were only one day out, on a broad reach. We talked it over. The vote was unanimous. We came about and headed back.

Later I discovered what had fooled me. The master battery switch connections were reversed. When we thought we were using the working batteries we were actually using the reserve. And because the windlass, searchlight, depthmeter, and radio were wired directly to the working batteries, we had been draining both banks instead of just one. (We have since bought a small, portable generator, one of our smarter moves. It powers drill, sander, or saber saw, and has rescued our battery from impending death several times.)

The electric circuits righted, we set sail for the Galapagos a second time. The first few days were beautiful sailing to a beam reach. The third day out the head broke. This was my first time repairing it at sea, and the rolling swells conspired to make the job dirtier and more difficult than ever. Three hours later the new part was installed, the head was back together, and I had made the usual apologies all around for my language.

Nancy and I were sitting below, reviving over a hot cup of tea. Suddenly Nancy gasped and pointed wordlessly at the companionway ladder. Smoke was pouring out from behind it!

The motor was off; the stove, too. What was it? I swung the ladder out of the way. Through the acrid, dense cloud I could see wires, glowing red. I grabbed the nearest thing at hand, a hammer, and ripped out the burning wires.

As soon as the smoke had cleared, the source of the problem was evident. We had been taking a lot of spray, and a small leak in the mizzen boot had allowed water to get into the depthmeter amplifier, causing a direct short. There was a fuse in the amp, but none between it and the battery. The power cord, in a dying moment of glory, had incandesced like the element of a toaster. Each of us had a colorful comment about the way the instrument had been installed.

The wind stayed brisk, even freshened a little. We asked ourselves if we were sailing *Sea Foam* too hard. We were close-reaching under full sail in 20-to-25 knot apparent winds. We had sailed her this hard many times, but that was near home, safety, and a marine hardware store. Nancy, always the most cautious sailor on board, was bugging me to reduce sail. I was on the point of giving in when the eyebolt to which one of the jibsheet blocks was shackled snapped off. The sheet slackened, the jib flapped wildly. Philip quickly winched it in, and the sail filled, the only difference being that the sheet now rubbed on the corner of the cabin trunk.

"Easy to fix," said Philip. "We can just lash the block to the bulwarks at a scupper, at least till we get a new eyebolt. No problem."

Hardly were the words out of his mouth when there was a sharp *crack!* The jibstay was suddenly a wide, graceful arc instead of a nearly straight line.

"Into the wind—the dolphin striker's broken," yelled Philip.

He and Chris got the jib down in seconds, and I went forward to look at the damage. It was true. The dolphin striker was sticking out at a crazy angle. The jumper stay to the tip of the bowsprit was hanging in the water. A swaged stainless-steel fitting had just cracked apart.

I felt a sickening wave of depression wash over me. Was *Sea Foam* turning into the one-horse shay? How many of her aging fittings—and maybe even fastenings, I thought morbidly—were crystallized? Would we awaken one night to the snap, crackle, and pop of metal, a floating disaster? Or, worse, a sinking pile of junk?

"Everything looks fine, now that the strain is off the jibstay," said Chris, and I returned to reality. If the wind would ease, we could jury-rig something and still be able to use the jib, at least in light airs. We'd have to. *Sea Foam* had a hard time going to weather as it was. Without a jib she would virtually heave to and go nowhere. The three of us stood on the foredeck discussing how we would support the tip of the bowsprit using a block and tackle and the anchor windlass. Having worked it out, we went back to the routine of watch-and-watch sailing.

Peace lasted till dusk, when Chris tried to turn on the running lights. Nothing. We had been having a nagging problem keeping the bulb contacts free of moisture and corrosion, but usually applying a little carbon tetrachloride and twisting the bulb back and forth had restored contact. This time, however, all the lights were out—masthead, stern, port, and starboard. They had all been wired economically through the same fuse.

It had been a wet sail, and I figured I knew what the problem was. Two hours and three fuses later I found the connection where the wires had been twisted together and poorly taped. Water had gotten in and shorted the circuit. Until months later, when I was able to get materials for completely rewiring all the running lights, I never was sure when I turned them on if they were going to light or not.

Sometime later I was awakened by a loud crash. I struggled sleepily up the companionway to find Philip at the helm and Chris already on deck.

"Wha's a trouble?" I mumbled from another world.

"Spinnaker pole fell down," said Philip.

The fitting on the pole end had broken. I'd guessed from the sound that it must at least have gone right through the deck, but aside from a dent there had been no damage. Chris secured the pole on deck as I headed below to warm bunk and deep sleep. In the morning we took down the other spinnaker pole from the mast, where it had been secured vertically, and lashed it on deck. We were no longer going to risk being bombed by an 18-foot, solid-spruce missile.

It was our fourth day out, and all day long we waited to see what kind of disaster would strike next. In the afternoon the wind eased, and we were able to jury-rig the bowsprit and raise the jib. Everything seemed solid. The bowsprit was well-enough supported that I figured we could safely fly the jib in winds up to 20 knots.

The sixth day out we passed a huge sperm whale. It was dead, floating high in the water. Fortunately we were upwind of it. Hundreds of birds were circling, and schools of fish were everywhere, churning the surface to foam. We caught a mahi-mahi and had a banquet of fish stew and banana cake.

The day before landfall, I fixed our position at 1400 as being 50 miles northeast of Tower Island, and planned to sight it at midnight or thereabouts. Tower is 210 feet high. By 0100 we hadn't seen a thing, and a heavy overcast blocked out all the stars. There was a faint mist which seemed to rise from the surface of the sea.

Remember, Herb babe? Remember that night? It's the landfall of your very first ocean passage, and you're depending solely on your shaky celestial navigation. Think about it. By your calculations you are playing tag with some very hard islands and you can see nothing. Nancy is at the helm. You are sailing under staysail and main, loafing along at about three knots. You look into blackness and see more blackness. Remember? No sky, no horizon, no land. Your world is a pocket, zipped tightly shut, and Sea Foam *is in it.*

With no visual reference beyond your boat, you soon feel totally blind. You strain your eyes, at first confident that you'll see land in time to avoid hitting it. You strain, still seeing not one thing, and gradually your confidence erodes. Where you thought you could see a mile or so, it now feels more like two feet. Your palms begin to sweat. You want to heave to, but the currents here sometimes reach a speed of four knots, and you feel in better control making slow progress under sail, so you want to keep sailing and *you want to heave to. You keep sailing.*

Finally, about 0300, the mist clears, but the sky remains overcast. Somehow you can barely make out a horizon, the sky being an infinitesimally lighter shade of black. Against this, to the west, you almost make out a huge, jet-black mass that interrupts the straight line of the horizon. Almost. After looking away and looking back again and catching it in your peripheral vision, you finally are sure. Land ho, softly, to yourself. And thank you, Lord. Must be very close if you can see it, you think. Very close indeed.

I stayed on deck till sunrise. The shadow took color, perspective. It was Marchena, 1100 feet high, and no less than 12 miles away. We never did see Tower, which we'd left about 18 miles to port.

We crossed the equator wearing parkas and mittens, the cold a result of the Humboldt Current, and tossed kind Neptune a warming jigger of gin. Our landfall, the island of Baltra, was barren and desolate, with a few run-down shacks for the officials who had been banished there, but we thought it beautiful. The little bay was a meteorological phenomenon. It seemed to boast 30-knot winds all the time no matter how calm it was outside. But it protected us from chop and swell and seemed comfy as a womb.

We had made it. We'd passed our initiation as blue-water sailors. We'd coped adequately with emergencies. Most important, our idealized concept of the cruising life had been tempered by reality. A good night's sleep and we were more eager than ever to explore, to learn, and to grapple with whatever might come. We hadn't changed our minds.

ELEVEN

SCALDIS HAD ARRIVED in Baltra before us, and her crew was eager to continue their quest for cinematic fame and fortune. Consequently we were all dismayed to find that we'd probably be tossed out of the Galapagos on our ears. New government. New policy. New restrictions. Over 50 yachts had cruised the Galapagos that summer, thanks to a policy that had required no advance visa. Life is timing, and we'd blown it.

Phil Walker decided to fly to Quito, the capital of Equador, where he would sweet-talk for *Scaldis* and include us as part of their movie-making project. Phil knew some people he hoped would impress the authorities, including some bigwig on the staff of *National Geographic*. The big guns in his arsenal of logic were that he had invested a ton of money in this film, that he had left the U.S. at a time when no advance visa was necessary and had been told so by the Equadorian Consul in L.A., and that in our journey down the coast we had not learned that there were new rules. We agreed that the argument was irresistible and cheerfully waved him goodbye, after which we retired below to sit around and think positive.

In just two hours Phil was back. The weekly plane had been overbooked by 40 people. Our prospects had taken a great leap backward. We talked it over and decided to check into Wreck Bay, the administrative center for the Galapagos, where we would throw silver-tongued Phil into the fray locally.

Nancy and I discussed our situation. We'd learned that if you came here without permission, you would be as if interned; that is, you could stay indefinitely as long as you never moved the boat except to leave the islands for good. We were determined to stay and keep writing letters forever, or until we got permission, no matter what. The Galapagos had been the most cherished goal of our planning, our dreaming. Nancy's chin was out three inches, and I knew from looking at her face that I wasn't going to give up easily.

There is a technique that we have used again and again for various purposes. Refined and honed to surgical sharpness, we now call it the Ignorant Visitor's Ass-Planting Technique. It has yet to fail.

One relates to this technique the way a sailor relates to luck: you can't depend on it, but you must have it. It is far better to be prepared with the right papers and the right negotiables, but things are different in every country and every bank, and conditions can change radically while pokey sailboats are en route.

We have had numerous successes using the IVAPT. One involved getting an extension of our visa in New Zealand. Initially denied, we wrote back with "Yes, but . . ." The "but" can be whatever: necessary dental work, repairs for the boat, an incapacitating anything (but never admit to a lack of money, as that frightens authorities into immediate action).

It helps to address your letter to an immigration office in the wrong town, or to customs. It also helps to write by hand, making key words illegible and misspelling flagrantly. Eventually one of four things will happen: (1) they actually believe one of your excuses; (2) you are such a nuisance that someone runs out of patience and grants your request; (3) you use up so much time that you're ready to leave anyway; or (4) they come pick you up with the wagon. This last is the only thing that will prematurely thwart a "yes, but" campaign.

It is essential to maintain a pleasant, respectful, and polite mien, no matter what; to put completely out of your mind the tiniest doubt that your request will be granted; and to be irritatingly, patiently *reasonable*. Reasonableness, which has nothing at all to do with reason, is demoralizing to the enemy. (Here I have this perfectly good check, and you have money, so it's inconceivable that we can't, as reasonable men, get together. Given enough time and discussion, I'm sure we will.) Success comes in direct proportion to your determination to see the matter through.

Our most satisfying skirmish was with the Bank of Hawaii in American Samoa. Because we thought it was part of America, after all, we assumed that a cashier's check drawn on the Chase Manhattan would be negotiable. With unaccustomed foresight, we arranged to have one waiting for us in the mail when we reached Pago Pago.

"They won't cash it," we were informed by several yachties on our arrival. "They wouldn't cash mine, and I had to wait 30 days for it to clear." This cannot be, we concluded, as I rubbed our last, lonely penny between thumb and forefinger.

The teller was a pretty, plump Samoan girl. I almost won with my initial blitz by informing her that I was so broke I would have to move in with her if she wouldn't cash my check. In Polynesia, requests for hospitality can*not* be denied. The poor girl stared in terror at the prominent wart (since removed) on my left cheek, at facial lines deeply etched by overindulgence at the past night's welcoming party, and at my rampant, ungroomed beard. Samoan girls hate beards. Her pen trembled over the corner of the check, but superego in the form of the bank's rules prevailed, and I lost by a hair.

We invaded the carpeted executive area in force. The managers were all busy, particularly when they learned from the teller what the purpose of our visit was. Perfectly all right, we'll wait. We sat down in front of a huge, unoccupied desk. It was noon. Nancy got out sandwiches, and Craig pulled cans of soft drinks out of a brown bag. I piled three months' accumulated mail on the desk and started to read through it, letter by letter. Nancy produced an embroidery hoop. Craig curled up with the local paper.

We relaxed for two hours of air-conditioned comfort and correspondence. Finally, a harried assistant manager came over.

"Is there someone helping you, sir?" He knew perfectly well there wasn't.

"We're in no hurry," I said, pleasantly. "I have a cashier's check for $1,000 drawn on the Chase Manhattan Bank, and we're just waiting for someone to initial it so's we can get some money."

He was on the point of giving me the "it is not the bank's policy" bit, but he hesitated. Craig had crushed the five empty pop cans and made a neat row of them on the desk. There were a couple of crusts—Nancy hadn't cleaned up from lunch yet. I was only halfway through my pile of mail.

"Do you have any identification, sir?" the assistant manager asked morosely, and the day was won.

Sailing from Baltra, we arrived in Wreck Bay on the island of San Cristobal at 6:30 in the morning. The officials arrived at our boat at 8:30. Although they hadn't done one thing a minute earlier than they normally do, because we arrived early we were charged overtime. The illogic of this escaped them. By the time we left Wreck Bay, permission in hand, we'd been nickel-and-dimed for nearly $100.

A typical case of low-grade gouging was our treatment by the Wreck Bay Bank. (The name alone rings with institutional confidence.) The first day we went in to change money.

"What's the rate of exchange?" I asked.

My question provoked more consternation than I would ever have expected. The four men, all stooped and bent from hunching over their desks for the last 60 years, held a muttered conference in the far corner of the room. Resolving the problem in a shade under 30 minutes, their spokesman hobbled to the counter.

"Twenty-three sucres per dollar," he said.

We cashed a twenty and stormed the commercial area, determined to spend it as fast as possible. It took us three days. Oranges, the best we'd ever tasted, were half a cent. Limes, one cent. Avocados, four cents. Papayas, ten cents. And a full quart of icy beer was 32 cents. It was going to be hard to get rid of money in any other way than to give it to the officials.

We finally managed to spend the twenty, and made our way back to the Wreck Bay Bank.

"I'd like to cash a twenty," I said. As none of the four men looked up, I'd spoken my shameful Spanish into thin air.

"I said, I'd like to cash a $20 bill, U.S."

The Speaker of the Bank looked at each of his fellow moles in turn. Then he looked at me, gave me a negative nod.

"Whaddaya mean, 'no'?" I said in English, then corrected myself and tried it in Spanish. Who knows what came out. It was enough to get me another no from the S of the B.

"Not for 23 sucres," he explained.

"For what, then?" I asked.

You'd have thought that they hadn't worked all this out beforehand. Maybe S of the B forgot. He went to each fellow *croulant* in turn, then came back to his desk, sat down, and resumed work. It was as if he knew I wouldn't go for it, and didn't care.

"For what, then?" I asked once more.

"Twenty-one," he said, not looking at me.

Nancy and I looked at each other. As the island wasn't crawling with banks, we saw no alternative.

"We're getting screwed," said Nancy, "so we might as well relax and enjoy it."

"There's a sucre born every minute," I said, figuring that one non sequitur deserved another.

Before leaving Wreck Bay we had to cash several more twenties. I cashed them all at once for a blazing 19 sucres per. Had I cashed one at a time, who knows how deeply the bank would have gouged. As it was, we got our own back. Expatriates in Academy Bay were happy to pay four and five sucres over the official rate for U.S. dollars.

High in the hills behind Wreck Bay is a village called El Progresso. In private we called it Regresso. A tired, ancient bus, a converted flat-bed truck, ground its way up the tortuous trail several times a day. The village itself was a collection of poor, dilapidated shacks housing an infinite number of children, chickens, and pigs, with an occasional shy parent showing his or her face. Cole created a near-riot with his Polaroid camera. The inhabitants' pleasure in seeing themselves, usually with their hands covering their faces, caused a human river to flow from hidden huts, each individual demanding to have his picture taken. Cole used up $20 worth of film; then, to stem the tide, he pretended to have run out. Without this white lie he would still be snapping away, the Pied Piper of Polaroid, giving, at a small cost to himself, about two million dollars worth of pleasure.

Set back in a grove of huge orange trees laden with ripe, fat fruit was the once-stately house of Cobos. Cobos, we were told, ran the Galapagos for years as his private fief, a mini-tyrant of limitless cruelty. The wooden building, now dangerously decrepit and boarded up against intrusion by the curious, beckoned us with the fascination of a haunted house. We wandered through darkened rooms, up cobwebbed stairways, into musty attics. One of Cole's sons, luckiest of souvenir hunters, discovered a book. It was inscribed to Cobos from "William Robinson, yacht *Svaap*." Time was foreshortened, and for a moment we could imagine the house as it must have been, the reception that Robinson might have had. We were reluctant to break the spell, to leave. Even more reluctant to spend the night in Regresso, however, we rushed to catch the last bus, and rattled our way back to bay and boat.

A few days later, Phil Walker did it! Sliding in on *Scaldis*'s coattails, *Sea Foam* was in. How Phil managed it must have been a form of magic. I was present during two attempts at a radiotelephone conversation between him and the Ecuadorian mainland. Because of the weak signal, static, and other interference, I would be hard put to relate one complete thought that was exchanged. By some electronic osmosis, Phil did the impossible, and the local authorities were instructed to grant us permission to cruise the islands as we wished. We were the last boats to get such a blanket permission for several years. Our wave of good luck was still running strong and, delighted to be on the crest of it, we set sail for Hood Island the next morning.

TWELVE

W E ARRIVED AT HOOD ISLAND in the afternoon after a pleasant day's trip. Shaped like a peanut shell, Hood is the southernmost island in the Galapagos and, only 600 feet high, one of the lowest. We anchored behind two islets in a dent in the north shore, just off a wide beach of white sand.

All hands from both boats went ashore. Beyond the beach the soil was sandy and arid, but dense, stubborn growth made an inland stroll unattractive. We walked along the shore, escorted by a couple of raggedy, unkempt mockingbirds, so tame and bold that we had to guard against their pecking our bare toes. Some animals, like monkeys, provoke laughter. Our beggarlike guides with their erratic, pogo-stick, two-footed hops tickled us hugely, and kept us chuckling and pointing like kids at the circus all the way up the beach.

Our goal was a party to which hundreds of seals had been invited. We intended to crash it. The party was divided into groups which we soon learned were harems complete with off-spring and a king bull. Lesser bulls, involuntary celibates, hung around the harem waiting for a chance to challenge the king. In the meantime, they baby-sat, patrolling the water's edge for straggling pups. Some of the kings were territorially possessive, and their aggressive rushes, though awkward, represented a voluble, 400-pound deterrent. Other bulls were more lethargic, and we were able, cautiously, to approach mothers and pups.

Phil W. set up his movie camera. Hunkering along the sand and acting sealish, Ivor made friends with a mother. Craig was patting a tiny pup. As Phil extravagantly spent 16mm frames, Cole photographed him at work. On top of Phil's wide-brimmed straw hat sat a mockingbird-clown, supervising the whole operation.

Nonhuman and human creatures related with Disneylike lack of shyness, studying each other with open interest. For the animals, birds, and reptiles that thrived in the Galapagos, the environment was idyllic. But for humans?

Coming from the tropical lushness of Costa Rica, the islands of the Galapagos presented a moody landscape to my impressionable imagination. Away from the villages, a sense of lonely isolation enveloped me. Although the settlements and the high ground of the geologically older islands had enough water and soil for farming, most of the islands, particularly at sea level, were dry. Scrub growth struggled with gnarled obstinacy out of a thin layer of arid soil. Fields of naked lava attested to still-active volcanos. Rocky islets jutted like monstrous teeth out of the chill Humboldt current. Craters and faults, pockmarks and scars of an Olympian fever, pitted the terrain. With their grandeur and unique wildlife, the islands of the Galapagos comprised one of the highlights of our trip. But I could never rid myself of the feeling that I was an interloper, barely tolerated by the forces of an inhospitable environment which, were I to drop my guard, would consume me.

This admittedly subjective reaction was reinforced by a book that I finally finished late one night called *Satan Came to Eden* by a German woman named Dore Streicher. She and a Dr. Ritter had fled the disillusionment of post–World War I Germany and settled in the Galapagos, partners in search of an earthly paradise. What they found was hell.

According to Dore, their relationship was Platonic, their venture philosophical. The boat dropped them and their supplies at Post Office Bay on the island of Floreana. They explored the island and finally decided on a place to build. They called it Friedo. It was three miles from their supplies, but it had a spring, and water was precious.

Thus began a marathon. The trail lay mainly over a lava bed. They made two round trips a day carrying tools, lumber, corrugated roof iron. Their shoes were soon worn out, torn to shreds by the razor-sharp rocks. Dr. Ritter, a martinet, lashed Dore verbally through periods of exhaustion. Week after week, until a passing yacht moved their supplies two miles closer to their site, they continued to live like human mules with unbelievable determination.

Their feet became lacerated and infected. They wrapped them in rags and kept going. Dore had trouble with her teeth. Ritter pulled them all, made her a set of steel ones. Other settlers arrived on the island, and a series of mysterious deaths followed. Finally, Dr. Ritter died—Dore suspected he was poisoned—and she fled the island and returned to Germany. So much for Eden.

I knew that even the stark drama of Dore's understated tale could never, by itself, give me a true understanding of what she and Ritter went through. As drowsiness overtook me, I resolved to go to Floreana after leaving Hood and hike the trail of Dore's purgatory. I slept, and dreamed I was a seal.

The next day we moved the boats to the west end of Hood. Chris, Philip, Kim, and Ivor found some waves and spent the morning surfing with seals. The seals became so boisterous, grabbing the leashes and jostling the boards, that the boys were finally forced out of the water. We split up into small groups and hiked along paths that threaded the rocky, barren point. The point was a rookery for blue-footed boobies and for albatross, whose young retain their pinfeathers until their bodies reach full size, at which point they look like Big Bird on Sesame Street. The rocks near the water were inhabited by marine iguanas, two-foot-long blue-green amphibious lizards of prehistoric appearance. Blowholes punctuated the sky with exclamatory spume, and lonely cactuses stood guard on the barren flatland.

Scaldis had developed engine trouble, so we decided to stick together when we sailed to Floreana that evening. We weighed anchor just after sunset and laid a westerly course for Post Office Bay.

I have made bad decisions before and will no doubt make

others before I die, but this was one of my worst. It should have been a piece of cake. The nights had been clear. We planned to thread a passage between our only two hazards: submerged reefs lying 30 miles apart. Floreana was a high island, an easy landfall. If we happened to sail the 40 miles before dawn, we could hang off the entrance to the bay till first light. I was a little reluctant to start so early, but Cole was concerned about being becalmed without an engine and wanted to allow himself plenty of time. We were soon to learn why even experienced Galapagos fishermen insist on putting in at night.

Instead of light winds or none, we had a stiff breeze on the beam. One advantage of sailing fast is that current, if there is any, has less of an effect. I went to bed early with the delusion that we had things very much in hand.

Chris woke me at 2330. *Scaldis*, behind us, was nowhere in sight. However, no more than three or four miles ahead of us was a mountainous silhouette, and Chris thought we had picked up Floreana. It took me several seconds to check the bearing, then the chart. I was having a hard time accepting either of our possible positions. If it was Floreana, a following current had enabled us to sail 30 miles in four hours. If it was one of the high rocks that lay to the east of Floreana, we had been swept off course to the south 15 miles over the same period; if this was true we were very close to the southern reef and heading right for it. In either case, we were in real, sweat-producing danger.

After praying that we weren't already south of the submerged reef, we tacked north. If I had guessed right, we had 30 miles of open water between us and Conway Reef, the hazard to the north of our original course. Then, to add to our cup of misery, a heavy mist enshrouded us, and we were cut off from our single, mysterious reference. We reduced sail and jogged along at two or three knots.

The thought that what we had glimpsed might be Floreana nagged me. If it was, we shouldn't sail too long in this direction, or when daylight came we might have difficulty finding Floreana again in the fog. The fog was taunting us, occasionally rising for a few brief minutes to permit a glimpse of our landmark. Then it would descend, annihilating our vision.

I finally decided that what we were seeing *was* Floreana. When one of our glimpses put us to the northeast of it, we tacked and once more sailed slowly westward.

Then for over an hour the mist refused to lift. No one slept. Eventually we were all on deck. Eyes ached from trying to pierce the fog. When it finally lifted, not only could we see our original island, but several other smaller ones as well. The chart showed that we hadn't raised Floreana at all, but one of the high rocks east of the island. Once more we tacked northeast into open water, and I went below and slept for the two remaining hours of darkness.

When dawn came, the mist dissipated, and we looked in awe at the maze of high, rocky islets which we had blindly skirted. *Scaldis* was sailing up the east side of Floreana and had evidently spent the night *among* the islets.

"When did you realize we were in trouble?" I asked Cole after we'd anchored safely in Post Office Bay.

"When I saw the reef," he said. He was a shaken man.

"How the hell could you see a submerged reef in the dark?"

"It must have been the reef," he said. "The water was full of phosphorescence. The tide must have been high, but the turbulence over the reef somehow lit it up like a Christmas tree. We sailed right by it—maybe 100 feet away. Too damn close, I'll tell you."

With the chart we were able to trace where we'd been. In a 33-mile run we had been swept nearly 15 miles off course by a current running contrary to what was indicated on the chart. Once more it was pure luck that bought us the time to learn discretion.

After a large, nerve-settling breakfast we decided to pile everyone on *Sea Foam* and motor three miles to visit the pink flamingoes. These huge, shy, skittish birds live in a landlocked lagoon. After barely winning a tug of war with a seal that had taken a fancy to our sounding lead, we rowed ashore.

We crept through the low foliage, at times crawling on our bellies, with the skillful stealth of the Sioux. Reaching the edge of the foliage, we could see a huge flock of flamingoes. They were still too distant, a quarter-mile across the empty flats that border the lagoon. Phil's movie camera had a fine telephoto lens, but we wanted to approach as close as possible. We dressed ourselves in cut branches and inched across the open flats on our bellies. It was a muddy business, but our camouflage was successful. Phil started filming. The large, pink birds did their thing, balancing complacently on one leg. Before long, Phil worked his cautious way to my side.

"I'd like to get a picture of them taking off," he whispered. "I'll set up here, and you make your presence known and disturb them. Okay?"

When he was ready I stood up and doffed my bushes. The flamingoes, unconcerned, continued their one-legged vigil. Nancy, Craig, Chris, Philip, Conni, Kim, Ivor, Flo, and Cole arose from the ground like arboreal specters and shook themselves, causing a shower of falling leaves. The flamingoes remained pink and unperturbed, watching the funny people.

"Maybe they can't fly," suggested Conni.

Finally, by approaching to within five yards of the nearest group, and by stamping, yelling, and waving our arms, we managed to convince the flamingoes that we were nuisance enough to justify a brief 200-yard flight. Phil got his shots, and I borrowed his pen to cross "skittish" and "shy" from my guidebook.

After a day of rest, the day I'd been anticipating arrived. We started from Post Office Bay, up the lava bed toward Friedo, following the path that Dr. Ritter and Dore Streicher had traversed so many times. We were carrying lunches. I was wearing hiking shoes with hard rubber soles and thick rubber cleats.

At first the path threaded the trees, an easy pastoral stroll. Before long the terrain turned rougher. By the time we reached the lava flow my respect for Dore and Dr. Ritter had deepened considerably. Halfway up the lava flow it had increased to pure awe.

Molten lava solidifies capriciously. Some flows are smooth, a natural highway. Others are an obstacle course of tumbled boulders. Without water or wind to polish them smooth, the boulders on Floreana presented a surface as hospitable as a shark's open mouth. Balance was essential; a fall meant a disaster of laceration. Still strong, we hopped and leaped from boulder to boulder, razor-like surfaces raping our shoes.

After a half-mile, the lava bed gave way to a dirt path. The footing was easier, but the going was now more steeply uphill. The temperature soared, approached 90 degrees. By 1:00 we had walked far enough to have reached our goal, and it was obvious that we'd taken a wrong turn. We ate our lunch and started back.

Our tired, weak-kneed descent down the lava flow took us about three times as long as the ascent. Nancy and I, fearing a misstep, dropped far behind the young. We moved gingerly, handing each other down from the tops of boulders like two *Leisure World* arthritics helping each other off a bus. Back on the boat, I looked at the soles of my shoes. There wasn't a cleat left on them, and the thickness of the soles had been reduced by half. Nancy's new sneakers went into the trash can, her blistered feet into a bucket of warm water and Epsom salts. Over a period of weeks, Dr. Ritter and Dore had made that trip two and occasionally three times a day, burdened with supplies. I had barely made it once carrying a canteen and a tuna fish sandwich.

Our sail to Santa Cruz was one of those pleasant surprises the wind god can bestow when he's of a mind. We left Floreana at 7:00 A.M., a traumatic event for Nancy, as the taunting and goading of the whole crew is required to get her functioning before noon. By leaving early, we hoped to cover the 31 miles before dark, expecting light winds and an unfavorable current.

We powered out of Post Office Bay to find a steady, 15-knot wind on our beam. *Sea Foam* flew, crystal water-curls peeling from her prow. Every so often an obstreperous chop would challenge her, only to find itself beaten to exhilarating spray. The Currentmaster pooh-poohed our chart and tilted the seas in our favor. We were secured and at anchor by 11:00 A.M., shaking our heads in disbelief at our passage time of just over four hours.

Having nearly exhausted our supply of Costa Rican gin and vodka, we were in the market for something cheap to restock with. Someone told us of a local rum called Puro, so Nancy and I walked back into the poorer part of Academy Bay to forage in the little shops. When I heard the price, 62 cents a fifth, I determined to buy a dozen cases.

"Let's just buy one bottle and try it first," suggested Nancy.

"Christ, at that price, how can we lose?"

"Let's just buy one bottle," she resuggested.

"Oh, come on. If it's booze, what's the difference? It can't be all that bad."

"Let's just—"

"Nancy!" I snapped.

"—buy one bottle," she finished, giving me a heart-melting, protruded lower lip.

I should put away male dominance once and for all and *listen* to her. She knows things I'll never know. In certain areas her intuition is unerring, and one of them is shopping.

I tramped back to the dock, one bottle in hand, Nancy two paces behind me. Wordlessly, we rowed out to the boat, where I poured everyone a drink of my discovery.

"To love and marriage," I toasted sardonically.

I could get the glass no closer to my nose than four inches. I, who pride myself on learning to enjoy esoteric dishes (except for the overripe eels I threw up in a Left Bank restaurant, and the hyper-salty anchovies I couldn't finish after having just lectured my date on her prosaic palate)—I, who had learned to drink in the Deep South, using a corrosive called White Lightning—*I* could not get the stuff close enough to sip.

"Maybe we should try mixing it with something," said Nancy.

We tried everything, from orange juice to soy sauce. I finally was able to gag down a sip (the only one on the boat who could), but there was no way to make the Puro palatable. Philip promptly found a marking pen and drew a skull and crossbones on the bottle. In spite of subsequent dry spells, the fullness of that particular bottle was to remain unthreatened.

Exactly a year later we found ourselves dry, broke, and in a country where liquor was expensive, and we were reduced to brewing our own papaya *sake*. As a result of our experiments, here are our suggestions:

1. Take a clean, five-gallon jerry-can.
2. Fill it with some sugar, rice, ripe papaya fruit, and fresh water.
3. Shake vigorously three times daily for six days.
4. Let settle for four days.
5. Pour off the clear liquid into another container.
6. Throw it away.
7. Wash out jerry-can with a solution of baking soda.
8. Borrow money, buy booze.

People back home were often reluctant to write us letters because they felt their lives were humdrum compared to ours. It took me years to convince some of them that this was not the case. Forgotten routines, news of people whose company we missed, and the details of land life were no longer ordinary to us. Because I, too, tend not to write about a typical cruising day, forgetting that it's far from ordinary to the people back home, I'll describe our brief visit to Isla Bartholomé. Signified by no disaster or unusual occurrence, it was one of many similiar interludes that stylized our cruising life.

We met *Scaldis* at Baltra, took on fuel and water, and sailed to Bartholomé together, anchoring in the protected cove. It was late afternoon. Pinnacle Rock, a towering, stalagmitic sentinel, cast a long, thin shadow. The cool of the evening breeze stroked our skin while blowing away lazy bugs. We sat in *Sea Foam*'s cockpit, sipping cocktails. Phil and Cole, their light-sensitive minds appraising the surroundings, drew our attention to the island as the colors changed from fawn to gold to umber to rust and, finally, to the rich purple of shadow. We ate dinner in the cockpit: freshly caught red snapper, cooked in butter, was seared and fried quickly in a hot pan to conserve moisture. Stars peeked enviously through knotholes in the night sky. We went to bed early.

And slept late. After breakfast we rowed to the beach, which was significant for its total lack of litter. We planned a barbecue for the evening, hoping the boys would be successful spear-fishermen.

Nancy and I climbed a commanding hill that gave us scenic supremacy. We exulted in our hour of mastery, momentary directors of the drama of rock, sand, water, and sky. Surfeited with imaginary power, we descended the hill and, hand in hand, scavenged firewood for the picnic. The work made us hot. We left our clothes on the beach and waded into deep water. Nancy squeaks when immersing her body in anything colder than a hot bath. For nearly an hour she squeaked constantly.

We walked on the beach until we were dry, and then dressed. Cole appeared from somewhere. Having started just after sunrise, he was still taking pictures of Pinnacle Rock. We survived the evening by eating succulent barbecued fish faster than the mosquitoes could eat us. Nancy and I rowed out to *Sea Foam* and crawled into our bunk. Salty and sunburned, we drifted into contented sleep, scratching, scratching. . . .

THIRTEEN

WE LEFT THE GALAPAGOS in early October 1973. Our passage to the Marquesas Islands of French Polynesia took 24½ days, and for the last 16 days of the voyage we never touched the twin headsails. Our biggest enemy was boredom, which we combatted by reading, playing games, kibitzing at Craig's morning school sessions, cooking new dishes, watching porpoises, catching fish, debating (some cynics might say arguing), taking baths on deck in a child's inflatable dinghy, swinging in a bosun's chair slung at water level from the bowsprit, writing daily in our journals, putting sunburn medication on previously unexposed skin, and for practice doing more navigation than necessary. Life was unremittingly pleasant. As a second introduction to crossing oceans it gave us confidence and allayed the fears that always went with sailing away from shelter into the empty, endless horizon. We should have recognized this passage for what it was, a gift from the gods. Instead, we took it for a typical voyage. Only subsequent experience would reveal how far we'd been led down the garden path.

For a week out of the Galapagos, *Sea Foam* and *Scaldis* had stayed together. Because neither boat had self-steering, there was always someone at the helm. With both boats burning navigation lights, there was no added danger in sticking close. But one night Cole decided to power to charge his batteries. I was on watch, and the crew was asleep. I figured there was no need to wake everyone with the diesel when we could just as well charge the batteries during the day. *Scaldis* powered over the horizon and we hadn't seen her since.

Both Cole and I had been furiously taking sights and radioing our positions in an attempt to get back together. Twice we had arrived at coordinates so close that we should have been able to see each other, but even a man aloft had been unable to see the other boat. We zigged and zagged, raised and lowered sail, and otherwise departed with erratic zeal from normal, goal-oriented passagemaking. It wasn't that being in visual range was all that important to any of us. It was the principle of the thing. Two master mariners like us should have been able to do a simple thing like find another boat.

In our defense, we had not been able to get star fixes because of cloud cover. We were thus limited to navigating by the sun, which required a calculation based on dead reckoning. (Noon shots were impractical as the sun at its meridian was almost directly overhead.) Current and drift, when added to my inexperience with the sextant, introduced enough of an error to keep the two boats farther apart than the few miles within which one yacht can spot another at sea.

The first two days we had tried to use our running fixes as references from which to lay closing or intersecting courses. The third day I had virtually flattened our working batteries by constantly transmitting so that Cole could home in on us with his RDF. He finally got his act together and took a bearing, then spent the afternoon sailing 20 miles in what must have been the reciprocal direction.

That night Cole sighted a freighter a couple of miles to his north, heading east. A half-hour later, I spotted the same ship passing us to the south. By comparing notes, for the first time we got a clear idea of our relative positions. We were highly confident that tomorrow...

At 2:00 P.M. the next day I turned on the radio. "*Sea Foam, Sea Foam—*" It was Cole, doing semipermanent damage to the radio's speaker.

"You're very strong," I said. "Must be just over the next wave. What's your position?"

Cole gave me his coordinates. I looked at the worksheet where I'd jotted down the position that Philip and I had agreed on.

"Is Conni on watch?" I asked Cole, suddenly wary. Conni was

crewing on *Scaldis* during this passage. Ever since she'd failed to observe the liner *Princess Elizabeth* towering over us like the Miami Hilton 250 yards off our quarter, I had lost faith in her myopic qualifications for lookout.

"Yeah, it's Conni's watch. Why?"

"Because she's blind without her glasses and she won't wear 'em," I said. Then, calling topsides: "Hey, Philip. Have a look around—*Scaldis* must be about to hit us."

"I just sent Kim aloft," said Cole. "If you're around he'll see you."

"What do you mean, 'if we're around'?" I snarled into the mike. "Philip's just gone up the ratlines, and if your calculations are even halfway accurate we'll have you in sight in a jiffy."

Ten minutes later, Philip came below.

"There is no other boat out there," he stated flatly.

"Cole, old man, I hate to say it, but your navigation is hopeless. We are occupying *identical coordinates* and yet you're nowhere in sight. How do you explain that?"

"I'd say that you don't have the foggiest idea what the hell you're doing," he replied in friendly fashion.

I thought that was a little harsh, inasmuch as he was the one who didn't know where he was. I told him so.

"Look," said Cole. "I just took a peek outside. We're about a mile south of a huge black cloud."

I actually went topsides to look. There were at least three clouds he could have been talking about.

"Let's face it," I said, back on the radio. "We could spend the next *month* chasing rain clouds. If we can't get together with sextant, compass, RDF, and all that—"

"You're right," he said, and *Scaldis* sailed on ahead, leaving shorter, plumper *Sea Foam* in her wake.

We continued to maintain an 0800 sked on the radio. Even now, after 35,000 miles of Pacific passagemaking, I am far more comfortable at sea when we can keep radio contact with someone. I believe that a ham radio capable of transmitting and receiving on the amateur bands is much more useful than a marine radiotelephone. (Few of the yachts we met in the Pacific could afford the new SSB radiotelephones; overseas phone calls via KMI, the San Francisco relay station, were expensive; and half the time the KMI operators appeared to ignore the weaker, 12-volt battery-powered signals from the South Pacific.) Yachties who'd invested roughly $3000 and up found themselves with virtually no one to talk to, whereas those who had become hams had spent a quarter as much and could tap into a huge, international party line.

Of course, party lines can have their disadvantages. In Academy Bay we had met an American who owned and operated a local hotel. He was also a ham operator, and one night a week he gave unstintingly of his time, skill, and rig to get local residents in touch with loved ones. He told me the following story of a young man who'd arrived in the Galapagos on a visiting yacht the previous summer.

Tom, the young man, discovered that a genito-urinary problem which he thought had been cured was flaring up again. He became so concerned that he insisted on flying home for treatment, until his father, the boat's skipper, heard about the ham in Academy Bay. On the appointed evening, Tom and his father arrived at the hotel early, scheduled to be first. While waiting for the airwaves to settle down, roughly 15 people drifted in and took up positions around the lobby, hoping for a shout home.

"I'm starting to get through," called the hotel owner from the radio shack, a tiny, airless room just off the lobby. "Come on in and we'll see if we can set up a phone patch."

Within minutes he worked electromagnetic magic, and Tom was on the horn with the family GP.

"What's the problem, son?" asked the doctor cheerfully. Clear as a bell.

"Could we shut the door?" asked Tom. His father shut it.

"I think I've got gonorrhea, or something like it," said Tom in a low voice into the mike.

"You'll have to speak up," said the hotel owner. "He'll never make out what you're saying. And don't forget to say 'over.'"

"I think I've got gonorrhea," said Tom, somewhat louder. "Over."

"Sorry, son—didn't get that. Could you spell it phonetically? Over."

I know dozens of extremely intelligent people for whom the prospect of spelling "gonorrhea" would be terrifying. To spell it phonetically with a live audience—not to mention countless electronic eavesdroppers—would bring them to panic. Tom recognized a hopeless situation, spelling not being his strong point, and something in the web of his inhibitions snapped with a loud "fuckit."

"Hey, Doc," he shouted, "I think I've got clap: Charlie, Lima, Alpha, Pappa. Over."

There was a poignant pause.

"I see," came the doctor's voice through the speaker. "What are your symptoms?"

"I drip," said Tom, stronger with each word. "Over." He was beginning to enjoy himself.

"Please repeat. Please repeat. And speak slowly. Over."

"MY PENIS," he roared. "IT DRIPS: DELTA, ROMEO, INDIA, PAPPA, SIERRA. OVER!"

His father stole a quick glance into the lobby, all hope of discretion blown away. Only loyalty and love kept him rooted by his son's side. The doctor asked a few more questions, then recommended a new, broad-spectrum antibiotic that the local doctor could administer. He convinced Tom to stop worrying, and to keep him up to date by whatever means he could, but preferably not by ham radio.

While on the subject of ham radios: One of the worst passages of our sailing career was a 1350-mile jaunt that should have taken us two weeks and ended up taking us six. We left Pago Pago on December 3, 1977, bound for Tarawa in the Gilbert Islands. Two days later a companion yacht, *Edward Richmond*, left Apia, West-

ern Samoa, bound for the same place. In addition to checking into the Pacific Maritime Mobile Net every evening (a ham
net which logged the positions at sea), we agreed to a morning
sked with *Edward Richmond*. Seven days out of Pago Pago our
transmitter burned out. From then on we could listen but we
couldn't talk.

Roughly halfway to Tarawa we encountered the most perni-
ciously hostile weather we've ever experienced, before or since.
The wind blew straight out of our destination at speeds of 30 to
50 knots. The sky, when it wasn't a pastiche of grays, took on the
doleful color of acute jaundice. For three solid weeks our only
respite from constant squalls was brief, suspenseful periods of no
wind at all. The equatorial current, normally good for a 25 to
50-mile-a-day boost westward, was reversed by the constant westerly winds. Our worst day we lost 100 miles. Our best days we
stayed even. An unplanned Christmas at sea was irrigated with
Nancy's unwonted tears and scored by recorded carols broadcast
from lonely Canton Island. (The Sailing Directions declared
that entering the Canton lagoon, the only place we might have
put in for shelter, was dangerous in a strong westerly blow.) Day
after day we slogged to windward with grim stubbornness. By
January 1 the weather had eased, but it was 16 more days before
we reached Tarawa.

Edward Richmond encountered the same winds we did. After
a week of it her skipper did two things: he turned and headed
for Hawaii, and, concerned over our radio silence, he put *Sea
Foam* "on the board" with the Maritime Mobile Net. From then
on, unable to assure everyone that we were all right, we listened
to nightly broadcasts requesting information as to our where-
abouts.

This dilemma made me recall my youth when I was courting
the future mother of my children. For years I had been scarring
my karma by lying to concerned parents as to why I was bringing their daughters home so late. In this case, however, I fervently
wanted to make a good impression.

Promise after sincere promise to be home, this time, at a

reasonable hour, was broken by the karate chop of avenging fate. If we went sailing, we were becalmed. In the motorboat we broke down. We were twice lost in the fog. Once, in a heavy old rowboat, we were left high and dry by the tide. The Coast Guard learned to recognize the voices of both sets of parents and developed a special "there, there" phoneside manner just for them.

So it was no surprise to discover on reaching Tarawa that not only had the Net, all cruising yachts, the Coast Guard, and the authorities of the Gilbert and Tuvalu (formerly the Ellice) Islands been alerted, but also if we had been missing for 24 more hours my mother would have called out the U. S. Navy. Her clout went untested, for which I'm grateful, but for a while thereafter I was troubled by a recurring dream.

(*Sea Foam*, in mid-ocean, is beating her lonely way to windward. The Fleet steams up, decks swarming with grinning gobs. An aircraft carrier the size of a small city peels off and pulls alongside.)

ADMIRAL: "Ahoy, *Sea Foam*!"

ME: "Hi there, skip—anything we can do for you?"

ADMIRAL: "Hey, man, we been lookin' all *over* for ya."

ME: "We've been right here, sailing along, being intrepid."

ADMIRAL: "Well, you been out here a long time, and your momma's worried." (Fade.)

FOURTEEN

ALTHOUGH FATU HIVA struck us as the most spectacularly beautiful island in the South Pacific, at least some of its impact must be attributed to contrast. After nearly 25 days of nothing but ocean, the island's magnificence was a mind-blower. And it seems to me ironic, in retrospect, that by a chance of geography Fatu Hiva should have been our first glimpse of Polynesia. If cruising the South Pacific is a banquet of scenery, the menu was ass-backwards. Fatu Hiva should have been the cherries jubilee and the snifter of Napoleon, not the antipasto.

Because they are geologically young, none of the Marquesas have coral reefs. All anchorages are open coves and bays—interruptions in the island's perimeter—and as such are vulnerable to bad weather from certain directions. We were anchored in Hana Vave Bay, on the western side of Fatu Hiva, a deep indentation in towering granite protected from all but westerly weather. Because of the trade winds, 90 percent of the weather came from the east, and the bay was calm and sheltered. The island's height, however, could cause gusts to scream down from the mountainside at speeds of up to 60 knots. These williwaws lasted only about a minute. Their sudden violence tested our nerves, but they were also bug-eliminators, and before we finished cruising in the Marquesas we came to wish that all the bays had them.

The village of Hana Vave lay strung out on both sides of a path which led up into a valley. Instant friendship, instant smiles. No hidey-face, peek-a-boo. Gifts of bananas, mangoes, papayas. The people of Progresso in the Galapagos had clung to a life of poverty, struggling for what little they had. The Fatu Hivans lived in a self-tending cornucopia of such sufficiency that they could neither use it all nor give it all away. This had to make a difference in how they viewed the world.

A native family paddled out in their pirogue (outrigger canoe) to visit. They brought us our first *pamplemousse*. So many firsts! Marquesan pamplemousses were enormous grapefruit with the coloring of limes, and the pulp inside was a sweet, juicy combination of both fruits. Another first: ripe mangoes, picked off the tree and eaten then and there, fruit with energy-producing sweetness and a juice that quenched thirst as effectively as a mountain spring.

The lady laughed a lot. She was young, fat, and toothless. Her husband, maybe 23, still had a few teeth, but it looked as if he used typewriter ribbon for dental floss. Besides smallpox and syphilis (the old-time whaler's contribution to Marquesan culture), Western civilization had thrown their diet out of balance by introducing prepared and refined foods.

By way of revenge, a couple of young lads paddled out to *Sea Foam* with their ukuleles. Although many of the Polynesians we met were truly talented players and singers, they all *thought* they were. Their favorite song was a Marquesan version of "She'll Be Comin' Round the Mountain When She Comes." Of the three chords (four if you want to get elaborate) our troubadors knew only two, but they did know two other chords which they felt would do just as well. The same standard of quality control applied to tuning the instruments, and to the concept of metric scan. Since then we spent pleasant afternoons in the company of fun-loving, entertaining, talented natives, but 90 percent of the time it was my karma to draw the Gong Show losers. Initially, I was unaware of my fate, and I would sit in *Sea Foam*'s cockpit tapping my foot and grinning like a fool, suffused with a sentimental bonhommie usually reserved for family Christmas Eves.

There was a total of six yachts in Hana Vave during our stay. Enough, felt the villagers, to warrant a hula. A hula turned out to be a dance, held in the village in the open air. A couple of guitarists laid down a good beat. Another first: the *tamure*, a wild, rhythmic, man-woman dance of abandon that usually ended, to gales of laughter, just short of intercourse. Native children learned the motions as soon as they could walk. I tried, felt 45 and foolish, and resolved to drink more before the next hula.

The mood of Hana Vave was hypnotic. One evening we sit for two hours in the cockpit, silently absorbing the spectacle around us. The bay welcomes the sunset with open arms. Golden light and purple shadow work sorcery among the planes and angles of towering stone. The water is a mirror. The music of ukuleles drifts out from the village and gentles the occasional skittish thought. The sky is perfect, the woolly clouds are perfect, and for a brief moment I, too, am perfect, one small, clear note in a pyramid of harmony.

It is wise not to keep a list of missed opportunities. Reading it could drive you to drink. We came to Omoa, Fatu Hiva's other village, on the southwestern tip of the island, because the people there made the finest, most exquisitely decorated *tapa* in all of Polynesia. (Tapa is a fabric made by pounding the bark of breadfruit or paper mulberry trees, after which it is hand-decorated using natural dyes.) Concerned about money, we decided to dicker and deal with .22 shells. Forewarned, we'd brought hundreds of shells, bought in California at a cost of about a penny apiece.

"Don't offer too many shells," we'd been advised. "They'll do anything for just a few. Give 'em too many and you'll spoil 'em, create inflation for people who come later. Fifteen or twenty shells will have them at your feet, humbly grateful. Hang tough, man. Bargain, bargain." Tapa was going for about $20 for a piece about one foot by two, but loyal to the cabal of interracial commerce, I started by offering five bullets for a small tapa that Nancy liked.

Polynesians are extremely polite. The lady I was dealing with smiled and offered us all some ripe papaya. We ate, and I raised my offer to ten shells. It was a hot day, and she sent her son to open some green coconuts, from which we drank, thirstily, fighting the midday heat. I raised my offer to 20 shells. She smiled, and gave us a stalk of bananas to take back to the boat.

"Je vais vous donner cinquante (50) cartouches," I said, breaking the faith. She smiled and gave us a basket of mangoes.

Fifty shells were all we'd brought ashore.

"To hell with it," said Nancy. "We'll pick up some tapa at one of the other islands."

These words, along with "No need to (do it) (buy it) (hike it) (visit it) (climb it) (dive for it) now—we'll be back this way and we can do it then," must be chiseled into the tablet of self-delusions. No other island made tapa. By the time we got to Tahiti we were even broker, and the price for Omoan tapa had tripled.

Driven by a craving for fresh vegetables, cold beer, and ice cream, Sea Foamers set out for Atuona on the nearby island of Hiva Oa. Atuona is a picturesque village with a bakery, stores, and a pastoral hillside graveyard that contains, among other things, the remains of Paul Gauguin. We checked in with the gendarme, then moved in a phalanx toward the commercial area. The beer was Hinano, another delicious first, and ice-cold. Craig made a beeline for the only Marquesan junk food: *fidi-fidi*, a doughy, deep-fried pastry with the taste of old grease and the consistency of rubber. Craig adored them.

Nancy and I split from the group and hitch-hiked back to the anchorage with a truck full of Marquesans. It was a holiday weekend, All Saints' Day, and everyone was in a festive mood. One of the Marquesans was a school teacher, who declaimed that he disliked the French because they sat around drinking wine from glasses, looking down their noses, and toasting "au succès." Nancy and I took the hint and drank from the bottle, toastlessly. We offered the Marquesans some cartridges if they would get us some fresh vegetables, unavailable in town. They took the cartridges and disappeared, to reappear on the beach an hour later with a huge basket of contraband they'd stolen from a Frenchman's garden. Another first: illicit vegetables taste as good as the other kind.

Few bays in the Marquesas have water clear enough for good snorkeling. We set out for one that did, an uninhabited bay named Hana Moe Noe. We cruised in and dropped anchor. Before ten minutes had passed, there were wasps all over the boat.

(*Sea Foam* seems to hold a mysterious attraction for wasps. One day in New Zealand I was doing something to the main boom when a wasp flew out of the furled sail, buzzed my left ear ferociously, and sped away. I peeked into the folds of the sail and saw hundreds of wasps, all in a soporific state. I looked in the furls of the staysail and the mizzen. Hundreds more. We were on a mooring and the wind was light. I raised mizzen, main, and staysail. Thousands of comatose wasps speckled the gently undulating fabric. I went below and donned bright yellow foul weather gear—pants, jacket, hood, and gloves—and a diving mask, trusting my beard to protect my chin. People on the dock, several hundred feet distant, turned to stare. They saw a wildly attired eccentric single-mindedly attacking his sails, flailing madly about the deck with a broom. They were too far away to see the wasps. Later on, in the pub, no one would believe that I'd seen them either.)

In Hana Moe Noe, the wasps invaded the cabin en masse. Philip, forewarned and deathly allergic to their sting, had sailed on another yacht for the day. He needn't have worried. We went about our business as usual, albeit in a cloud of wasps. The only casualty was when Chris sat on one. I would have reacted just as the wasp did.

Three of us went snorkeling, Chris begging off because of a fresh cold. Nancy, Craig, and I swam across 200 yards of open water to the north shore. Over a sandy bottom, the water was transparent at a depth of 40 feet. I was extremely nervous, as a man from another yacht had reported seeing a hammerhead shark at the entrance to the bay when he had dived there.

Someone once pointed out that one's first meeting with a shark underwater will most likely separate the chicken from the sea. I had yet to encounter one. My guardian angel was no doubt putting off this confrontation, knowing that it might well have ended my snorkeling career.

After an uneventful hour of exploring the rocky shore and not seeing much, we swam back across open water to *Sea Foam*. Just as we were approaching and I was convinced that this time, thank you very much, we would not be munched, a large shadow glided out from behind the hull. For ten seconds I knew that the hammerhead had returned to get me and that it was all over. The shadow drew closer and I recognized Chris in his wet suit. He couldn't understand why I was angry that he'd gone swimming after he'd said he wasn't going to. I couldn't understand his objections to my saying he looked like a hammerhead. Another first: I learned I can sweat under water.

On the northwestern corner of Hiva Oa is a huge valley called Hana Menu. Overlord of the whole valley—and sole resident, along with his family—was a young man named Ozanne. His father in Atuona on the other side of this mountainous island had given us a letter to deliver to him.

The afternoon sail from Hana Moe Noe to Hana Menu was one of those wild, exuberant rides that makes the heart sing. The sky was munchkin blue, the ocean a playground of whitecaps. The wind blew 30 knots from the starboard quarter, and *Sea Foam*, skirts hiked up around her waist, danced across the waves. The massive cliffs of Hiva Oa sped by, a land reference that heightened our feeling of speed. We sailed into the bay bearing gifts in the form of a 30-pound wahoo, caught on the trolling line as we rounded the point.

We took the fish ashore as a gift to Ozanne. Soon safaris were arranged. While Ozanne and two others rode off on horseback to shoot wild cattle, the rest of us headed five miles up the valley on foot to visit a waterfall. I carried my .22 in the event Ozanne's dogs raised a pig or a goat.

I am not much of a hunter. Once, at a friend's home in Maine, a persistent crow had been driving me crazy, starting his interminable cawing at dawn. His tree was several hundred feet from the house. I could see his perch from the bathroom, and took to waiting there every morning with a .22 rifle laid across my knees. My opportunity came, and I knocked Mr. Crow off his limb with one shot. It was a cold fall morning. I walked toward my prey, gun in hand. A bloody, erratic trail scarred the thin mantle of new snow. At the end of it lay the dying bird. He stabbed me with a pain-filled stare, and something tangible passed between us. I finished him off, but he didn't die in vain. The few times I had been tempted to shoot an animal since then, I'd been transfixed by the memory of an accusing eye.

It was because of this that I wondered what I was trying to prove as I set out, gun in hand, up the Hana Menu valley. In my mind I saw how it would be: the dogs would scare up a prey and, with the help of native beaters, would chase it across the path in front of me, where I would reluctantly shoot it. My aversion to killing was only exceeded by my aversion to expending energy.

The first mile or so was easy and pleasant: broad paths threaded leafy shade, and if there was any slope it was unnoticeable. We had been walking barely half an hour when the dogs started barking. They had cornered a goat in the precipitous rocks that bordered the valley.

The three Polynesian men with us looked at me, first expectantly, then scathingly. They turned and ran dogward while I, motivated by their scorn, moved off lethargically through the vines, thorns, and creepers, a caricature of lethal determination.

By the time I'd broken through the underbrush and climbed up the canyon side to a point of no advance, I realized that I was in the wrong place. To get where the action was, I had to retrace my steps. Before I'd done so, I heard Nancy's call.

"Herb—come on back. It's all over."

I stomped back to the clearing. A goat hung from a tree limb, and one of the Marquesans already had it half-butchered. As I reached the clearing, another Marquesan ran up with a second goat draped over his neck. They had each gotten one, having leapt on the cornered beasts and slit their throats with knives.

Relieved that the hunt was over, I left the emptied gun behind, and we continued up the path, eager to visit the waterfall we'd been told about. The going got tougher. Instead of a path, we were now climbing up a river bed, clambering over rocks, hopping over pools, and scrambling over fallen logs. The day grew hot, even in the shade. Mile followed mile, and though we'd often hiked over rougher terrain, we were glad to reach the end, to cool off in the chill water, to stretch out in the shade by the falls and linger over lunch. The water crashed down over the rocks into a deep pool, and even the sound refreshed. As we looked up at the falls, a trick of perspective made the water seem to escape straight from the sky through a gate of trees. Five stars, if you want to add it to your waterfall guide.

Ozanne had shot a bull. By the time we passed his house near the beach, the skin was staked out to dry and Ozanne had left in his runabout to take the beef to his father's store in Atuona. The French government, in order to keep the wild cattle from being wiped out, at that time (1973) allowed the locals to shoot cattle during one year and prohibited it the next. Firearms and ammunition were controlled, and visiting yachts were asked to declare both when they came in. Because yachts at that time were not searched, most everyone lied and retained cartridges for trading. The Marquesans used the shells to provide themselves with meat. Too much of this might eventually wipe out the supply of wild goat, pig, and beef, but at the time of our visit there was plenty, and trading in cartridges seemed to be mutually beneficial.

When we went to Ozanne's house for a feast, we were served fresh goat meat. The Marquesans don't eat the liver, so we got it. Goat liver was the sweetest we had ever tasted, far milder than beef liver, and a surprise, as goat meat itself is inclined to be gamy and strong-tasting.

One afternoon we invited Ozanne and three young boys to go

fishing on *Sea Foam*. The seas were moderately rough, and as we trolled back and forth off the northwest corner of the island, I could see that our guests were feeling ill. Craig has always had the same problem: he can spend all day in a runabout in rough weather without a qualm, but subject him to the slow undulations of a sailboat in a swell and he greens up like a golf course in springtime.

Before long we caught our first fish, a wahoo. We'd been trolling with three lines and suddenly had hook-ups on all of them. The only fish we landed, however, was the one closest to the boat. The hooked wahoos darted back and forth at top speed (40 mph). Their mouths open wide, they cut the taut, longer lines with their razor-sharp teeth. For the rest of the day we trolled with one line only.

Chris was gutting the wahoo and was about to toss the entrails overboard when a vicelike grip stopped his arm in mid-toss. Polynesians hold as delicacies the parts of the fish that we normally throw away. As soon as our guests realized we didn't want these tidbits they divided them up with gusto. Molars popped fish eyes, which were then chewed and savored. One man ate the liver. The most seasick of the young boys was given the still-beating heart, an honor that made his eyes shine with 20 times their normal candlepower. Soon they were all talking and smiling, their discomfort gone, and *I* was the one who felt ill.

When we arrived back at Hana Menu, Ozanne kept the fish heads for soup and stew. When you think about it, Marquesans and Americans could live happily ever after with the same practical arrangement that Jack Spratt had with his wife.

Our overnight sail to Nuku Hiva was on the wind—wet, lumpy, and uncomfortable. About midnight I heard the electric windlass motor start. Since Chris slept in the fo'c's'le, where the switch was, I figured he was responsible, and I accused him.

"I'm not doing a damn thing," was his indignant reply.

The windlass stopped whining. I went topsides and stared at it. Several waves, pounded to flying spray, tried to make me feel unwelcome, but I persisted. Unlike my car when I used to take it to be repaired, the windlass misbehaved on cue, suddenly starting all by itself. This time it didn't turn off.

I glared at it, hoping for the gift of X-ray vision, a flash of insight. Nothing. I went below and turned off the main switch at the battery (our running lights had shorted out again anyway). I later found that water had gotten into the solenoid, shorting it to ON, but at the time I blamed a Marquesan poltergeist, a diagnosis I failed to sell to my skeptical crew.

In Taiohae, Nuku Hiva, we discovered no-noes at the same time the no-noes discovered us. Tiny, invisible mites, they can devour a whole human being in short order. Many an unfortunate yachtie remembers the Marquesas only for the no-noes and the misery they caused.

Scratched no-no bites provide a beautiful foothold for staph infections. Staph is always present on the human body, but even more so in warm climates. Any open, untreated sore is subject to staph infection. Staph thrives in saltwater in the tropics, the temperature and salinity being sufficiently similar to the blood's, and people with cuts are advised not to go swimming. Once you witness not only the localized inflammation but the overall debilitation that staph can cause, you will never risk its virulence unnecessarily.

We were lucky two ways. First, none of us were plagued by the pus-filled sores that afflicted many yachtsmen and Polynesians. Second, Nancy was our sacrificial no-no zinc. Whenever I went ashore alone, all exposed flesh was violated. Whenever we went with Nancy, the no-noes ate her exclusively. She took to sweating out her shoreside expeditions in long pants, long sleeves, shoes, socks, and a bandana, all exposed parts covered with greasy, foul-smelling, ineffective insect repellent. If I stayed near her I was immune, even in trunks. I took her everywhere and she worked perfectly, although her disposition was temporarily crippled by what she pointedly termed the fucking injustice of it all.

FIFTEEN

I T WAS MY WATCH. I could barely make out the towering blackness of the thunderheads against the inky sky, and it was
only during flashes of lightning that I could see the shadow
of Ua Pou slowly shrinking behind us. Cozy below in warm
bunks, the family slept soundly while I rigged preventers during
the slatting, rolling, light airs, and then hastily reefed the mizzen
during a nasty squall. Between times I brooded at the helm,
drip-drying between deluges, and wishing I'd postponed our departure.

We were on our way from the Marquesas to Ahe, one of the
northern Tuamotus. Philip was due back at college soon, and we
had suddenly found ourselves pressed for time. As a result we
were sailing to the Tuamotus—"Les Iles Dangereuses"—with no
moon. Because of unpredictable currents, about 20 yachts a year
go up on Tuamotu reefs. Story after story of wrecks happening
to sailors of great experience and local knowledge haunted me,
and I could feel a strong case of nerves coming on.

Daybreak was dreary, squally, and rolly. No one felt well. At
one point we had some soup, but that was all anyone wanted. A
noon sight put us a little farther north than I expected, so I
adjusted my dead reckoning accordingly. At that point, my main
concern was to get through the day.

The next morning everyone felt better. Nancy worked in the
galley all day preparing a huge feast for Thanksgiving: roast
chicken, mashed potatoes with gravy, cranberry sauce, fresh
tomato, fresh avocado with dressing, and nine loaves of bread—
three regular, three cinnamon, three banana—all this while the
boat was rolling wildly. The minute we hove-to for dinner, the

seas calmed, the sun shone, and we cheerfully demolished the major part of what she'd made.

After dinner we raised the twin headsails. Everyone shot sun lines, and the duplication of effort served once again as a check on our results. All seemed well, and my nerves relaxed, momentarily lulled by a sense of well-being.

The day after Thanksgiving was Nancy's birthday. The weather was magnificent. Everyone was cheerful. However, we had become certain that we would not reach Ahe during daylight on the following day. Slack water, which was desirable for negotiating the pass into the lagoon, was supposed to occur about three hours after sunrise. Consequently, we had to be near enough at dawn to reach the pass at slack water, yet heave-to far enough away that we wouldn't be washed ashore by a freak current. At this point we seriously considered changing our destination to Takaroa, so situated that we would arrive at dawn the next day, but everyone had their hearts set on Ahe.

That evening the twilight skies were clear, I shot the stars and somehow came up with a triangle the size of Rhode Island.

I was frantic. The results were absurd. I reworked and replotted everything. Either I had read the sextant wrong in each case, or I had come up with the worst series of sights in the history of navigation. I finally gave up and grabbed a short nap before my watch.

Nancy was tired and grateful to see me when I arrived, scratchy-eyed, to relieve her. She kissed me and went quickly below for some much-needed sleep. Before she had time to undress, however, I called her back.

"What day is it?" I asked her.

"Friday, November 23, my birthday."

"Are you sure?" I said. "What day did we leave the Marquesas?"

We traced our way back to a date we were certain of.

"It's not Friday, it's Saturday, and you, my love, have *got* to steer while I go below and rework the star shots. I know it's unfair, but—"

"That's okay. It's too important to be put off."

This time, with the tables for the proper day, the triangle came out satisfyingly small. We were 12 miles south of our DR. Had we turned south and headed for Takaroa, as we had considered, we would have hit it right on the nose—at 3:00 A.M. of a moonless night.

"No harm done," said Nancy generously. "As a matter of fact, if we'd tried to have Thanksgiving on the right day, nobody would have felt like it."

Which was true, of course, but it didn't make me feel much better as a navigator. The wrong day! Good God, I thought, of all places—the Tuamotus—to pull such a stunt!

At twilight the next day we were 18 miles north of Ahe, precisely where we wanted to be. We hove-to for the night. In the morning I woke before dawn to shoot the stars in order to find out how far the current and wind had pushed us. Radio WWV, Hawaii, gave me the exact time. I started the stopwatch, went on deck, got some good shots, returned below to work them out. Then I realized I had failed to write down the time as it came over the radio. I knew the hour, and the stopwatch gave me the second, but there was no way to know for certain what the minute was.

Furious at myself, I solved the problem using the minute I thought I remembered and worked out a position. A one-minute difference in time would move our position 15 miles east or west, so I bet on the position 15 miles west of the past night's position; although we had been hove-to, I figured that the equatorial current added to the trade winds must have pushed us west *some*.

An early sun line would lie nearly north and south on the chart, giving me our longitude and determining which of my possible positions was the right one. At 7:30 I got a good sun sight. I wrote down the time. I verified the date. I took the sextant reading and wrote it down. (I've been known to take a reading, then change the sextant to fit it back in its box and forget what the reading was.) I worked the problem and had Chris verify my arithmetic. The line of position showed that from the time of our evening fix to our fix the next morning, *Sea Foam* had not drifted at all. So much for hunches about the capricious Tuamotu currents. Finally, a thin line of treetops appeared on the horizon, seeming to grow right up out of the water as we approached. We'd managed to find Ahe.

These two blunders taught me some important facts about myself and sailing. I am not the same person at sea that I am on land. At sea I tend to be nocturnal and sleep restlessly. Working arithmetic in a pitching cabin is likely to make me giddy. Pressure, absent on shore in a learning situation, impinges and accumulates at sea with each stupid mistake. All these factors combine to make me far less sharp at sea than I normally am. Not realizing this at first, I tended to trust myself as I would on land—to my chagrin.

Hunches are apt to be downright dangerous when it comes to navigating. It's best to check your navigational instruments regularly, and then trust them, no matter how strongly your intuition dissents. I learned this once and for all in the Gilbert Islands in 1977. We were approaching what we thought was Tarawa, middle island in a north-south chain of three close neighbors. Tarawa, however, was a port, and as we drew near we could see no boats, no pier. It had to be the island to the north or to the south of Tarawa. The lay of the land and the fact that we couldn't see Tarawa to the south (the tip of the island was blocking it from our view) had me convinced that we'd raised the southern island. My conviction was undeniable and dead wrong. Even though a sunshot put us north of Tarawa, indicating an incredible three-knot northerly set, the illogic of that possibility blew my cool. As a result we wasted three hours sailing north instead of south, and finished by spending an unnecessary and unpleasant night at sea trying to keep a lighthouse in sight while hove-to in 30 knots of wind. Had I trusted the sextant, we'd have been comfortably in port that afternoon.

There was no slack water at Ahe when the Sailing Directions had said, but we didn't care. We started the diesel and, making seven knots through the water, inched our way in the pass against a six-knot outflow. Once inside, the serene, stunning lagoon made it all worthwhile. We dropped anchor near the pass and swam and dove among coral heads in water of such transparency that one could see clearly for 150 to 200 feet. Then we motored south to the village. That night I slept 14 hours straight.

In 1977, for the first time, the number of yachts that visited Ahe during one year equalled the number of the village's inhabitants—something under 200. In earlier years, a visiting yacht was a rare occurrence, and each one was celebrated with a feast. When we visited, they were getting several yachts a month, and were throwing one feast a month in honor of whatever yachts were there. Our feast was special. In addition to the six yachts anchored by the village, the Aheans were hosting some French dignitaries in celebration of an agreement reached regarding pearl farming in the lagoon. The project promised to bring Aheans additional income far in excess of what they earned from selling copra.

Spruced up in our slightly mildewed best, we rowed ashore to the town meeting hall. Forty of us sat down at tables laden with lobster, pork, *poisson cru* (raw fish marinated in lime juice), cooked fish, rice, banana *poi*, coconut bread, punch, and coffee. The French contributed bottles of rum and wine. Musical groups using guitars and ukuleles played dinner music during the meal, dance music later. The singing was first-rate. In terms of gaiety, fare, and entertainment, it was the best native feast we've been to, before or since. (I am told that in spite of intimidating numbers Aheans still warmly, cheerfully, and impartially welcome all visiting yachts.)

One evening Papa Toa, Ahe's chief, and Peri, assistant chief and interpreter (he spoke French), came out to *Sea Foam* to visit. We sat around the saloon drinking tea and coffee. Peri had to interpret everything Papa Toa said. Small talk wound down to a halt. Nancy yawned a couple of big ones. It was time for them to go, yet they stayed.

Finally it came out. We were going to Papeete. Peri's wife and their grandchild were flying there, but Peri couldn't get on the plane. Would we take him with us?

"We're already five on board," I said.

"I can sleep on deck, or on the floor. No problem."

I looked at the others. Peri had told us he'd done some sea time. It was only a three-day trip. The Aheans have given more pleasure to yachts than we could ever repay. To hell with the inconvenience: take him.

A couple of days later, Peri was back. His wife, Te Va, couldn't get on the plane either. Could she come, too?

I had seen Te Va. She was quite stout. But once you've been persuaded to say yes to something, it is easy to be talked into saying yes to a little more. That's what they taught us in Fuller Brushmen's school.

"I guess so," I said. "Craig and Philip can double up for three days."

Peri left. Nancy looked at me, a sudden panic in her eyes.

"Do you suppose that means she's bringing the baby, too? She sure as hell isn't going to leave him here."

The Sunday we were to leave, Peri arrived aboard three hours early. No way were we going to be allowed to leave without him. With Peri were: Te Va, 300 pounds and a bad knee; their grandson, barely five months old; seven large cartons of pearl shells, to be sold in Tahiti; three suitcases; a bag of clean rags to be used as disposable diapers for the baby; and three cartons of food, including coconuts. We all gulped, moved over a little further, and managed, somehow, to get everything stowed for sea.

We left the pass just before 5:00 P.M., passing two other yachts as they entered. Lose one, gain two: good luck, heroic Ahe.

The pass between Arutua and Rangiroa is about 20 miles wide. The coconut trees on the northwest corner of Arutua were our only landmark as we approached from the north. Currents made the pass dangerous, so we wanted to negotiate it in daylight. In order not to arrive before dawn, we just loafed along due west under mizzen and staysail, barely making steerageway. At 1:00 A.M. we turned and headed south.

We raised all sail, and even though the wind was very light, on a broad reach we were making five knots. The seas were flat. Te Va stayed on her bunk except to go to the head, once daily. The baby stayed there with her. No matter what time of the day or night the baby woke up and cried, Peri was there, instantly. He changed diapers, discarded used ones over the side, and once a day warmed up a thermosful of formula on our stove. He slept on deck, and sat up with me on my watch, taking half the helm time. I couldn't have asked for more considerate, helpful passengers.

The baby delighted Nancy. She dandled him, cooed at him, gave him his bottle, hugged and patted him for burps. At one point I looked at her with my eyebrows raised a concerned, questioning quarter-inch.

"No chance," she reassured me. "Grandchildren only. But isn't he cute?"

He was. The son of a Tahitian mother and a Chinese father, he was a piquant genetic cocktail of the sort that gives many Tahitians their striking physical beauty. His features bore no clue, however, to the mysterious origin of his name, and I was hard put not to laugh at Nancy's doting, "There, there, Pedro."

After we passed between Arutua and Rangiroa, the wind dropped to nearly nothing. During the next 20 hours we made only 40 miles. We had barely enough fuel to make the rest of the trip under power, but I was determined to get to Tahiti as quickly as possible while the calm weather held. With Te Va and Pedro aboard, rough weather would have been a nightmare. We powered all day and all night. Philip sighted Tahiti at dawn. A breeze came up, and for the last 40 miles we suspended our love-hate relationship with the engine.

We reached Papeete Harbor by noon, tied up to the quay, and managed to get Peri, Te Va, Pedro, the seven boxes of pearl shells, and the three suitcases ashore without mishap. And every second day, for the next two weeks, gifts of fruit appeared mysteriously on our fantail.

SIXTEEN

PAPEETE, THE MAJOR PORT and port of entry of French Polynesia, is located on the northwest corner of the island of Tahiti. We found the harbor itself safe in all but the most vicious of northwesterly weather. The main street ran along the south shore of the harbor. Midway was a tiny park, the De Gaulle monument. To the east of the monument was the quay, the high-rent district; to the west, the shore was a rocky embankment, the low-rent district. Yachts in the high-rent district tied up close enough to the quay that a gangplank served for going ashore (neap tides were 12 inches, springs 18 inches). They could, if they chose, plug into 110-volt or 220-volt shore power. Sailors in the low-rent district had no access to shore power, and because they didn't tie up close enough to use a gangplank, they had to use a dinghy to get people on and off the boat. *Sea Foam*, with two brief exceptions, could always be found in the low-rent district.

Arriving sailboats disgorged crews that had been kept cooped up together for weeks. Often people exploded out of yachts like shrapnel, manic with gratitude that they'd neither gone crazy nor killed each other. They came from Hawaii, the U.S., Mexico, Panama, Canada. A few came up from New Zealand. Papeete was the scene of decisions, crew swappings, mate swappings, divorces, marriages, recriminations, congratulations, discoveries of pregnancy, fistfights, arguments, reconciliations, renunciations, and commitments. Things came to a head. Those who didn't adapt to cruising, who didn't find a satisfactory portion of the rewards they'd hoped for, went back where they came from, some of them sadder, some wiser. Many continued past Tahiti, feeling that the anxieties and interpersonal stresses caused by passagemaking were

amply rewarded by what they found after they arrived. Tahiti
was a threshold. Many who crossed it would decide that they'd
be happy to cruise for the rest of their lives.

The Societies offered tremendous variety within a relatively
small area. You could be entirely by yourself, or you could tie
up to the main street of a town-becoming-a-city. You could tie
up in front of any one of a number of tourist hotels, each with
its own atmosphere, or, with a little initiative, you could find and
visit a village that rarely saw a foreign yacht. We found places
where there was no one, and for brief periods of abandon left
all our clothing in the locker. Tiring of naked loneliness, we'd
rejoin the social whirl and swoop ashore every night dressed to
the nines. We met residents: Tahitian, French, expatriates from
everywhere. We potlucked and fishfried on tiny, uninhabited
Motu Tapu in Bora Bora; rafted up with several yachts for cocktails and dinner; and participated in Dutch-treat junkets to the
Bellevedere in Papeete (a hillside restaurant that will collect
you in a bus, feed you all you can eat and drink for a fixed price
in a setting that commands an unparalleled view, and return you
to your yacht waddling, weaving, and not too much poorer).
Sometimes we tucked into landlocked bays. Other times, during
the hot, humid summer, we anchored on the windward side of
a lagoon where we were secure in calm waters protected from the
sea by the coral reef, but cooled and kept bug-free by the constant trade winds. In Bora Bora we found the most spectacular
snorkeling in the Societies; in Huahine, shells and surfing waves;
in Raiatea, inlets with rivers to paddle up; in Tahaa, villages
which have remained basically the same for ten generations. We
alternated between elemental and luxurious life-styles in a rhythm
that pleased our sense of proportion, all in a setting of unqualified
magnificence and a climate that rarely deviated from perfection.
The question in my mind was never whether the Societies were
worth a visit, but whether we visitors had sufficient imagination
to be worthy of their promise.

When we first saw Tahiti, we watched it grow out of the western ocean into a towering cone of gold, frontlit by the firelight of

sunrise. From that moment on it was a heady brew of scenic grandeur and concentrated charisma, Mutiny-on-the-Bounty mystique and grass-skirted romance. Two subsequent visits proved that a first can't ever be a first again. But the wistful nostalgia this knowledge aroused was balanced by another feeling, the feeling that with each successive visit we were coming home. The breathy excitements of a new affair were replaced by a comfortable intimacy, an affectionate familiarity, and a possessiveness that occasionally took the form of jealousy. At least it did for me.

Toward the end of our third visit I became interested in getting the facts regarding the increase in the number of yachts that were invading *our* Polynesia. The figures from the Port Captain's office were much as I'd guessed: 190 foreign yachts in 1974; 220 in 1975; 262 in 1976; over 300 in 1977. Prior to 1974, pleasure yachts were not tabulated separately, but the official estimate was 160 yachts in 1973. Projections for the future boggled the mind....

Log, June 3, 1990: "We're approaching Ahe in the Tuamotus. We're beaming in on the Universtat-Constellar grid. Photocell pickups translate to print-out screens the intentions of passing yachts, transmitted by computerized, flashing running lights. Every yacht is on a beam reach, guaranteed by South Pacific Nuclear Trade-Winds Control, and the constant flow of traffic is regulated by Circulation Nautique, nerve center of the No-Longer-Dangerous Archipelago. As we approach the pass leading into the lagoon, specific instructions are flashed on the illuminated scoreboard, sold used to Ahe by the New York Mets back in 1985. Signals gleam red. The signboard puts us on hold.

"The holding pattern is crowded, but the waiting boats circle carefully and skillfully, sliding past each other in a graceful arabesque. Outgoing traffic, seasonally heavy, suddenly ceases. Signals glow green. We file in, bowsprit to boomkin. Once inside the lagoon, we diverge into four files and proceed with flotilla precision to the village.

"The original villagers have long since been transferred to remote atolls, prohibited to visitors in order to protect the cultural purity of Tuamotan life; but Southwest Casting has staffed Ahe with hypnotically trained personnel who re-enact the generous hospitality of the original inhabitants. We proceed to an assigned mooring. Jet launches collect us, and a wave of humanity surges ashore to soak up tropical experience.

"The bar opens at 8:00 P.M. The feast is at 9:00: frozen *poisson cru*; synthetic *poi*; instant taro root; and a light wine made from reconstituted coconut milk. The turnstile at the entrance to the great hall accepts credit cards. Hosts and hostesses are charming and gracious. Entertainment is live.

"The next day the yachts leave the village and spread out over the great lagoon to designated anchorages. A week is spent in isolated splendor, no neighbor closer than 500 meters, an organizational triumph. If one should prefer diversion to solitude, however, there is always the trip to the pass in the glass-bottom hydro to watch professional divers play among incredibly lifelike sharks. . . ."

"Everyone's sailing down here," I mused authoritatively one evening. "Tahiti's turning into a marina."

"So what?" rejoined Nancy. "More people, bigger parties."

"Paradise is overcrowded," I persisted. "SRO. No room at the inn." I waved my wine glass, imagining myself conducting muted cellos, minor chords.

"Nsns," answered Nancy, a dozen pins in her mouth, her right hand revving up her chartreuse, handcrank sewing machine. "Thr's plnty'v rm. Besides," she continued, pinless, "if there weren't lots of yachties I wouldn't be selling all these shirts and we'd be back on beans and rice." She was referring to Nancy's Originals—shirts, skirts, tops, and pants which made imaginative use of the inexpensive, brightly imprinted flour sacks available locally. She had started a rage. Fifty percent of all yachties in Papeete in July 1977 boasted a flour-sack shirt in their wardrobe. Picnics in the park looked like the stockroom of a bakery. During the hot, humid nights you could walk down the quay and see all the yachties sacked out on deck. Days, thanks to Nancy, you'd see them decked out in sacks.

"Okay. Okay, okay, okay." I could tell by the tone of her voice that when I spoke she heard not muted cellos but a solo bassoon. "But here we are, gunnel to gunnel at the quay. And look at the trouble we had squeezing in among all the other yachts last time we were in Huahine. I'm not sure it's worth it to come here any more."

"Of course it is," she said, because for her it always was.

Nancy's optimism to the contrary, the population explosion of cruising sailors was both a burden and a blessing. Always threatening was the possibility that yachts might become a bore, or worse. A case in point happened in the anchorage at Punaauia. Tired of the constant parade of sailors which passed her yard, roused her dog, and disturbed her family repeatedly with drunken, midnight shouts of "row in and get me," a Tahitian woman put up a barrier to the public-access pathway. A yachting Ms. with laundry, sure of her rights, stepped over the barrier and started up the path. The Tahitienne ran out to defend the land with an uppercut, knocking the lady and her laundry to the ground. A bit put out, Ms. Yachtie climbed to her feet and decked the aggressor with a right cross. Having gathered her scattered laundry, she retreated to her husband, who had observed only the end of the fracas from the dinghy and, not knowing his wife had acted in self-defense, punished her bad behavior by tossing her in the drink.

Next day the Tahitian lady admitted that she was *fiu* (up to here) with yachts. Her house had been ripped off and she was sure a yachtie had done it. She and her opponent made up, and a guarded truce was maintained, but her attitude was no longer that of the garlanded girl paddling out with welcoming gifts of blossoms and bananas.

Nevertheless, arriving in French Polynesia four years later we still found: a government which welcomed us, in spite of the crowd; which made constant efforts to streamline the check-in and -out procedures; which allowed duty-free importations to yachts in transit; which uncomplainingly handled the extra work of transient mail; which provided mooring facilities, water, electric power, showers, laundry facilities, and trash collection for our 36-footer for a mere $1.50 a day; and which considered the three greatest sins a yachtie could commit to be gun running, dope trafficking, and exhibiting a bad disposition.

Partly as a result of increasing yacht traffic we also found: a greater-than-ever choice of provisions at prices no worse than Hawaii's; a growing selection of marine supplies; diesel and electronic labs; haulout facilities; two yacht clubs; and an army of merchants delighted to get our business.

And away from the city we found that the island of Tahiti and the leeward islands, although peppered with visiting yachts, continued to offer some of the most beautiful cruising grounds in the world; that they were thoroughly and accurately charted; that all of the popular and some of the out-of-the-way places were marked with a complete system of buoys and beacons; and that with a small amount of adventurousness we could still enjoy a cove, lagoon, or motu by ourselves.

But the fact remained that the better-known, more popular anchorages were full of boats—lots of them. To blasé locals we were just another one of the bunch. No longer did we receive, gratis, the formerly abundant traditional hospitality. At least half of our friendships with locals we initiated ourselves. We were accepted and befriended, but no longer lionized.

A French friend found the yacht situation overwhelming. It used to be, he told me, that an occasional yacht anchored in front of his beachfront home. He enjoyed the aura of romance it lent to his lagoon, and enjoyed meeting the intriguing, adventuresome people aboard. Since then the yachts have often numbered a half-dozen or more, adorning his erstwhile Utopian panorama with nude, soapy bodies, a foliage of flapping laundry, and a soundtrack of noisy generators and outboards—all virtually on his doorstep. We felt that we and other sailors could prolong our welcome by being sensitive to local feelings, by not congregating in places where the mood couldn't absorb great numbers.

With lots of yachts around us we struggled not to fall into the biggest trap of all—social exclusiveness. Partying with our friends was the easiest and most natural thing to do. To the French and Tahitians we could thus appear standoffish, cliquish. It took real energy to get past the hurdles of differing language, custom, taste, and (most of all) sense of humor. But more often than not our efforts were rewarded with a new friendship, and perhaps even an ally if the question should come to a vote: yachties, yea or nay.

Nancy saw no problem. She agreed with a Tahitian lady we met. On the southeast end of Tahiti, past the point where the road ends, we found a tranquil cove. Bow anchor out, we backed toward shore, our eye on a palm tree. This lady appeared, seemingly from nowhere, as I rowed ashore with the sternline.

"Okay if we tie up to your tree?" I asked in my best French.

"Why certainly," she replied, apparently amazed that I should ask. "The world is for everyone, n'est-ce pas?"

Later on in the cabin I had Nancy cornered, glued once again to her sewing machine.

"All right, you absolutely have to admit that if boats continue to swarm down here, the whole thing is going to be ruined. I mean, imagine a NO VACANCY sign on the Pearly Gates, an OUT OF WINGS sign at the commissary, sharing your harp, being pushed off your pink cloud . . ." I could have gone on, but Nancy interrupted.

"Dn't b rdcls," she squeezed through the pins. "Th mr th mrry'r."

Which, even now, is the state of the *Sea Foam* standoff. However, during our first visit in 1973 none of this had occurred to me, and though we were beset by economic vicissitudes, our 11-month stay in the Societies was pure cruising delight, as yet not infected with the bacteria of possessiveness.

SEVENTEEN

KIM WESTON AND OUR SON CHRIS, convinced that *Sea Foam*'s standing rigging was far too loose even though it was designed to be sloppy, spent two days when we were in Bora Bora tuning every stay and shroud. We left Bora Bora in beautiful weather and 20 knots of wind, our destination nearby Raiatea.

We were flying, full and by, mizzen, main, staysail, and jib drawing *Sea Foam* across the swells at an angle that suited her rhythms. When *Sea Foam* sails hard on the wind it is war, chop and swell insisting "you won't," fat hull valiantly maintaining "I will." Each rise and fall is a battle that *Sea Foam*, battered to a complete stop, loses as often as she wins. But when she's just off the wind, direct confrontation is avoided. We slide over the watery hills and valleys in a harmony of speed and spray, while wind and rigging sing a counterpoint of dissonance and resolution that makes the blood race.

We were one hour out when there was a loud snap, and *Sea Foam*'s rigging sagged like a holed balloon. Kim's yell from the foredeck had a touch of panic in it.

"Into the wind! Come up into the wind—the bobstay's broken!"

The bobstay runs from cutwater to bowsprit, pulling the bowsprit down against the upward tension of the forestay and headstay. When it failed, the bowsprit rose a foot, and all fore-and-aft support of the masts was lost. I rounded up into the wind and hit the starter button. The diesel responded immediately, enabling me to keep *Sea Foam* in irons, the sails flapping and spilling the suddenly dangerous wind. We got the sails down in less than five minutes, but it seemed like an eternity. The unsupported masts were probably moving no more than a foot at the tips, but it seemed to me they were waving like the arms of a signal-man, semaphoring a life-and-death message.

"What happened?" I asked. I couldn't believe that the half-inch chain that was our bobstay had failed.

"It's the fitting," said Chris. I went forward to have a look. The stainless steel tang to which the bobstay was attached had torn away from the stem, taking half the deadwood with it.

"We're lucky we didn't lose the masts," said Kim. "Jesus, I'm sorry."

"Forget it," I said. "It's more my fault than yours. Besides, better to have it happen here than far from land in mid-passage."

I wasn't being generous. It really *was* my fault. This fitting was the one I should have removed in San Diego and replaced with one bolted conventionally, fore and aft through the stem. The one that had pulled out had been bolted athwartships, across the grain of the wood. This was the worst possible way to stress the wood, an open invitation for it to split.

After giving the mainmast as much support as we could by using the jib and staysail halyards as forestays, we powered the 35 miles to Huahine. Even with no sail up, the masts moved around alarmingly. We would have to concoct something more solid for our 80-mile leg to Papeete, where I'd arranged by radio to have *Sea Foam* hauled out. Besides, for me it was worrisome to rely solely on the motor at sea.

In Huahine we rigged a huge underbelly sling, a long chain that led from the stern samson post in a great loop under the fore-foot. To this we attached the bobstay with a turnbuckle, having first wrapped the giant loop of chain with carpet and rags at points of chafe. The rig supported the bowsprit fine. Although we never had to test its strength unduly, we were able to power-sail to weather all the way from Huahine to Moorea, the masts steady as rocks.

While in Moorea we anchored in Robinson's Cove, the Society Islands' challenge to Fatu Hiva's scenic supremacy. Bow anchor out, stern lines to palm trees, we were snug, completely sheltered from the ocean and watched over by towering sentinels of granite.

It was a grace period wherein we collected our spiritual reserves. We knew that in one week we would be entering the cruiser's purgatory: living aboard one's boat in a shipyard.

The first time we ever hauled out *Sea Foam* was in San Diego, just prior to our departure. Little prepared as we were to accept the fact that boat maintenance is a never-ending struggle, the excitement of the voyage ahead of us carried us through. Even though we slept aboard and were awakened early by the yard workers, we went to coffee shops and restaurants for all our meals, and for cleanup we drove back to our marina (we still had our car) to enjoy a sauna, steambath, shower, and swim in the pool. Having worked hard for our tired muscles and grime, we took the luxuries as our due. None of us realized that these were the vestiges of our old way of life, and that no matter where we went in our travels, never again would our bodies be so pampered nor a haulout so pleasant.

Our next haulout was in Costa Rica, where we first became acquainted with boatyard trauma. First of all, we were charged at the rate of $30 a day—a very high price for Costa Rica in 1973—which put pressure on us to get the job done fast. Second, we had no way to escape from the boat, so we ate there, slept there, and took sponge baths from the fresh water we had on board. Third, we were right next to a construction site where the workers started at dawn, quit at dusk, and spent most of the time in between watching the girls sand and paint in brief costumes. Fourth, we had to put up with an outrageous outhouse.

The abomination stood high off the ground on precarious two-by-four legs, the theory being that the tide, having come in twice a day for a long time, would continue to do so, thereby keeping the area under the privy clean. The theory was okay, but the designer had forgotten that most of the time the tide was out. Furthermore, the structure was enclosed only from the floor up, so that both privacy of the body and publicity of its product were guaranteed. Droppings fell six feet to the sand, accompanied by noises which were megaphonically amplified by an unfortunate coincidence of acoustics. The most polite thing you could say to someone would be "How did you do?" implying the lie that you hadn't noticed, but with time we hardened and took to greeting emerging performers with boos or applause as they merited, the workers next door looking on with bewildered amusement.

In Papeete, the facilities in the boatyard were primitive but not trauma-producing. The shower was a hose, but there was clean, fresh water and plenty of it. The toilet was one of those French "bombsight" toilets, a hole in the floor with a place to put each foot, but it was private, and most of the time it flushed and was kept clean.

One time the boatyard toilet did clog up, and we were forced to walk to the next-door yard to use theirs. The owner was so unpleasant about it that I finally went to our yard owner to demand that he get his toilet fixed. Amazingly enough, he produced a key to a real, just-like-home toilet reserved for live-aboard customers like ourselves, the existence of which he'd forgotten to mention. The yard workers were still out of luck, as the hole in the floor stayed plugged up for days, but we yachties were in good shape.

Wingy got really upset about the head. Wingy was the one-armed, toothless Tahitian who lived in a shed in the yard. He served as night watchman and did whatever odd jobs needed doing. I never saw him at a loss when it came to doing anything a man with two arms could do, but Wingy was still treated by the boss and the other Tahitians as a second-class citizen.

In the evenings after work, Wingy and I used to sit in front of his shed, sharing a beer and making conversational sounds, none of which were comprehensible to the other. Wingy spoke basic Tahitian and what must have been Pig-French. Sometimes we'd end up with him mumbling in Tahitian, of which I know four words, and me in American, in which his vocabulary was zero. Nothing was decided about the future of the world, but many cocktail parties boast chitchat of as little import, and at least ours was never argumentative.

The boss got after Wingy to get the head working, and Wingy

tried, I'll say that for him. He was like a doctor who issues only one prescription, no matter what the patient's complaint. With the toilet, Wingy's one method usually worked. It consisted of sticking a running hose down the hole and then going away and doing something more pleasant. After a while—at the propitious moment, in Wingy's mind—he would return, snatch the hose from the hole, and uttering the Tahitian equivalent of *"voilà!"* he would flush the toilet. Usually, he would be rewarded with success, but this time he achieved nothing. Wingy persisted, varying the time of applied water from short, sneaky little squirts to an eight-hour marathon. One evening, three days and at least 30,000 gallons later, we heard something lurching its way up the rickety ladder that provided access to *Sea Foam*'s deck.

It was Wingy, swaying with each step in a giant arc from side to side, a half-empty quart of Scotch clutched under his stump. He eventually made it halfway, and I was able to lean over and rescue the bottle. Freed from his burden, Wingy scampered up the last five rungs in something under four minutes. Nancy said I was callous to grab the bottle. She should try helping a one-armed, ladder-climbing drunk from above.

Having reached the cockpit, Wingy repossessed the bottle, took a long swig, sat down hard, and insisted that Chris and I join him in a drink. There was about half a bottle left. Knowing that if he finished it he'd be an overnight guest, and knowing also that a Tahitian doesn't know how to recap a bottle be it beer or booze, Chris and I selflessly undertook to save him from himself. We drank, and after an hour of increasing camaraderie we were able, through Chris's incipient Tahitian and my French, to piece together Wingy's simple story.

Which was that he'd quit. He was damned if he'd spend the rest of his life cleaning out stopped-up toilets. He didn't care what happened, the yard would have to get along without him. They couldn't treat *him* like this. Confirmed underdog-lovers, Chris and I were with him all the way.

Having been declaiming instead of drinking, Wingy was sober enough at the end of an hour to make successful descent a possibility, whereas Chris and I had done enough of a number on ourselves to insist on helping him. I sent Chris down first so that if Wingy slipped he wouldn't fall on the hard ground, while I gave advice from the deck.

In the morning Wingy was gone. The next morning a plumber arrived with a brace of helpers. Even with the aid of a power-driven snake, it took them nearly a full day to clear the pipes. Meanwhile, the carpenters and shipwrights were making their own coffee, sweeping their own shavings, and fetching and carrying everything. After an absence of four days, Wingy came back to his old stand and was welcomed effusively by his fellow workers. His bearing was erect, and he had a new and unmistakable gleam of independence in his eyes.

The bobstay tang took shape. The wood for the stem was scarfed in, and a strap of quarter-inch stainless steel six feet long was throughbolted and lagscrewed into the stem. The tang was another strap of stainless steel, welded and throughbolted to the first. Perhaps it was overkill, but it comforted us to know that this particular piece of hardware would no longer be one of the rigging's weakest links.

Our two weeks in the boatyard—or more precisely, the bill for our two weeks in the boatyard—forced Nancy and me to confront a problem that we had pushed aside during the previous months. Our money had been disappearing at a rapid pace. After paying the boatyard bill, we had $200 left to our names. The question of how we were going to finance continuing on to New Zealand—or anywhere, for that matter—was demanding an answer.

"What'll we do?" I asked Nancy one drizzly morning, demonstrating once again my qualities of dynamic leadership.

"One step at a time," she said, her usual rejoinder. This, in a nutshell, typified our working relationship. In times of trouble I looked into the future and saw pitfalls and obstacles, accumulating in the process enough apprehension and indecision to hypnotize myself into a statue. Nancy would remind me that to get from here to there required a series of individual, manageable tasks.

We tied up for a time in the low-rent district in Papeete, and Chris and I picked up jobs varnishing and painting other yachts, each drawing down a staggering $12 a day. Nancy and Conni found sewing jobs. When work at the quay ran out, we moved to Punaauia, where I got a job painting a boat for $20 a day. Not only was this a substantial raise, but as a fringe benefit, most days I could swim to work. Conni connected with a boutique which gave her more sewing than she could handle—the excess she spun off to Nancy. My first cruising article sold, a minisuccess that to me was heady wine, and I sent off a second, and a third. Chris had moved off *Sea Foam* and was crewing on a 40-foot sloop for an elderly single-hander. Chris's plan was to save enough to fly home, or to get a berth on a yacht that was sailing there. It appeared he would have his choice.

It was a time of peace for Nancy and me, a time of doing our own things. Little by little we were accumulating enough to provision for our passage to New Zealand. And if you have to work, it is some consolation to be in a beautiful spot. Our setting was dreamlike: *Sea Foam* sat in a mirror surface, while ten boat-lengths away the ocean self-destructed on the reef, pulverizing its blueness to whiteness, and the sun shone.

EIGHTEEN

IT WAS IN PUNAAUIA that I first recognized the Old Anchorage Resident syndrome. We'd planted our hook in a small area in front of the Auberge de Pacific Restaurant, and there was only room for three or four boats to swing in this particular hole. I found myself viewing newcomers as intruders—with suspicion and mistrust. In subsequent conversations with other yachties I discovered that all Old Anchorage Residents (OARs) feel the same way about newcomers (Newks). During the time that a Newk is anchoring, the mutual assistance pact to which most yachtsmen subscribe is put in abeyance. Newks are watched by OARs covertly but attentively, and how a Newk copes will determine his acceptance by the OARs even more than when or how long he runs his generator. The way this actually works out, however, was a surprise to me.

The Polynesian Psychological Society has documented the depth of animosity that OARs hold for Newks. At the quay in Papeete, one drops anchor anywhere from 150 to 250 feet off and ties up either stern or bow to the quay. Sailboats, most of which are notoriously unmaneuverable in reverse, make of this a tricky task even on a calm day. When the wind comes up it is usually a cross wind, and the difficulties increase geometrically. The PPS observed the efforts of 1,000 yachts and came up with the following results, using civilians as a norm against which to contrast the OARs' performances.

Situation 1: Newk drops anchor and backs in smartly on his first attempt.

a) Civilians catch well-thrown docklines eight times out of ten. Though they often have trouble making the line fast, they generally succeed in doing something which is adequate for the moment, the end result being that the Newk's anchoring is smoothly and expertly completed.

b) OARs who you *know* could walk a bowsprit in a gale with one hand full of sail ties and the other one full of shackles *miss* catching the dockline 90 percent of the time, doing it in such a way that the line thrower appears incompetent, and nearly always causing such confusion that the Newk has to repeat the backing-up procedure, doing it poorly because of his irritation.

Situation 2: Newk drops anchor and makes a couple of awkward attempts to back in, finally getting close enough to get a line ashore, maybe.

a) Because of the increased difficulty of the throw and the increased psychological pressure on the line catcher, civilians miss the line 50 percent of the time.

b) OAR's success average *increases* to 50 percent.

Situation 3: Newk butchers the operation in every way. The anchor is put down too close to the quay and has to be raised and re-set. The chain fouls repeatedly in the locker, requiring great yellings and swearings from poop to foredeck. The backing maneuver is only completed after several near-disasters, much gunning of the motor, and constant crises of fending off.

a) Civilian, tired of waiting, has gone home.

b) OAR increases his average to 97 percent success, making one-handed retrieves that would have left Willie Mays standing agape.

Situation 4: Newk, hanging off his anchor in a 20-knot crosswind about 25 spaces from his intended slot, his dinghy painter wrapped tightly around his propeller shaft, calls for help.

a) Civilian neither hears nor notices his plight.

b) A phalanx of OARs in a flotilla of tenders motors out to shepherd the poor fool in.

In follow-up interviews, the marine psychologists determined that OARs were totally unaware of the jealousy and resentment that inhibits their coordination. When shown the statistics they were amazed. I discussed this with a sailor-psychologist who is skilled in self-awareness. He confessed to the following:

"I'll never forget one time here at the quay when *Siren Song* came in for the first time. A 50-foot racing cutter with no engine and a crew of incredible skill, she dropped anchor under full sail and continued toward the quay at about eight knots. With perfect timing the foredeck crew dogged the anchor rode as the helmsman put the tiller down. It was a tremendous shock to me suddenly to realize that I was intoning a silent prayer: 'Please, Lord, let their rode part, their windlass brake fail, the rudder jam—anything, but let that show-off SOB sail headlong into the cement.' I, a man who refuses to fish because he cannot bear the agony of the hooked worm, I am hoping for a disaster. But it never came. Not only did *Siren Song* snap around in perfect position, but the afterdeck crew, disdaining the helping hand, *lassoed the bollards!* As you can well understand, no one spoke a word to them the whole time they were in port."

The converse is also true. The most welcome Newk is he whose best efforts never exceed what one might expect from Laurel and Hardy. I remember sitting in Hana Vave Bay on the island of Fatu Hiva with four other yachts. It was night, one of the blackest, when God has dropped the cover on the cage and we parrots must sleep. Outside the bay, a mile or two off, were the running lights of a yacht. Knowing that it would be impossible to enter safely in the total darkness, a couple of us turned on lights to guide our brother in. Once in, however, brotherhood ended and the OAR–Newk relationship took over. The acoustic perfection of the bay enabled us to overhear the loving exchanges between wife at the helm and hubby in the bow.

FEMALE VOICE: "How far in are we?"

MALE VOICE: "Who knows?"

FV: "I think we should go in a little further."

MV: "I can't see a damn thing—let's drop it here."

FV: "What's the matter with you? I don't want to anchor half-way out in the middle of the goddamn ocean."

MV: "I don't care. I can't see well enough." (Sounds of chain in hawsepipe.) "Reverse!"

FV: "I still think we should go farther—"

MV: *"Reverse!"* (Sounds of reverse.) "Neutral!" (Antisounds of neutral. Sudden cessation of chain-hawsepipe sounds.)

FV: "Oh, *shit!* Did you forget to make the end of that chain fast? You *ninny*. I told you . . ." (Harangue continues to the accompaniment of suppressed OAR laughter.)

The next day, bright and early, an OAR appeared with scuba gear and made a successful dive for their ground tackle. The Newks were deluged with invitations to cocktails and dinner in gratitude for the entertainment they'd provided, and for demonstrating that their competence was no threat to the rest of us.

During the period of our inchoate skill, we on *Sea Foam* worked out a conservative routine. We would motor slowly around the anchorage in the manner of a dog that sniffs about a bed of leaves, scratches out a depression, turns around several times to get the lay of his bed, then snuggles down, belly to warm earth. Where you drop the anchor will determine how far you have to row ashore, how you'll feel if the wind blows up, how close to or far from your neighbors' noises you are, and other considerations which will contribute to enjoying or not enjoying that particular anchorage. It is a decision so sensitive and so critical that I can safely say it has been the cause of more near-mutinies on our boat than any other situation.

We used to be consistently guilty of using incredible amounts of scope. When we bought *Sea Foam*, she carried a 40-pound Danforth-type anchor. It would not dig in unless we put out 7:1 scope or better. We never felt secure with it unless we put out 10:1, which may account for our being called "swingers" in the anchorages we carved a broad swathe through. From California to New Zealand and back we diligently sought anchorages with a maximum depth of 30 feet so that our 50 fathoms of chain would suffice. To provide ourselves with enough margin of safety for swinging room, we always found ourselves much farther out than anyone else and spent much of our port time rowing.

Our tendency to drag continued to mystify me. My anchor *looked* like others of the same type. It certainly weighed enough.

Devotees of this type of anchor swore by it. If I'm dragging and other people aren't, I'm doing something wrong, right? I felt deficient, inadequate, both judgments reinforced by my scornful crew. We always had more trouble setting anchor than anyone else, and when the night winds came up, if anyone was going to drag, it was *Sea Foam*.

I re-read the experts. Chapman: "5:1 minimum, 8:1 normally. Chances are you'll never need more than *15:1!*" (Italics mine.) Royce: "4:1 general purpose, 8:1 for storms." Hiscock: "3:1 at high water." Still not making the proper deductions, I increased our usual scope to 15:1 and continued to compile a miserable record. At a depth of 30 feet, I had to plan on a swinging circle with a diameter of slightly more than one-fifth of a mile. We began to eliminate some of the smaller anchorages we'd hoped to visit. As for Hiscock, I was convinced that my anchor wasn't even touching bottom when I had a mere 3:1 out.

Two anchors on the same rode (the system we had used in Ensenada) provide as near a sure thing as there is in the anchoring game, but the system has its disadvantages. Too many changes of wind direction can make a fouled-up mess. And it's difficult to get all that ground tackle back aboard, particularly in deep water when you're hauling up the weight of both anchors and considerable chain. Consequently we only used this method when conditions were extreme. However, with just one anchor out, if the wind came up at night I could count on a severe case of nerves.

The seeds of my enlightenment were planted while we were anchored in Punaauia. Often, while swimming back and forth to work, I would gaze fondly through my dripping mask at a young valkyrian naiad who, thick blond mane to her hips, sunbathed nude on carefree, cloudless days. The 38-foot sloop on which she lived was anchored to a plow in eight feet of water by 20 feet of chain. Surely, I schemed, on the first blustery day it will drag, I will leap into my jetfins, churn down the lagoon, save this maiden from destruction on the reef, and reap the hero's harvest.

I kept vigil in vain. If the wind blew over 30 knots my nymph would go to the bow and let out another ten feet of scope, retrieving it when the wind died down. Eventually I arrived at the conclusion that not only was she capable of taking care of herself, but she knew more about anchoring than I did. The finale of my fantasy was written on the day that *Sea Foam*, having wrapped some of her 8:1 scope around the fluke of the fisherman, dragged past my heroine at about four knots. "Need any help, Dad?" she asked with a faintly derisive smile.

It was two more years before we finally acquired our own plow anchor, a 45-pounder. Our lives completely changed. No longer did we make at least three attempts before the anchor grabbed hold, covering more miles in reverse than many yachts do in forward. Instead we entered anchorages confidently, dropped the hook, paid out moderate scope, backed down, and stopped. We were moored, tied to the bottom as if rooted. It will take us years to live down our old reputation, perhaps because we haven't done all we might to dispel our ill fame: after acquiring our plow we twice arrived in prosperous anchorages with our purse thin and our liquor locker dry, and promptly staged an artificial debacle. The hospitality engendered by our ineptitude exceeded my highest expectations, and the guilt that accrued was, I reckoned, a fair enough price to pay.

Two days before Bastille Day we moved *Sea Foam* to Papeete Harbor and found a slot right in the center of the high-rent district. Being tied up to the main street of a city in the throes of its own version of Mardi Gras insures involvement. "What the hell," said Nancy, summing up, "if you're gonna go to a party, go to a party."

Bastille Day, July 14, is celebrated in Papeete over a seven-day period. Daytime is crammed with native races, contests, and tournaments of all kinds. All the nights but one are devoted to the dance competition: teams from all the islands, beautifully rehearsed and costumed, vie for first place and a world tour. Phil Walker from *Scaldis* had once more talked his way into the good graces of the powers that were and had passes to everything. Two friends from California appeared out of nowhere and gave us three days' worth of passes they couldn't use. Nancy and I, previously resigned to attending only the freebies, suddenly found ourselves celebrating like visiting royalty. Two of the passes got us to the Governor's Ball. We danced every dance; joined groups of strangers and smiled at them as they spouted unintelligible argot at an insane clip; and walked home as the sun was coming up, arms around each other's waist, in that lockstep you learn if you love someone shorter (taller) than you. Good parties are Nancy's fountain of youth. She sheds 20 years. I felt pretty good myself.

During the week, *Sea Foam* was moored in one of the most advantageous locations for watching the fête. We hosted hundreds on a bring-your-own-sandwich-and-beer basis. Men's and women's canoe races were held in the harbor right off our bowsprit. There were individual races for each class, from single-paddlers to 16-paddlers. In addition, there were sailing-canoe races and hydroplane races. My heart swelled at the volume of cheers, shouts, and squeals that came from thousands of native throats urging special champions to Herculean efforts. Such loyalty, such village patriotism!

"Don't be naïve," said Nancy. "We could cruise for the rest of our lives on one percent of the money that's changing hands."

Being tied up in Papeete's high-rent district, we were able to enjoy the unaccustomed luxury of a gangplank. But when we were in the low-rent district, we were forced to get ashore via dinghy. Usually I rigged an outhaul, a long, continuous line that ran through a block on *Sea Foam* and another block on shore. This meant that transportation was always available, and we were relieved from the frustration caused by dinghy deficiency.

Dinghy deficiency resulted from our having given far too little thought to selecting a tender or tenders for *Sea Foam*. Our original thinking was molded by economics and ignorance, both of which could have been overcome with a little imagination. As it was, with a crew that never numbered less than five, we endured two years of cruising with only one ancient, four-man inflatable. Month after month we made two trips whenever we all wanted to go ashore.

When we got to New Zealand I took a steady job as a carpenter, which required leaving *Sea Foam* at 7:00 A.M.—often, in the winter months, in the darkness of a raw, cold, drizzling rain. I watched Nancy, whose lot it was to ferry me ashore, gradually deteriorate psychologically. Her usual bubbling banter disappeared, and our relationship was reduced to a series of sullen silences. Finally a friend with an extra skiff took pity, and I was able to row myself ashore. Nancy was once more able to sleep, and although the weather didn't improve, sunshine came back into our lives. When the time came to return the skiff to its owner we promptly bought an identical one, wondering how we'd existed without two tenders. Subsequently we cruised for another two and a half years with Nancy, Craig, and myself aboard. Even with only three of us we found two tenders a luxury-turned-necessity, giving us the flexibility to go separate ways.

To date we have never had an outboard. I have always enjoyed rowing, but whenever possible I've given this privilege to the crew. Never having become dependent on a motor, we don't miss having one. The few times I've caught myself envying outboarders are far outnumbered by the times we've watched friends fiddling with just one more refractory machine. The most recent instance occurred off the Royal Suva Yacht Club during our second visit to Fiji in 1978. A young couple left their yacht, happy and smiling, headed for some pre-dinner cocktails at the yacht club bar. Their tiny outboard pushed their fiberglass pram along at an effortless three knots. Before they'd covered one-tenth of the quarter-mile distance, the motor quit. In the sudden silence, the English language's most popular scatological expletive reverberated through the anchorage.

"Honey!" shushed his wife reprovingly.

"Sorry. Lost my head. I'll have it going again in a minute."

He wound a rope around the flywheel and pulled a mighty

pull. Nothing. Another try was followed by yet another. The motor responded with those lifeless chuffs that are totally devoid of encouragement.

Still in control of his temper and, he thought, the situation, he ran through a rudimentary checklist: gas in the tank; gas cap vent open; gas shutoff on; choke no longer choking; sparkplug dry. Wind, pull; wind, pull; wind, *pull*. Nothing.

The offshore breeze carried them several hundred feet past their yacht, and they were drifting at an alarming rate toward the pass and open ocean. The skipper went through the checklist again, angry haste causing clumsiness and delay. Having pumped the priming button till a kaleidoscopic wedge of petroleum slick spread out from the pram's stern, he wound and pulled, wound and pulled. I could see through my binoculars that his face was flushed, his breathing labored. The couple was too far away to be heard, but due to a skill in lip-reading which I developed during my acid-rock period, I was able to follow their conversation.

"Do you want me to row?"

He snapped around to glare at her, his face contorted.

"No! This sonofabitchin' thing's gonna start or I'm gonna know the reason why."

"Maybe just to keep from losing ground?" she asked meekly.

He snarled an answer which I missed, but his wife got out the oars and started rowing. Hubby then fell into a fit of mindless starter-yanking, only occasionally backlashing his sweating oarsperson across the face. Knowing that the evening would be a dead loss unless either the engine started or someone rowed out with some booze, Wife began intoning an unorthodox silent prayer, which, she confided to me later, was simply, "Please, God, let the fucking thing start." Mercifully, He did, albeit 30 feet from the dock.

The small-outboard owner often knows his engine intimately. There is a tendency for him to feel its problems as if they were the problems of his own flesh, and to defend its eccentricities with the unreasoning loyalty of kinship. He at times will lie shamelessly about its reliability, its economy, its long service. ("That sweet-runnin' little jewel? She's been cruising with us since '75.")

A typical member of the species once joined us along with his wife for dinner and drinks aboard *Sea Foam*. When it came time to leave, his wife offered to row the short distance back to their boat.

"Naw, we'll power," said her husband, plopping determinedly into the sternsheets.

We monitored their progress aurally. The buzz of the engine was punctuated four times by intervals of silence. The next morning I asked him what had happened.

"Aw, the line filter's a little dirty. All I had to do was take off the gas cap and blow into the tank—build up some air pressure for a minute or two, you know—and the sweetheart started right away." He seemed in good spirits despite the fact that his breath smelled like a gas pump.

Little-outboard owners are much like little-dog owners. Accompanied wherever they go by their yapping pets, the masters are tender and solicitous when their charges behave, scolding and finger-wagging when they don't. Big outboarders are a different breed. Broad of shoulder, wide of stance, their eyes are mere slits, and their hair, if they have any, flows behind them as if whipped by imaginary airstreams. They talk out of the corners of their mouths. Either they overload their dinghies with passengers and bulldoze through the anchorage at 12 knots, trailing a surfable wake, or they load light and, planing like rocketing bugs that barely dent the surface of the lagoon, they scream off into the vanishing point of imagination. Mechanical problems rarely arise for big outboarders, and those that do are dispatched quickly with the impersonal, calculated confidence of a trainer of Doberman guard dogs. A big outboarder is abstracted during most conversations, and the only way to pique his interest is to talk about trading up to a more powerful outboard.

Scaldis boasted one of these superdinghies. It was lovely to share in the convenience and extended horizons that a fast boat provides. With only arms and oars as resources, we would have missed the picnics on faraway beaches, snorkeling excursions to distant reefs, and successful fishing trips trolling in the passes. Often we sped miles to the nearest village to mail letters or to pick up fresh produce, ice, and beer. Only half of these trips had to be made just to buy gas.

We once spent a month with a yacht that had a sailing outrigger canoe. Several times Nancy and I had the use of it for the day. Aesthetically, the sailing canoe was a quantum leap forward. We explored large areas of the lagoon too shallow for *Sea Foam*'s six-foot, six-inch draft or too distant for a rowing expedition, and saw places we'd never have seen while thoroughly enjoying the process of getting there. One evening we were becalmed on the homeward leg. Nancy and I later agreed that had we been stranded in an outboard I would have spent hours getting greasy and losing my temper. As it was, with only one small paddle as an auxiliary, we threw over an anchor and watched Midas work his magic in the western sky. Supper was picnic leftovers—bread and cheese, some red wine. Later the romantic setting led to amorous experiments which the narrowness of the canoe spiced with challenge and risk. Finally, when the full moon reached the meridian, a land breeze sprang up and wafted us, sleepy but content, back to *Sea Foam*.

In spite of all we had read on the subject of cruising, we completely failed to grasp what the life is actually like until we'd lived it for a while. People cruise at different paces, just as people live at different paces ashore; but we, and by far the majority of cruising yachts, have observed the following. 1) Nine out of every ten days, month after month and year after year, are spent at anchor. 2) Once moored, anchored, or tied up to a quay, a tremendous inertia keeps you there. Things that are lashed for sea are unlashed, and things that have special places for a passage are left out for convenience. Half-finished projects lie on deck under tarpaulins. 3) As a result of (2) it requires anything from a half-day to three days just to ready the yacht for a day-sail. A day-sail in protected waters is most sailors' favorite diversion, but because of the effort required to ready a yacht-home-workshop for an outing, the majority of cruising yachts tend to stay put.

Taking these factors into consideration, we've come to the conclusion that a cruising couple needs several tenders. Number one should be a small inflatable, a light, stable utility boat to be propelled primarily by rowing. Number two should be a fiberglass dinghy designed for sailing, with the largest hull you can carry on deck. Number three: a planing inflatable with a husky outboard. Four: a surf-sailor. Five: a kayak. Six through ten: whatever else you can cram aboard. Admittedly, this solution is expensive, but freedom and mobility are two of the objectives that drive most of us to sea. If you are like we are and spend 90 percent of your time at anchor, the only answer is a veritable fleet of small craft.

Sea Foam, Scaldis, and several other yachts all met in Huahine for the filming of the grand finale of *Aroha.* We were staging a Tahitian double wedding, followed by a traditional Tahitian feast.

Random memories:

. . . Taking an inflatable to the shallow lagoon northwest of the Huahine Bali Hai Hotel; sitting there at anchor, preparing to don fins and mask, when a lovely Tahitian girl swims alongside, having materialized, apparently, out of thin water. From the tub that she is towing she takes oysters, opens them expertly, and hands one to each of us with half a lime. To our unbelieving thank-you's she responds with a wide you're-welcome smile and swims away. . . .

. . . Nancy and I, the morning of the wedding, walking along the road searching for frangipani; finding none until we reach a small cemetery, where there are thousands of blossoms; Nancy tripping blithely among the graves, gathering, gathering, while I nervously pick up a few so that, should this sacrilege draw the wrath of a Polynesian god, Nancy will have company. . . .

. . . Phil Walker, in the course of filming the wedding in the outdoor cathedral of palm trees, zooming in on the book from which Papa, the master of ceremonies, is reading the service. The camera focuses on a full-page, full-color, front-view male nude, and the wedding is interrupted while Phil recovers. Papa explains that he always performs the service from memory. When asked to read it, he had to improvise, and selected, as a prop, an anatomy text with a pretty cover. . . .

. . . Eating on the beach off banana-leaf plates; drinking wine from bamboo cups; the whole group walking fully clothed into neck-deep water, successfully checkmating the mid-afternoon heat. . . .

. . . Running when the rains come and finding shelter in a copra-drying shed; the band resuming, the guests bravely boogeying like hunched-over gnomes in the five-foot headroom. . . .

. . . Collapsing, exhausted, on *Sea Foam* about midnight, while small scattered groups continue to make party sounds till dawn.

Nancy and I invited a young California girl named Marci to crew with us to New Zealand. She had flown down to join *Scaldis* for a few weeks, and her soupçon of cruising life had merely whetted her appetite for more. We had lost Chris and were about to lose Conni. We had grown fond of Marci in the brief time we'd known her, and she was willing to chip in for food. But it was a big decision for her, and she was hesitant.

As a get-acquainted day that might help her make up her mind, we invited her to sail the 35 miles from Huahine to Bora Bora with us. We caught a fish going out the pass. The seas were moderate, the sky blue, the wind fresh on the port quarter. *Sea Foam* was on one of her best points of sail, and the day's run was relaxed and dry. Neptune, the Great Seducer, was making all the right moves. Although Marci didn't give us a definite decision until a week later, by the time we motored into the Bora Bora pass in the golden-yellows of a brilliant sunset, we knew she had been won over.

Following a few more days of underwater filming, *Scaldis* set sail for an island-hopping return trip to Papeete. Conni, Chris, and Philip had left. Marci moved aboard. The rest of the cast dispersed. The stage hands were striking the set; the janitors sweeping the theater. After a successful year's run, the play had finally folded, leaving Craig, Marci, Nancy, and myself to contemplate the western horizon, suddenly feeling very much alone.

NINETEEN

OUR MONTHS OF CRUISING in the Societies had made us loathe to leave. We never tired of snorkeling in clear water, exchanging stares with brightly colored fish, exploring coral kingdoms, finding shells. We were accustomed to fresh produce, fruit, ice cream, and cold beer on demand. We'd made many friends. We were pampered and spoiled, and we'd gotten soft. After nine sheltered and gregarious months, the open ocean seemed lonesome, forbidding, and endless.

We took one more day to go over the rigging, another to scrub *Sea Foam*'s already pristine bottom, yet another to pick up those few provisions we'd overlooked. Still we procrastinated. It was Friday, and no sailor leaves on Friday. Then it was the weekend, and we couldn't check out. And then we got a wire from Chris in Papeete asking if he could sail with us—he'd had a falling out with the man he was crewing for over his boat's seaworthiness. Three recent haulouts had failed to remedy a serious leak in her strip-planked hull. So we had to wait for him.

During these days of hemhawing, a rat that had joined us in Papeete left in the middle of the night. He must have jumped overboard and swum ashore, a most unratlike exit. I spent some time considering the possibility that Rat might know something we didn't.

I don't consider myself superstitious, although I will never pointedly call attention to this by walking under a ladder or failing to throw a pinch of salt over my shoulder at appropriate times. Not leaving on a Friday is merely common sense: the environment out there is threatening, hostile, unknown; it contains enough potential violence to squish you and your boat between thumbwave and forefingertrough like a grape. Granted that leaving on Friday will have no influence whatsoever on your fate, who in his right mind would take any chances?

The other occurrence that gave me misgivings was Nancy's petal larceny. Polynesians have strong feelings about some transgressions, and reputedly the spirits of the dead have powers of retribution. Propaganda or no, we had heard a large enough assortment of apocrypha to respect the *maraes*, ancient sites of ritual cannibalism. Though we would have loved a souvenir, stealing relics has an exceptionless legend of terminal vengeance, and we constantly avoided the temptation. But Nancy had collected hundreds of blossoms from a cemetery, and I had no idea whether this was okay with the Purloined Tiki Tribunal or not. I suspected not.

But the day comes when there are no more available excuses, and if you are ever again to look at yourself in the mirror, you must take the plunge. For us, this point was reached on a bright morning early in September. We left with all systems go, the barometer high, no weather warnings, and a 15-knot beam wind.

Sea Foam slid gracefully along the crests and troughs of a gentle swell at six knots. All of us, misled by the brilliant day, were cheerfully and eagerly looking forward to Tonga and Fiji. Fourteen hundred miles wasn't so far. *Sea Foam* would lap up the distance. The ship's company would function like a well-oiled machine. A piece of cake.

Six hours later we were in a full gale. Nancy, Marci, and Craig were sick. The seas were continuing to build. The wind switched to our quarter, and trying to keep *Sea Foam* from broaching was a constant battle. We couldn't change course to run downwind until we were certain we'd passed Mopelia, a small atoll southwest of Bora Bora. The mere thought of passing upwind of coral reefs with less than 1000 yards visibility made my ulcers bleed. We gave the atoll a berth of 20 miles. I would have been happier with 100.

The shrouds screamed like banshees in the rising 45-knot winds. Black skies attacked us intermittently with drenching rain. We had nothing up but the tiny staysail. Chris and I took the bulk of the watches, while Nancy, though ill, took part of a watch when she could. Marci was too inexperienced and Craig too sick to be able to help. If we hadn't been so busy, that first night would have been terrifying. Even as it was, it seemed interminable.

It is difficult to say which is worse during a storm, daytime or night. At night, with all light blocked off by the overcast, our world shrank to the red glow of the binnacle. Sitting at the helm, you responded to the push and pull of the waves entirely by feel. You couldn't see the bow, let alone what was ahead of you. You took it on faith that you had a clear way. The alternative to this form of faith was madness. And if you hadn't done your homework on the integrity of your boat, you gained firsthand knowledge of hell.

Daytime was almost worse. Looking over his shoulder, the helmsman could watch a mountain of water bearing down on the stern like an implacable avalanche. Time and again it would seem as if the wave had to engulf us; but each time, *Sea Foam*'s broad counter lifted skywards, allowing the huge, angry mass to flow harmlessly beneath us. At first it was as if each wave was testing *Sea Foam* to her limit in a desperate struggle for survival, but as she continued to rise buoyantly over wave after wave, we realized that she was taking the seas much more in her stride than we were. And when we finally were able to run more downwind, the motion of the boat and the task of steering became easier.

But the wind, if anything, blew stronger, whipping the tops of the waves to stinging spindrift. The spray and the rain found hidden weaknesses in our supposedly waterproof foul weather gear. Standing watch was a sodden experience. If the wind had been from a different direction we would have turned back, never again to trade cozy comfort for adventure. As it was, we were committed. Marci learned quickly, and soon was able to stand watch without supervision. Craig began to feel well enough to do his share. Discomfort is a privilege, I would remind them as I went below.

We listened regularly to the general weather reports on station WWV. Nothing was said about any storms in our area. It had to be a local storm—our private pocket of misery, not worthy of mention in the overall picture. That meant it shouldn't last very long, we thought. But there was no sign of any weakening of the howling wind, and once again I found myself brooding about stolen flowers.

It was the second night out that I first heard them—clear, unmistakable, and emanating from the sound of the wind. I nudged Nancy, half-asleep in the bunk beside me.

"Hear that?"

"What?" she said, suddenly wide awake.

"Voices," I said.

"What voices?"

"The voices in the wind," I said, regretting for the first time my habit of telling Nancy whatever's on my mind.

"You're kidding," she said, looking at me intently for some sign that I was.

"No, really—the wind, the sounds in the rigging—they're voices singing. Don't you hear them?"

"Honey," she said, rolling over to go back to sleep. "Whatever you do, don't tell the others."

Hardly encouraged, I went topsides for my watch. Wind and waves were gale force. There was no relaxing at the helm, but after I adjusted to the rhythm of the giant swells and began to steer more or less automatically, I was able to concentrate on the voices. Their volume diminished somewhat if I wasn't paying attention to them, but they never stopped.

There was no possibility of turning them off—I tried. I concentrated on celestial navigation theory, but though the voices receded they were still there, singing unceasingly.

"Go away!"

The sound and intensity of my own voice startled me, but the choir—for that's what it was—paid no attention. My nerves, already tensely resisting the psychological onslaught of the storm, felt as if they were piano wire stretched to the breaking point.

"You're going bananas, Daddy-o," I said to myself. It was not a comforting idea.

"Hang on," I thought. "The crew needs you." I chomped a little harder on the bit of sanity. For the remainder of my watch I continued to play mental games, like trying to remember long-forgotten names of classmates, or the reasons we went cruising in the first place—anything to keep the music turned down. And when I finally crawled into my bunk, sleep only came after counting numberless whitecaps to the rhythm of a great chorus.

It wasn't so bad in the daytime. There were things to do, the DR to plot, food to fix, dishes to wash—Nancy wasn't quite up to the galley yet, as the boat was pitching like a cup in the hands of a high roller, and we were the hapless dice. The presence of others, conversation, and the difficulties involved in doing the simplest tasks kept the sound of the singers to a nearly sub-liminal level. But whenever I stopped to listen, hoping they had gone, I could hear them softly in the background.

The third night out was, if anything, worse. We couldn't believe that there was nothing on the radio about our storm. Only *Sea Foam* seemed to be in her natural element. With her 36-foot length and nearly 14-foot beam, she was plowing down the back-sides of the swells like an eager, buxom bodysurfer at Waikiki Beach. But the strain of 50 hours in a gale was beginning to tell on the rest of us.

During my watch I discovered I was too worn out to battle the voices. After all, they were harmless. Perhaps I, as an ex-musician, was subconsciously organizing the overtones of the wind in the shrouds. Perhaps the fillings in my teeth were picking up some far-out, telepathic, Polynesian wavelength. No explanation made sense, but the question had ceased to bother me. I relaxed and began to enjoy the music. The voices filled my mind with grand, wordless cadences, endlessly repeating the same, stately chord progressions. As I listened, the tension within me gradually relaxed. By some sort of mental jujitsu our situation was transformed. Instead of being against Nature, we'd joined her. Instead of being a speck engulfed in hostile violence, we had become a part of the great dance of the storm.

During the next day the winds decreased slightly, but the skies remained overcast, the seas huge. I risked asking the rest of the crew if any of them heard the voices too, but none of them did. Far from being upset that the skipper was freaking out, they got great pleasure out of teasing me.

"How can you hallucinate when there's no stuff on the boat?"

"Your grog's catching up to you—you're *hearing* elephants."

The kidding went on and on, but it was cheerful and in fun. One way or another my singers (I was getting fondly possessive of them) were lightening the burden we all shared.

For the next three days we were able to fly a reefed mizzen with the staysail. The winds had diminished to a constant 35 to 40 knots, and the sky broke up for a few minutes just often enough for us to take morning and afternoon sunshots. During the six days of the storm we'd sailed a distance of 840 miles, half of which was on staysail alone. Every one of us had a vulgar comment to make about the "constant, gentle trades."

The seventh night I came on watch to find that the seas had calmed down, the winds were 15 to 20 knots, and Chris had un-reefed the mizzen and raised the main. The skies were cloudless. I sat at the helm in an unusual silence. The rigging was quiet; the voices had gone. I could summon them back at will, but I could dismiss them, too. They were no longer an undeniable presence, and now sang for me only by request.

The first clear night after a storm is more beautiful than other nights. Escaping the storm's fury lightens the spirits, leaving your mind free to wander in the infinite indigo of the night sky. One marvels that his tiny efforts have even minutely affected his destiny. It's no wonder that sailors are a superstitious lot. I happily concluded that we hadn't angered any evil spirits by picking a few frangipani blossoms.

Our landfall, Eua, is an island 1000 feet high and ten miles long, and is the only ground in southern Tonga that rises above 200 feet. We hove-to five miles off the end of the island at 1:00 A.M. and at dawn headed straight for the East Pass. By mid-afternoon of our thirteenth day we were tied up securely in

Nukualofa's tiny small-boat marina. Soon after an early supper we were all sleeping like logs.

I was rudely awakened at 6:00 A.M.

"Hey, Hon," said Nancy, affectionately gouging me with her elbow. "I hear your voices."

'Someone's singing," mumbled Marci from the main cabin.

"Herb—" began Craig.

"Yeah, I hear them," I interrupted. Out of tune, amateurish, the voices were nevertheless approximating the music I'd heard at sea. Sleepily, I grumped topsides to investigate.

"It's the Eua ferry," offered a man on the quay. "About three weeks ago, overloaded, they capsized trying to enter the Eua breakwater in a storm. Eight were drowned. They still overload the boat, but now they always sing two or three hymns before they leave."

"I'd be the last to begrudge them that," I said, heading back to my bunk for a few more hours' sleep. "I just wish they'd rehearse."

I often wonder why cruising people persist in exposing themselves to the dangers of the sea. The answer that satisfies me after a landfall (that the simple pleasures are sweeter after they have been risked) must be replaced by a different answer just prior to leaving the pass (a sense of cosmic fitness: it's *time* to leave). But at sea, when the wind is shrieking curses from the upper spreaders and the hull is shuddering with the absorption quotient of a punching bag, there is no answer whatsoever to the sailor's lament: what the fuck am I doing out here?

The voices have never come back. There have been times when I've needed their inspiring grandeur, their moving strength, but I cannot even fabricate them in my mind. Incidentally, I stumbled, quite by accident, on a volume in the Tongan library. Written in Western notation, the book contains some of the songs I heard sung by the voices in the gale. You'll find it filed under *music*. You may also find it where I did, as, in strict accordance with Polynesian logic, it's cross-filed under *aids to navigation*.

TWENTY

W E SPENT TWO WEEKS in the town of Nukualofa in southern Tonga. Tonga is an independent monarchy and a member of the British Commonwealth. Time begins in Tonga, because although Tongans are east of the dateline, they have persuaded the dateline delineators to squiggle the line eastward to include them. Most Tongans are poor. The head of the family that befriended us worked at guarding the king for a wage of $5.00 a week (recently bumped from $3.50). Tongans don't starve, however, at least not conspicuously, as they are all members of one or more families that own acreage where indigenous foods are grown. The king himself lives very well, thank you.

Nukualofa is low and flat. Of interest: a monument resembling Stonehenge, origin unknown. We rented a car, and besides the monument, we visited the blowholes. Nancy has told me that visitors to Honolulu hop a plane to the big island of Hawaii, hire a car, and drive all the way across the island just to see one blowhole, after which they must stay over in a hotel. In Nukualofa, you can hire a car after lunch, visit four dozen blowholes, and be home for tea. We stood on the rocky shore, and as far as we could see were high natural fountains, sparkling towers of spray squirting in a ballet of random rhythms.

Many yachts approach Fiji from the east-northeast, sailing down a wide channel among smaller islands—an easy approach, in clear weather. But the weather becomes less consistent as you proceed west, and the occurrence of squalls or gales is unpredictable. One 40-foot fiberglass sloop was sailing "the alley" when the weather deteriorated. Squalls were fierce and nearly continuous. Although the couple had a vane, they kept watch. After a particularly violent and persistent squall, the weather cleared and they found themselves *inside* an islandless circle of coral. They anchored and slept. When morning came, they explored the full length of the eastern reef, but found no pass large enough for their boat. On the western side, they finally found the one pass out of the lagoon. Their boat had been blown right across the reef at high tide, perhaps on a particularly large wave. They hadn't noticed a thing.

For every miracle, of course, there are plenty of disasters. Government records in Fiji show that during the period from 1975 to 1978, 200 boats went up on local reefs. We had been warned of the dangers, and whenever we were presented with a choice of courses while cruising in Fijian waters, we tried to choose the chicken way. This didn't guarantee our safety, but we hoped that our efforts would affect the balance of the Great Scales.

We were 15 miles off Suva Harbor with the powerful red range lights in view. We had no chart, but I had looked at someone else's, as had Chris, and we thought we had a good picture of what to expect. The wind had risen, and the choice was either to heave-to off the pass in a steep, three-foot chop that was extremely uncomfortable and showed every sign of worsening, or to enter a strange harbor in the dark with no chart. The vote was unanimous: go for it.

Our choice was not as frivolous as it may sound; avoiding discomfort was given little weight. What concerned us was that if we didn't enter the harbor we'd be heaving-to off a lee shore and a submerged coral reef. We had the range lights by which to maintain position, but what if the weather closed down, as seemed likely? The pass, though long, had lighted buoys on either side. Having entered, the one hazard between us and the Suva Yacht Club was also marked with a lighted buoy.

We negotiated the Suva Pass, riding the range lights as if we were on rails, and our midnight opinion as to the location of the Royal Suva Yacht Club was substantiated at dawn. I have never questioned the wisdom of our decision, although several skippers whose opinion I respect have since told me I was nuts, an opinion unsupported by anything more persuasive than an arbitrary rule of thumb: "You just don't enter a harbor for the first time in the dark with no chart." A Fort Knox of golden adages, I reply with "the proof of the pudding . . ." Nobody wins.

Suva fascinated us. Prince Charles arrived in honor of their centennial, and the huge celebration in the park was ceremonious and varied—all Polynesian countries were represented by dancing and singing groups. Reasonably priced Chinese and Indian restaurants abounded. The central market place was a teeming hub of locals, and was packed with handicrafts and produce. Shops and pawnshops offered hours of contentment for browsers. And I could have stood on a street corner forever, contentedly watching the slender beauty of Indian women dressed in colorful saris, and basking in the warmth of ready Fijian smiles.

We spent 18 days in Suva, then left for some island-hopping to the east. On the way we stopped at our very own island. Called Thangalai, it lay midway up the east coast of Viti Levu just inside the coral reef on the right side of the pass. It was small, an emerald amulet in a setting of platinum sand. We were the only people. We anchored *Sea Foam* in the lee of the trades and rowed ashore. Nancy and I found ourselves alone, picking over shells that the sea had washed up. The sun was hot, so we shed clothes and went swimming. The snorkeling wasn't that interesting, and we began to clown around, kissing underwater, masks getting in the way. (If you laugh underwater it's a mistake.) We waded ashore. Still feeling playful, we walked into the woods and made love under a coconut tree. Because of bugs and leaves it was hardly ideal, but as punctuation it was perfect, a flagrant apostrophe that made the island uniquely ours.

We spent the second day on Thangalai gathering papayas, breadfruit, and coconuts. All land belongs to somebody, and one of the many ways that cruising people fail to endear themselves is to help themselves without asking. But common sense is tuned to degrees; with no one to ask, and overripe windfalls everywhere, we didn't feel that our thieving would deprive anyone. We took what we could use.

The hurricane season was approaching. One rogue storm had hit Fiji in late September two years before. Usually, locals feel fairly safe until December 1, with January and February being the months of greatest frequency. It was now October 14, and the barometer was falling with purposive consistency (the purpose, I was sure, being to make me nervous). We spent a worrisome night as the wind swung from east to north to west, blowing and raining like stink, the lee shore chuckling greedily in the chop just astern of us. With dawn, the rain and winds stopped. The barometer reversed its plunge and exulted like the market in '28. By 10:00 A.M. we were on our way in weather that smiled, rocked, and comforted, maternal antidote to nocturnal fears.

About South Pacific hurricanes: they can be lethal, and they can be capricious. They demand the utmost respect. However:

1. Most of them fail to exceed wind-speeds of 70 knots. This speed is reached only near the center, and only during part of the storm's life. Seventy-knot winds are brutal, but there are still things you can do, and unless you're unlucky you'll survive.

2. Even the most virulent hurricanes cut a relatively narrow lethal swathe. Depending on the storm's breadth (not necessarily a function of wind-speed), winds 100 to 200 miles from the center will have decreased to 20 to 40 knots.

3. Hurricanes are pretty fair about sticking to their season, although an occasional rebel confounds prediction.

4. The odds of finding yourself in the path of the one hurricane out of four that exceeds 70 knots are slight; out of season, almost nil. If life is a roulette wheel, for once you are the house. (Example: Ovalau was hit by one hurricane in the last 20 years. Anemic and underfed, the storm caused minimal damage.)

We were flirting with the edge of the season. For much of my life I had strayed from saintliness, and I was giving God a good chance to get back at me. Neurotic ganglia, the DEW-line of my paranoia, sent continuous janglings of alarm. I spent most of my time listening to weather reports with one eye on the barometer and the other on the hurricane holes we'd marked on our charts. But no matter what the degree of my anxiety, neither tomorrow's threats nor yesterday's fears stood a chance against a today of beautiful sailing.

And we had plenty of those. The islands of Makongai, Wakaya, and Ngau all lay within a day-sail of Levuka, and their lagoons offered shelter and variety for the most discriminating gunkholer. After a few days in one anchorage, we would leave at dawn and be in our next anchorage long before light and good visibility ran out. Even the wind god made an effort to square past injustices. In moderate seas under puffball skies, everywhere we sailed we had the wind on our beam.

Ngau was our last stop before returning to Suva. We anchored in a protected bay in front of the village of Waikama, mostly because Marci, an anthropology major, opted forcefully for a peek at Fijian village life. The minute we stepped out of the dinghy we were surrounded by six dozen children of all ages. Our progress along the shore toward the village lacked only a flute and a Pied Piper to blow it. When we reached the village we discovered all the men in the process of building a house for a couple of newly-weds. Two-by-fours and galvanized nails replaced lashed bamboo as framing, but thatch was still used to make the roof and walls. A single room measuring 15 feet by 20, the house was completed in a total of two days.

The village women prepared a hearty noon meal for the house-builders, and we were included. I remember two kinds of boiled cabbage, one with fish and coconut milk, the other with hot peppers and meat. Green tomatoes with a spicy salad dressing. Tapioca. Cooked fish. All washed down with exotic Tang.

At that time Waikama was a relatively poor village. Having no outboard of their own, once a week the villagers rented an outboard-powered punt from a more affluent neighboring village and went fishing out on the reef. We offered to take them twice, our self-interest lying in the hope that we'd learn about local fishing techniques. On the first expedition we loaded 21 villagers aboard. By towing a dory, we were able the second time to transport 31 of them, a *Sea Foam* record that still stands.

In gratitude for an excellent day's catch, the villagers invited us to drink kava with them. Fijians still believe that through kava they can talk to their ancestors and ask for specific favors, like good fishing or a fair wind for a particular voyage. In the villages where the traditional Fijian life-style continues, kava is never drunk without the ritual that goes with it. All the men (Nancy, too, by virtue of guesthood) sat in a circle. A village woman sat in the middle and mixed water and kava powder, ground from a local root, in an enormous wooden bowl two feet in diameter. The result was ready to drink when it reached the appearance, aroma, and taste of a mud puddle.

The mixer dipped half a coconut shell into the bowl and served the chief first. He clapped once (thank you), then took the shell and drained it. Everyone clapped three times in unison (approval). I was next, male guest of honor. The shell held ten large gulps. I took curtain calls for a feat that I thought was worth far more than a niggardly three claps. They gave Nancy a half-filled shell. I expected a vomitous "tilt," but she made it after 30 swallows and three illegal recesses.

I had been told it would be rude to leave before the huge bowl had been drunk dry. As the shell circulated again and again, I became awash, bilges and ballast tanks brimming. The only physical effect was a slight tingling around my lips reminiscent of the waning effects of Novocain. If it weren't for the solemn and impressive dignity of the ceremony, I would have preferred to recreate the sensation at the dentist's. (I hate the dentist's.)

Nancy and I have resolved to bring at least two aspects of our cruising life back to land. The first is a calendar we've made of every holiday in every country we've ever visited. When we get home we intend to celebrate them all. (Could you come by at seven for a party? It's Waitangi Day!) The other is the kava ceremony. I see a cold night in Maine. A small group is sitting cross-legged in a circle before the fire. I wear a necklace of shells, symbol of hosthood. Nancy sits at the kava bowl, refilling the drinking cup and passing it around. With each individual's draining of the cup we applaud. There will, however, be one essential change: the brew. Over the years good manners have demanded that I make at least two dozen attempts to acquire a taste for kava, all of which failed. And besides, I'm sure my ancestors, if they respond at all, would be far more likely to get through to me on rum punch.

Four Waikamans joined us on our trip back to Suva. We powered the whole distance over glassy swells with just enough wind aft to keep a cloud of diesel exhaust fumes hanging over the boat. Both Fijian girls were seasick. The two men felt better after eating the boiled head of a freshly caught wahoo. At Nancy's insistence they cooked it themselves, and at mine they ate it on the foredeck, out of my sight.

While in Suva Harbor we met a New Zealander who was waiting to make the passage home. He gave us a new slant on weather strategy.

"Everybody leaves too soon," he said. "Around about mid-October, people start getting nervous about the hurricanes and head south. What happens to 'em? They run into the end of New Zealand winter weather, which, though it may not be a hurricane, can be damned unpleasant. What I do, I hide in here till the first or second week of December. If the weather looks okay, I go for it. I make it home for Christmas and have a good sail besides."

I'd hate to recommend this gambler's judgment to anyone else, but that year it proved to be the best plan. All boats that left in mid-October ran into terrible storms and were blown way off course, and many suffered severe damage. We left November 5 and, what with headwinds and no-winds, took 15 days to cover the 1150 miles. The New Zealander left December 5, took eight and a half days, and never touched his sails the whole way. I leave it to you, fellow chamber-spinners in the Russian roulette of hurricane prediction.

The Fijian officials had commandeered my gun, a little plinker of plastic and steel that would shame any self-respecting rifleman, along with thousands of shells with which I was going to bribe and seduce natives all over the world. All during our intercultural foray in Fiji when I should have been bribing and seducing, my munitions remained locked up in the Suva police armory. Now we were about to leave for New Zealand, and I wanted my weaponry back.

I tried to reclaim the gun Friday afternoon prior to a Saturday leaving. Uh-uh. Get your gun, then cast off and *leave*. One hour's delay made customs nervous. Two made them paranoid. Three and they would be stomping your teak in hobnails, demanding to know what the hell was going on.

Saturday morning the one man (in a department of hundreds) with the key to the armory was home. It was his day off.

Sunday everyone was off.

Monday he played golf.

Tuesday, *Sea Foam*'s crew having spurred me on with Bronx cheers, catcalls, and other reminders of my inadequacy, I went to customs and, ignorant visitor that I was, planted my ass on their bench. I waited. "Just a minute," they said. I waited. "Right away," they said. I waited some more.

I watched a man deliver a huge red plastic bucket about 9:00 A.M. and hang it up high on the wall.

I watched the officials in the office make repeated trips to the bucket, each dipping and filling his own plastic cup.

I walked over and looked into the bucket. It looked like kava. By standing tiptoe I could get my nose over the edge. Smelled like kava. I dipped a finger and licked it. Yup. Kava, all right. I returned to the bench and once more planted ass. An idea glimmered.

It is essential, when using the Ignorant Visitor's Ass-Planting Technique, to keep your cool. You must be a sympathetic character. I have watched justifiably irate tourists fly completely off the handle, making fools of themselves and accomplishing nothing. The person who deserves the abuse is never there, having insulated himself with legions of callous flunkies.

I fixed a smile on my face that I hoped would pass for good nature. Thereafter, each time someone walked over and got himself a cup of kava, I muttered some doggerel and clapped three times.

I knew and they knew that everybody knew that they drank kava on the job. It was one thing to be discreetly open about it, but it was quite another to ceremonialize it as I was doing. The first three times I drew stern, shushy looks. I just smiled, acted stupid (which I find is becoming easier, I'm ashamed to say), and started clapping not only for each trip to the kava bucket, but for each swallow from a cup.

Their stern disapproval turned to embarrassment. Very soon I was clapping almost continuously, giving every impression that all I wanted, more than anything in the world, was to have a clapping good time with these wonderful guys. Soon a dour giant, stooped from the weight of his gold braid, who had thus far sat impassively in the corner, looked over at me.

"What are you doing here?" he demanded.

"I want my gun so I can leave Fiji," I said, couching my problem in terms I thought might by this time be attractive to him.

"Is that all?" he replied. He picked up the phone, and I had both gun and bullets in 15 minutes.

In 1975 and 1976 Fijian officials got serious. Without apparent formula, they ransacked visiting yachts from stem to stern, search dogs sniffing everything from sail covers to dirty underwear. One crew-cutted skipper, with a wife and three bestarched and pinafored daughters, had his boat torn apart with unsympathetic thoroughness. Fortunately for him, Suva was the first port in which he'd ever declared his gun. Therefore I would never recommend that anyone fail to declare his gun. I can only tell you that at the time of our visit in 1974 fewer skippers declared them than didn't, and that those who didn't declare them left when they pleased.

We finally got away, fully armed, on October 4. The sunset as we left was fantastic, and the sunrise the next morning was even more outstanding—150° of blazing color. With 1100 miles of open ocean to cross, the hurricane season underway, and us with only $20, I was most careful to log my praise of God's work, hoping that He would overlook the fact that the last sunset I'd graded, weeks before, was a scathing C–.

TWENTY-ONE

OUR PASSAGE TO NEW ZEALAND was an anthology of conditions. The first day out of Suva we rode out an interminable 50-knot squall in the Kandavu Channel under reefed mizzen and staysail, manning the helm in foul weather gear as much to avoid the acupuncture of stinging rain as to stay dry. From then on we battled headwinds, calms, and rain, with the occasional clear, broad-reaching day to encourage us. One night, tired of slogging to weather and unable to sleep well because of the hull's pitching, we hove-to. We got a much-needed night's rest, but it cost us 40 miles, and consequently this was the only time we did it. At 1400 Friday, November 15, I fixed our position at 256 miles north-northeast of Cape Brett, and predicted a Sunday landfall. It took us until the following Wednesday. But in spite of the frustration engendered by the constantly varying and often adverse winds, my sharpest memory was of the good days, and of the tropic–temperate transition: absolutely cloudless skies; the water a rich blue-purple, clear and bottomless; crisp nights with the air alive, the stars dancing. It was weather that stimulated rather than enervated, and it cheered us all. The midnight preceding November 20 we spotted the loom of Cape Brett, and at dawn we were powering toward misty land through the gluey surface of a static, windless ocean.

When my children were little, they used to love to be read to from a book called *The Magic Pudding*. It was a pudding born to be shared, with the ability to regenerate itself. On the evening before our landfall, our diesel tank registered 17 gallons, and I wondered if it would take us to landfall and into port. After powering for ten hours I measured it again: 17 gallons. True, it is difficult to get an accurate measurement at sea with a dipstick, no matter how gentle the swells, but I had taken several readings and selected an average. Our apparently self-replenishing fuel supply convinced us that our magic star was ascending.

A few miles off Cape Brett we spotted an empty Whaler-type powerboat drifting with the wind and current, complete with windshield, remote controls, outboard, and an anchor line that hung straight down from the bow. After towing it into port, we learned that the owner of the launch had posted a $200 reward for its recovery. When one's star is ascending, magic is not only possible but inevitable.

After clearing into New Zealand at Opua, we motored up to Russell, a picturesque resort town (still in the Bay of Islands) and anchored off the wharf. During New Zealand's summer—the northern hemisphere's winter—Russellites work like beavers as the town's population swells to 6500 partying, hotelling, motelling, camping, yachting souls. In the other months, its 650 year-round residents relax and count their money as Russell reverts to a sleepy country town.

We loved it both ways, and decided to make Russell our permanent base. There was plenty of work around, and the Christmas season was just about to begin. During the peak months of December and January that year (1974–1975), Russell was visited by over 200 boats, about one-third of which were from overseas. Many of the overseas boats went south to make Auckland their base, but we preferred not to live for any length of time in a big city. Others opted for Whangarei, a town of 30,000 located 15 miles from the ocean on a muddy river. Day-sailing there was impossible, and you were so much a part of town you felt you were living in a supermarket. In Russell we had country living and the Bay of Islands for day- or weekend sailing. The vote was unanimous to risk earning a little less and to enjoy living a great deal more.

Thanksgiving continued to be a moveable feast on our fouled-up calendar. This year we managed to celebrate it on a Thursday, but one week too soon. (Not one U.S. yachtie knew for sure when it was, so we played it safe.) There were no turkeys for sale. Chicken and pork were outrageously priced. We settled for a leg of New Zealand lamb, which they gave away for 39 cents a pound. Informed of our mistake in timing, we celebrated again the following week with roast beef at 42 cents a pound. We had not afforded either luxurious entrée for two years.

Kiwis (New Zealanders) are ardent boaters. Fizz boats (runabouts), sportfishers, and power palaces abound, but the New Zealander's greatest love is sailing. Herreshoff and Sparkman-Stephens designs are most popular, but there are also enough Rube Goldberg, designed-in-process-and-built-using-what's-around monstrosities to keep even the most jaded boat-watcher amused. The point is to get out on the water, no matter what.

Kiwi sailors tend to have a warped sense of courage, and are totally uncowed by weather that would keep normal people ashore. Earlier, in Tahiti, I had befriended a Russellite who had just sailed up from New Zealand. I had asked him how his trip had been, thinking I might have to make it myself someday.

"Ah, yeah. It was a bit of all right, eh?"

"Give it to me straight, Bill. What kind of a trip did you have?"

"Ah, yeah. Well, we left New Zealand, and right away we got hit by a bloody storm. Dismasted, we were, and had to turn around and wait while they put a new stick in. Ah, yeah. Well, we set off again, and the bloody weather stayed pretty wet. Good breeze— 30 knots, moved us right along. But we had to have someone on the bloody pumps most of the time. Ah, yeah. Slept in m' rain gear the whole way. Bloody boots, too. Bunks were too wet to take off clothes, and a little chilly. Ah, yeah. Not too bad, really, for winter, y' know."

Hardy they be, but prudent and considerate anchorers they're not. During the Russell busy season, every other day we'd catch some Kiwi trying to anchor his 40-foot icebreaker about 30 feet from *Sea Foam*. As guests in their country we tried to remain polite, but sometimes it wasn't easy.

One night we'd all gone to bed early. I was awakened suddenly by a loud thump and a grating sound on the hull. Still groggy, I rushed topsides. A 30-foot ferrocement something with a mast was crunching slowly along our port side. I hurried to fend off, swallowing swear words in view of the fact that the person on the deck of the assaulting craft was female.

She noticed the fact that I'd neglected to put on any clothes at about the same time I realized it myself. We glared at each other for a moment. Her rapier tongue was first to slash the silken evening.

"You dragged," she hissed.

There wasn't a breath of air.

"Bullshi— Not likely," I countered. Then I had one of my rare flashes of genius. "We've been here for weeks. We're on a mooring."

Which was a lie, but I was determined not to lose the argument over who was going to pull up what. She stared balefully at me for a moment, then turned on her heel.

"I'm getting my husband," she said, heading for the companionway.

"I'm getting my shorts," I threw at her departing back. I went below. Before I could return, I heard their anchor coming aboard, so I went back to bed. The next morning they waved and smiled, apparently having forgiven us for being in their way.

Pilecap. How could I have let this tale proceed so far without ever once mentioning *Pilecap?*

If I get things wrong, Pilecappers, you must forgive me. You are not in my logs or journals. Nancy's, Craig's, and my memories conflict. I will do my best with my recollection of first- and second-hand tales.

Pilecap was an English-designed and English-built, hard-chined, bilge-keeled sloop, perhaps 28 feet long. (Bilge-keelers have two keels, one on each side of the bottom, and can sit, balanced on their keels, on dry land.) She was owned and sailed by an elderly English couple whose names I never knew, so for reasons which will appear, I'll call them Father Christmas and Mrs. Windlass.

Pilecap was a legend before she became a reality in my life.

She had left from somewhere in Central America bound for somewhere in the Pacific Northwest. After having sailed nearly to Hawaii, running out of water and nearly running out of food, she made it, 73 days later. People were shaking their heads at this intrepid elderly couple who, for their parts, were pooh-poohing and tut-tutting and downplaying their adventure. This story came as words on the wind, part of the gossip that feeds the cruiser's grapevine.

I first saw *Pilecap* in Punaauia, Tahiti. I was on *Tolaki*, cleaning up after a morning's painting, getting ready to swim home to *Sea Foam* for lunch. *Pilecap* came puff-puffing into the lagoon at five knots, Father Christmas and Mrs. Windlass both in the cockpit.

Punaauia lagoon was one of our favorite spots, but it was tricky to navigate. It consisted of two deep spaces separated by a sandbar which, at high tide, was covered by six or seven feet of water, and dotted with coral heads. The French never charted it—the area on the chart was plain white. We had been told exactly how to handle it. We had chosen a tide that was against us, giving us steerageway under power at zero knots over the ground. We had posted a man in the rigging, and a friend in an outboard had guided us across the sandbar into the second deep space. *Pilecap*, to my horror, was steaming into the lagoon full bore with nobody even in the bows.

Somehow she powered past all hazards and across deep place #1, across the sandbar, across deep place #2, and right up on a reef which to my mind should have been unmistakable. The tide rose a few inches—enough—and *Pilecap* managed to back off the reef. She turned and puff-puffed back to the sandbar, threw over the anchor and put up an awning. Soon I saw tea and sandwiches appear, the sandwiches with their crusts trimmed. I was impressed.

Swimming by their boat, however, I realized that with the scope they'd played out, there were at least three shallow coral heads within the radius of their swinging circle. Trying to be helpful, I pointed this out. I also said there was room near us.

No sooner had I reached *Sea Foam* and pulled myself aboard than I heard the puff-puff of their engine, the rattle of chain coming aboard. I looked back at the little sloop and saw 4′ 8″ of doughty Englishwoman hand-over-handing their 5/16-inch chain, 6′ 4″ Father Christmas watching benevolently and approvingly from the cockpit. Soon the anchor was aboard, and they made the circuit of the lagoon, once more with both of them conning from the sternsheets. They puff-puffed out the entrance to Punaauia and out of sight. I later heard that they held Punaauia to be the most awful place they'd ever been in.

Pilecappers next distinguished themselves on the Fiji–New Zealand crossing. Several other yachts passed them, usually late in the afternoon. At this time, *Pilecap* always had her sails lowered, and both Father Christmas and Mrs. Windlass were taking tea, looking at the sunset. When asked if everything was all right with them, they would reply:

"Isn't it a lovely evening?"

"Hasn't it been a beautiful sail, so far?"

"Oh, yes, we always drop sails for tea, and for meals, and sometimes at night, too."

"No, thank you, everything is just fine."

I'd hate to put a number on the days it took them to make that passage. I remember it was sufficiently impressive that I thought it should go in the *Guinness Book of World Records* as the slowest non-traumatic crossing ever made.

When *Pilecap* arrived in New Zealand, they ran their little bilge-keeler up on the mud in Matauwhi Bay at high tide. I still haven't figured that one out. When the tide was out, she sat balanced on her twin keels on the mudflats. The dinghy was useless, and it was necessary to walk to shore across the mud. Both Father Christmas and Mrs. Windlass had hip boots, so it was rare that they were ever caught ashore with more water than they could wade back to their boat in. When the water was up they used the dinghy like everyone else.

My guess is that they felt more secure aground, that they didn't mind the inconvenience of mudflat-wading vs. dinghy-rowing, and that when the big winds came and we were all frantically checking our anchors, they were below sipping carefree cups of tea.

Naturally, it was Father Christmas who played Santa on a beach near Russell on Christmas Day, 1974. With charm, humor, and sweaty costume. A score of yachts got together and bought two whole lambs (eight dollars), which were roasted on a spit. Over the open fire was a sheet of corrugated iron, and hundreds of pippies, little mussel-like clams, were spread there to cook in the smoke. All the ladies brought a vegetable or a salad. Potatoes, wrapped in foil, were baked in the fire. Everyone brought an under-a-dollar present, and each was distributed by Father Christmas on a mysterious lottery basis. It was the only time I spent any time with the Pilecappers. They were both delightful. I hope they get wherever they are going, except I don't think they really care as long as they have a good time along the way.

In New Zealand, particularly in small towns, the hub is the pub. Even if they don't drink, the locals go there to shoot a little pool, pick up a little gossip, make assignations, and even get a job. If you don't drop by at least once a week they send someone around to give you a loyalty oath.

Each of us except Craig got jobs through the pub. Put out the word that you want work, and in a few days word filters back where work is. Within two weeks Nancy started getting sewing jobs, Marci became a waitress, Chris helped install a patio, and I became a sort of carpenter.

As a musician in Southern California, I had managed to achieve a luxurious, heavily mortgaged standard of living without knowing how to do very much. Now, freed from the fetters of a profession and a steady income, I was sorry I'd never learned a trade. All the way from California I'd watched my more talented fellow yachties pick up odd jobs—refrigeration, electronics, and engines are always breaking down to the dismay of their owners and the profit of those who can fix them. And all the way from California I'd read the abundant, help-wanted sections of the New

Zealand newspapers. Ad by ad, column by column, I came to the conclusion that the ad I sought was a pipe-dream: "WANTED— middle-aged ex-musician; good drinker; full of sea stories and bits of wisdom; excellent salary, fringe benefits."

Desperate, now, I tried to remember which do-it-yourself jobs had filled my days with the least frustration. As a plumber I had been a soggy failure; as an electrician, a spectacular one. But as a carpenter I had built some things that were only slightly askew, and I decided that carpentry was my best shot.

Sort of carpenters started at two dollars an hour in the Bay of Islands. I took quick stock of my tools: one bevel square, plastic handle broken; two framing squares, one bent, both rusty but cleanupable; one Teflon-coated, guaranteed rustproof saw, rusty; two hammers, one with a broken claw, the other with a cracked handle; and one carpenter's pencil, half dry-rot.

I arrived on the job with a new set of basic tools packed in a TWA carry-on bag, and discovered I'd forgotten one very important item: an apron. Carpenters wear marvelous leather aprons with huge pockets for nails and loops to hang your hammer, square, tape, rule, and chisel in. I reported to the boss with the pockets of my shorts full of nails, their points poking out through the fabric, and my tools hung from my belt on pieces of marline.

"You look more like a bloody sheepherder than you do a carpenter," he observed.

I hadn't lied about my experience. I was no journeyman, I had said, but I had built two houses back in the States. What I didn't say was that one of the houses was an eight-by-ten playhouse for my children. The other involved supervising the subcontractors who built my house in Laguna Beach. My practical experience was minimal.

My choice of hammers was a case in point. I had bought a 20-ounce beauty, a compromise between the Paul Bunyan, 24-ounce framer's special and the 16-ounce hobbyist's model. I found that everyone else on the job used 16-ouncers. Mine was perfect for rough framing, but unfortunately my first assignment was to nail down the composition flooring with two-inch nails. One swat with my mighty tool would fold the unresisting nail into a crinkled, artistically pleasing but structurally useless shape. Before I got the knack I'd strewn half a pound of galvanized debris in my wake.

The journeymen kept their pencils razor sharp with a couple of quick flicks of a chisel. My first attempt I demolished four brand-new company pencils before I achieved a beautiful, sharp, two-inch stub. But what to do with the by-product of my success, an awesome, incriminating pile of red enameled shavings? I scraped them up and stuffed them furtively into my pocket, later to toss them anonymously into the bay.

In a month I'd mastered pencil-sharpening and put in for a raise. I was delighted when I was bumped to $2.30 an hour. Journeymen only drew $2.70. I had arrived, my pleasure only slightly diminished by the self-appraisal that I wasn't good, but I was slow.

Before long, I found Chris a carpentry job with me. This was fitting, as he had gotten me my boat-painting job in Tahiti. Our relationship gradually changed from a head-butting competitiveness to a harmony of disagreement. Purgatory for me would involve being on a committee with Chris; for him, it was to crew under me. Ashore, we were finally friends.

Craig went into business for himself. Having found out that the Russell butcher was a shameless cheat, especially with foreigners, Craig offered a service: order meat through Craig, and he would buy it from the butcher across the bay, have it sent over on the ferry, and deliver it daily to each yacht for a ten percent commission. During the season Craig ran specials, merchandized indefatigably, and when the last foreign yacht sailed away he had saved over $150. He was only slightly troubled by dreams of the local butcher chasing him with a meat cleaver.

Craig flourished during our cruising. His nature was curious, and he loved to collect and classify. In New Zealand most of his profits funnelled into the coffers of a small but persuasive philatelic mail-order house in Auckland. He also had a marvelous collection of seashells, of which his knowledge was encyclopedic. He was in touch with shell dealers worldwide, and dealt with them like a Yankee trader. (One dealer offered 50 cents for Tahitian gold ringers, and Craig, in a fit of ambition, found, collected, cleaned, and mailed 600. The dealer bought them all, but at a reduced price, and Craig learned a valuable lesson about flooding markets.)

His resourcefulness was a lesson for all of us. One day, having found a downed balsa wood tree, he sawed it up and brought it aboard. With that and various bits found either on the boat or floating in the water, he made at least a dozen fully rigged model boats—schooners, ketches, sloops, trimarans, outrigger canoes, you name it. After he made roughly 20 matchbox sloops and launched them seaward to their destinies we called a halt, having ended up with 4000 homeless matches.

In Tahiti Craig earned all his own spending money by finding and turning in empty beer bottles for the deposit. Some stores refused to redeem bottles unless you could show a deposit slip for beer purchased from that store. Others refused to redeem them in large numbers, and Craig was interested *only* in large returns. He discovered that small Hinano bottles (redeemable) and Heineken bottles (no deposit, no return) were identical except for the labels. The problem: make little Heinekens into little Hinanos. Big Hinano bottles (unique) could be redeemed without labels. A mass production of label removal from the bigs and regluing onto the smalls ensued—a fraud which, after consideration, Nancy and I overlooked. Eventually, however, Craig's face became known to virtually every store in Papeete, and business dropped off. When Nancy and I were roped into the deception as bottle-returners, I put my foot down. One must draw the ethical line somewhere, even if it's dictated solely by inconvenience.

TWENTY-TWO

ONE MORNING I WAS SUMMONED to shore by a huge man with an outrageously bushy red beard. He was shepherd to a flock of young people who were traveling with the Outward Bound School. Outward Bounders, we called them, are everywhere, learning mountaineering, sailing, skiing, wilderness survival, and spelunking, and are usually city-dwellers trying to relate to the great outdoors. Here they were in Russell, just for the weekend, and they wanted to go sailing. I looked around at 17 hopeful, expectant people, sitting, for the moment, on their sleeping bags and survival kits; at John and Martha Ash, two New Zealanders who were also Outward Bound instructors; and finally back at Big Mike himself.

"You've gotta be kidding," I said.

"Frank Simon gave us your name," said Mike. "We were supposed to split up between you and *Wanderer*," (*Wanderer* was on the ways for a re-fit), "but we weren't told she wasn't available."

"You've gotta be kidding," I repeated.

"We wouldn't expect to sleep on the boat, of course, so all you'd be doing is sailing us to a beach where we can build a cooking fire and camp out in our sleeping bags. I'm prepared to pay you $100."

At the mention of money my eyes lit up. The Outward Bounders were already tossing their knapsacks into the dinghy.

"You've gotta be kidding!" This time it was Nancy, who had come topsides just as I had rowed alongside *Sea Foam*. Black Benny was overloaded with bodies and gear. Looking ashore, Nancy could see 16 more bodies wearing excited smiles and backpacks and carrying bedrolls.

We got everyone aboard and all the gear stowed below. Some-how we managed to weigh anchor, raise sail, and get under way. ("Hey, you, there by the mast, that line right there—no, the other one—pull on it and the sail goes up. All the way up, please. Well, pull *hard*er! Get someone else to help pull. Okay, make it fa— I mean, tie it to the pinrail—I mean that belaying pin—ah, shit, that wooden rail you're hanging onto.")

There was no way to move on deck. Mike had sailed before, but most of the students had not. With remarkably few fumblings and false moves, we reached out into the Bay of Islands. Everyone took a turn steering. Everyone had a camera, and shutters snapped like a swarm of attacking locusts.

The wind was perfect for a run down to Oke Bay, a beautiful, protected cove near Cape Brett. I was just climbing down off the fence of "Thank God there's no Coast Guard" (we were illegally overloaded) and "Wish to Christ there *was* a Coast Guard" (in case we sank) when it started to rain. The companionway bulged as survival school honor students tried to get below two at a time. Soon the main saloon was swollen and throbbing like the hold of a slave ship. I caught a look at Nancy's face through a porthole. She was boiling water for coffee, looking harried.

The rain stopped, people reappeared, and in the late afternoon we ghosted slowly into Oke Bay. Oke Bay is a large cove enclosed by hills and cliffs. It is uninhabited except for sheep roaming the hills. There are three beaches in the cove. One was unsuitable for the Outward Bounders because it was rocky; another would obviously be shrunk to nothing by an encroaching tide; but the third was small and perfect.

They must have thought so, too, the handsome young couple that was sitting alone on the beach next to a small fire. Their sloop nodded patiently at anchor. Their pup tent nestled in the long grass. The two young people were camping out in para-dise, enjoying absolute solitude and breathtaking beauty, the radi-ance of their love enhanced by the idyllic surroundings.

There wasn't enough light to go looking for another place—in fact, I didn't know of another suitable place close by. We dropped anchor. Bounders bobbed beachward, spreading out along the shore like an oil-slick. A volleyball net magically appeared. Clouds of frisbees gave the impression of a Martian air circus. Another fire was built. Sleeping bags were unrolled. Mob exuberance chopped rustic romance to a pile of wilting chips.

The young couple finished their meal, declined an invitation to enter the games, struck their tent, and took to the lifeboat. As they rowed past *Sea Foam*, Nancy and I were sitting in the cockpit, sipping toddies.

"Like to join us for a drink?" I called. It was the least I could do.

"No, thanks. Another time." The words were politeness itself, but I thought I detected a tinge of coolness in the tone.

Nearly a month later, I was introduced to the unfortunate couple in the Russell pub. It took two pitchers of New Zealand's 3.2 watery finest to lubricate their senses of humor, and one more pitcher to make us friends. I was grateful two ways: that I had a second opportunity to make amends, and that the couple turned out to be Americans and not New Zealanders.

We were delighted to be in a country where English was the first language, but slang made potholes in the freeway of understanding. One evening, sitting at the table with several New Zealanders, I was misled by the following summarized tale:

"Last night my cobber and me, we snagged a couple of sheilas. We all got pissed, and at the end I went crook. Later I tried to get this bird in the kip, but she told me to get stuffed. But she'll be right, mate. She told me to keep my pecker up, and she's promised to let me knock her up again tonight."

Pretty wild story, right? The translation, however, may not be quite what you think:

"Last night my friend and I, we picked up a couple of girls. We all drank too much and at the end I got sick. Later I tried to get this girl in the sack and she told me to do unto myself that which I had wished to do unto her. But she'll come around.

She told me to hang in there and promised to let me stop by her apartment again tonight."

New Zealanders are a gregarious bunch, and we made friends quickly. Once, in a state of camaraderie, I agreed to play a few gigs with the Russell Dance Band. Session #1 was for ten dollars, #2 for drinks, #3 for all the oysters I could eat, and #4 for ten dollars again. Sometimes we managed to finish our tunes at the same time, but usually we had to wake up the drummer and tell him the song was over. The only good thing about any of it was our introduction to a whole group of people we otherwise would never have met.

One night our sax player invited everyone to his daughter's twenty-first birthday party. Around midnight the host got out his sax. The Maori ferryboat driver grabbed a pair of spoons. The scion of Russell's oldest family brought his gutbucket bass (a do-it-yourselfer made from an empty five-gallon drum, a broomstick handle, and a single string). The postmaster, who doubled as Russell's barber in his spare time, sat down at a set of traps that had materialized out of thin air, and I sat down at the piano. "Honeysuckle Rose" and "Tea for Two" were the screaming favorites. The sax player's Maori wife sang "Won't You Come Home, Bill Bailey?" without the aid or need of electronic amplification. Nancy and I staggered home exhausted at 2:30 A.M., but the rest carried on until noon the following day.

Unable to put by enough extra money to see us comfortably around the world, New Zealand wages being what they were, Nancy and I decided to sail back to California. About this time (spring 1975) we became friends with an American couple, Ed and Laurie. Ed was one-third owner of a 55-foot schooner named *Samarang*. They had left California with great expectations. One couple peeled off in the Marquesas, the first possible place. The second couple made it all the way to New Zealand before divorcing. The agreement among the partners was that if two-thirds became disenchanted, the boat would be sold and the partnership dissolved. Now *Samarang*, with our son Chris as one of the crew, was to be sailed back to California by one of the other partners. This left Ed and Laurie with no boat, but still eager to continue sailing.

Ed, lanky, laconic, and easy-going, was a distance runner as well as an experienced sailor. His heart in repose (according to Laurie) beat only 30 times a minute. Laurie was a quiescent volcano of energy looking for a chance to erupt. Both had good senses of humor. They were older than our children but younger than we, and Nancy and I were sure we could enjoy them as cruising companions aboard *Sea Foam*.

Marci was sailing to Tahiti on another yacht, leaving only Craig, Nancy, and me. There would be plenty of room aboard. We came to an agreement on their share of the expenses for the passage back to French Polynesia. There the five of us would spend several months cruising the islands.

Meanwhile, life developed into a routine. I caught the ferry daily at 8:00 A.M., caught the 5:00 P.M. ferry home. We were building a three-story, A-frame house on a hillside across the bay from Russell. The roof was to be made with long, interlocking metal planks a foot wide, some of them nearly 50 feet long. They arrived at the freight yard in Opua, wrapped in bundles weighing 200 to 600 pounds.

I'd had a double hernia fixed five years before in the U.S., and I'd been assured that it wouldn't hurt me a bit to go on hoisting outsized martini glasses. At that time, the idea that I would do anything more strenuous would have struck both the doctor and me as unlikely. When we fetched the roofing, I played the role of a middle-aged stevedore and was rewarded with a dull pain and two bulges just above the groin.

The Russell doctor was English, newly arrived. I coughed obediently as he probed the left side.

"Hmm," he said. Doctors talk the same way everywhere. While I coughed and he probed, his two nurses checked me out visually, then returned to their tasks with an insulting lack of interest.

"Hmm," he said again, checking the right side.

He moved wearily over to his desk, fiddled briefly with his pencil, then spoke directly and distinctly to the office wall.

"You have a double hernia—," he said, confirming what from experience I already knew. My heart sank anyway. "And I certainly hope you didn't get it at work."

"I did. Why?"

"Because that means I've got to fill out a lot of stupid forms," he said, reaching into a drawer and pulling out a stack of printed pads.

Bolstered by his sympathy, I asked the big question.

"I suppose I'll have to have it operated on before I go to sea again."

"Absolutely. Peritonitis at sea would do you in, my friend." The thought gave him obvious pleasure, and he chuckled, probably for the first time that day.

He gave me instructions to fill out this form, take that letter to the surgeon at the Kawa Kawa Hospital, and to pay his receptionist $1.50 please (about two American dollars). At those prices I should have forgiven him his disposition.

The hospital sucked me into its maw on the appointed day. I was lying in my bed, reading, when an immense young nurse hove-to alongside, razor in hand.

"Come on in the loo and I'll shave ya," she offered, a big grin on her face.

Normally I'm not burdened with modesty. For some reason, however, this amazon startled me, and one of the strangers who inhabit my personality reacted with, "Please, can I do it myself?" Before I knew it I was sitting in a bathtub of warm water trying to shave myself without doing irreparable damage. I'd forgotten my glasses and I was damned if I was going to dry off, dress, and go back to my bedside table to get them. After 30 challenging minutes I was back in bed de-haired, unwounded, and glad to have done with it. One minute later, the nurse barged in and said she had to look.

"You missed here, and here," she said, moving my private parts around with the unfeeling purpose of a person going through a bowl of mixed nuts in search of all the cashews. "And you gotta shave more off your legs."

"I need a new blade," I grumped, and went back for another try, this time with glasses. Fill the tub, strip, get the soap, get the razor, put on the glasses, and try to keep them from falling off because I'd come to the hospital with the ones that did, and this time get every last goddamn hair. It didn't help a bit that the nurse stayed to watch, giggling unmercifully when my glasses fell off into the water. It wasn't till after the operation that I saw the funny side. By then it had happened to somebody else, to last week's me.

When I was well enough, we hauled *Sea Foam* out of the water for a whole month. There was a mountain of work to be done, work that was constantly delayed by rainy, raw weather. A friend designed and built us a windvane, which Craig christened "Speedy." In the kitchen of a friend's house we canned 120 pounds of beef and 24 pounds of chicken. The effort took two days, but we were repaid for months in terms of money saved and quality of meals.

After Ed and Laurie moved aboard, we left Russell for Whangarei for last-minute provisioning. Speedy worked like a charm. During the trip, Ed lost his contact lenses, and after a two-hour search we found them in the trash, mixed up with the coffee grounds. This was such a good omen, I thought, it spurred me to predict that our passage to the Australs would consist of nothing but fair winds and gentle seas. So much, as it turned out, for omens.

TWENTY-THREE

"**I**T'LL BE A SNAP," I had assured Ed and Laurie. "New Zealand to the Australs, then Tahiti and the Leewards. We'll have a windvane, seasonal predominant westerlies —all we'll do is eat, sleep, play backgammon, and sunbathe."

"Sounds good," Ed had replied, looking down at me appraisingly from the rarefied air he inhabits when he stands up. "How's *Sea Foam* go to weather?"

"Uh. . . ." I didn't want to start off our new relationship with a lie, but on the other hand I felt I should lead him gently into the truth of *Sea Foam*'s windward ability. Besides, I had a theory that all things are within reach, be you but patient.

"I figure you can go anywhere on a beam reach if you're not in a hurry. You're not in any hurry, are you?" I'd looked him right in the eye, hoping that attack would be as good a defense as any.

"Of course not," he'd replied. The lie we yachties lay on each other is that we really *don't* care—after all, we've got plenty of time and we love to sail, right? This lasts for about half a passage, after which everybody gets antsy and monosyllabic, and conversation, when it transcends necessity, dwells on what it'll be like when we arrive.

"*Sea Foam* is really beamy—roomy and comfortable." Actually, with nearly 14 feet of beam, she was built more like a bowling ball than a boat. "And you know you can't have everything," I'd finished brightly.

We were all highly experienced downwind sailors. Ed and Laurie, as part-owners of the now-departed 55-foot *Samarang*, had had a total of 20 hours to weather in their two-year journey from California to New Zealand. Nancy, Craig, and I had had maybe five days to weather as we made the same trip. About 98 percent of our total experience was downwind.

I've always felt that the invention of the ski tow severely compromised the morality (but not the pleasure) of skiing. On a rambling New Hampshire farm we had our own little mountain. We packed our trails on snowshoes, and our runs were well-earned rewards for hard work and a long climb. With that sort of nonsense in one's background, one doesn't sail all the way to New Zealand, sell the boat, and fly back. At least, not the first time. You buy back your run, tough mile after tough mile.

So it was that we found ourselves in Whangarei. Once more *Sea Foam* was stuffed with food, water, and fuel. Most of the little last-minute things were bought and stored. Days of errand-running, price-shopping, and parts-seeking had passed slowly by, and lists and tempers gradually grew shorter. Tempers can grow infinitesimally short, whereas lists never do, and there came a day when we were psychologically ready to leave, if not materially.

"Let's leave," uttered a random mouth speaking for a mind fed up with lying in a muddy river in the middle of a dirty, noisy city.

"Just another day or two," responded another mouth, speaking for a mind totally involved in readying his or her special domain. Just a few more things to find, get, stow, prepare, change, collect, mail, receive, buy, or make.

"Let's damn well leave," said one, said two, said all.

"Leave!" said Immigration.

We left. The plan was to float economically and easily down the 15-mile Whangarei River on a falling tide. It was a good plan, but it fell short in its execution. Customs was late. Some last-minute mailing took longer than it should have. Delay, postpone, just a minute; and finally cast off, bye-bye, *bon voyage*.

Three hundred yards from inception our voyage came to a squishy halt on one of the magical, moveable mudbars that populate the not-too-deeps of the upper river.

Customs men, strategically placed behind riverbank trees, surveyed us to make sure we didn't on-load any pot or off-load any duty-frees. Passersby snickered from the shore. Sea Foamers, veterans of cruising's many vicissitudes, finished lashing-down and make-ready chores, broke open a bottle of sherry, and wallowed in a three-course roast beef dinner. Finally at last light we floated free, and, taking only two hours longer than we should have, we ground down the river against a rising tide and nosed into open ocean. Mizzen, main, and staysail. Beam reach.

I had called the weather bureau just before leaving: a big front, northwesterly winds. Not bad, but at midnight the mizzen had to come down. At dawn we doused the main. The wind was as predicted, but it came in bucketfuls, bagfuls, barrowfuls, truckloads: 25 gusting 35, 30 gusting 40, 35 gusting 45.

At 1300, sixteen hours after setting sail, our windvane broke. One of the pins worked its way out of the gudgeons, and the auxiliary rudder twisted the lower half of its stainless steel bracket into uselessness. In order to free the rudder and bring it aboard we had to bring *Sea Foam* into the wind. Ten minutes and three bloody hands later it was done, but the staysail had flogged two large tears along its foot.

The wind had become more westerly, and there was no way to beat back to Whangarei against those seas, against that wind.

"Watch on watch it is, after all," I said, twisting my mouth painfully in an effort to smile.

Now we were running downwind under bare poles, heading a little south of east, creaming along at better than five knots. The winds increased: 40 gusting 50, maybe more. Watches were cold, wet, and scary. *Sea Foam* slid down one wave, blasted into the wall of another. She would rise up drunkenly, sending gallons of green and white water back into the cockpit; then she would stop, poised, readying herself to do it again. Steering demanded strength, total concentration. We were all so wet we felt amphibious. Our world was epidemic throw-ups; forced, appetiteless snacks; universal sog.

In order to stabilize the boat we raised a reefed main. The wind was now southwesterly, and we flew along at seven to eight knots, right toward the mark. We sorely missed the tiny staysail, normally our storm sail. We were sailing too fast, but we were still in control, and the motion of the boat was far less squirrelly.

We were lucky that the wind was blowing us in the right direction. *Sea Foam* has little choice in heavy weather. Lying a-hull with her full-length deep keel, she slams into the troughs with alarming frequency. She heaves-to like she goes to weather— somewhere around 70 degrees off the wind. We've heaved-to safely and comfortably in less violent weather, but in this case the waves were like implacable walls—towering vertical surfaces with occasionally breaking tops. I didn't want to lie to them nearly broadside, so we ran before them.

Sea Foam runs safely under bare poles, and the few times we've tried it she has handled well. But under bare poles her motion is erratic, non-rhythmic, much like a drunk with the blind staggers. With a little sail up—either staysail or reefed main—she runs with the wind 10 to 30 degrees off her quarter, and her motion is far more comfortable.

She has tremendous buoyancy both fore and aft. Her buxom stern is a raised transom with considerable overhang. Waves that look like they should engulf her merely lift her skyward. Aft from the cutwater her hull broadens quickly. When she surfs down into the trough she butts the oncoming wave like a goat butting a barn wall. Instead of cutting through the wave she rises up and over. Never a knife, always a cork, she rides the watery terrain like a runaway bus.

There is ostrichlike comfort in the running tactic, too. The faster one goes, the less intimidating the relative wind—until the helmsman loses his concentration and lets her round up into a beam reach, at which time the full vengeance of the wind reminds him of his naked vulnerability.

Our log for the passage reads like a catalog of sail changes. The wind never came from the same direction for more than 12 hours, nor blew at the same strength for more than six; and the sails, like a newborn babe, never failed to need our attention in the middle of the night.

The wind swung from north to west to south to east, so that after only four days out we found ourselves sailing due north. We'd read that there were nearly always westerlies further south, and that a downwinder could easily make easting in the roaring forties. I didn't want to blunder about in the Kermadecs, bob aimlessly in the calms and variables of the horse latitudes, or attempt to prove my beam-reach theory against the trades. So we tacked and sailed south-southeast to an east-northeast wind. And as the next five days passed, the wind veered steadily counterclockwise until, having sailed in a gentle curve to within 15 miles of 40 degrees south, we were finally able to steer the rhumb line to Tubuai.

Different events punctuate passages for different people. For Craig it was the fact that he'd thrown up 23 times in the first three days. I'm rarely seasick, but the few times that I've felt queasy my mind reverberated with plaints of "why me?" Craig is always sick for the first few days, but he never takes it personally, and treats each vomitous event with the detachment and professional interest of an actuary.

For me the trip was marked by the exact time each of us lost, more or less permanently, his sense of humor. Laurie was first. It was night. We were running with reefed main. The wind had settled down to a steady 30 knots. It was rough, the decks were constantly awash, and water was finding its way to the bilges through old leaks that had previously seemed small and unimportant, and through new leaks that were appearing for the first time. We were all tired, but each one of us was doing his share, persevering, enduring the watches, the cold, the anxiety, the eternal wet.

Suddenly a wave—a rogue, rebel, monster of a misfit—came out of the darkness dead abeam. *Sea Foam* was picked up, up, then thrown down nearly on her beam ends. The bilgewater sloshed up between the ribs and cascaded back over Laurie as she lay asleep in her bunk. A solution of 5 percent diesel, 80 percent saltwater, and 15 percent grime soaked her body, her bed, and what were left of her dry clothes. After that she slept fitfully and rarely smiled, and we all talked softly in her presence.

Ed was next. His normally resilient good nature was severely handicapped by unwonted seasickness. When one isn't feeling well, even the smallest additional chores loom unpleasantly difficult. Coming off watch one night at midnight he tried to pump out the bilge, but discovered that the electric pump wasn't working. In the process he discovered the trick our pump plays on the unwary—the same trick that, years before, had nearly sunk us on our way to Catalina. To pump the bilge you must open a gate valve which, on the port tack, is below the waterline. Then you run the pump. If for some reason the pump decides not to work that day, water syphons from the ocean into the bilge at an alarming rate. Ed, unaware, didn't realize what was happening until we had taken aboard a significant cargo of sea water.

"Never fear," I said, grinning my encouraging grimace. "We'll pump it out by hand, and I'll fix the electric pump in the morning."

The hand pump was the plunger type, old but reliable. It had been our main pump only weeks before while I was repairing the gatevalve for the electric. It had worked fine then. Confidently I grasped the handle, confidently pushed and pulled. My midnight grin sicklied o'er with the pale cast of panic. Nothing.

I watched Ed's face as the truth dawned. I watched the conflicting emotions play transparently across his face. With a clairvoyant flash, I knew exactly what his next line was going to be.

"I have lost," he stated definitively, "my sense of humor."

Deciding instantly that our abandon-ship gear would be far less comfortable than *Sea Foam*, I swallowed my fear like a parched prospector swallowing three tablespoons of peanut butter, summoned the remnants of my self-possession, and went to work on the pump. It required dismantling and re-routing the hose so that we could prime it. After that it merely required pumping. And pumping. And more pumping.

As we took turns sharing the burden, putting our shoulders to the wheel, I felt a great sense of accomplishment as the bilges slowly gave up their cargo. It didn't turn Ed on at all. Finally, when the pump started making noises like an urchin finishing a malted, Ed gave a couple of unintelligible grunts and crawled into his berth: tranquilizer, earplugs, fetal position, pillow over the head. In another flash—insight, this time—I knew I had lost his confidence.

My own sense of humor didn't disappear in a puff of disaster, but gradually seeped away as *Sea Foam* aged at an ever-increasing rate. We lost one backstay when a 50-knot squall hit us on a dark night and caught us with our twin headsails up. We lost another—the main running backstay on the same side—when a sudden wind shift on a pitch-black night broke the preventer and jibed the main. The mainsail frayed its leech to ribbons as a result of missing battens, and it was no comfort to me that it was my own fault: one of the items on the uncompleted list was batten material, and I had overlooked it. The mizzen had a three-foot tear in a seam—we had been raising it when a batten had caught in a backstay. The whole electrical system, a patchwork House That Jack Built, proved to be dangerously vulnerable to a wet passage and would have to be replaced. The windvane was broken. And in spite of baggywrinkles and other precautions, day by day I could see lines and sails fraying, chafing, and deteriorating. Nancy tried, with irrepressible good humor, to cheer us, but she was hopelessly outnumbered. If the sun had shined, the weather warmed, the breeze blown kindly, the seas calmed, there would have been the balm of pleasant sailing to heal the wounds; but as it was, the weather chiseled our attitudes into granite grimness, and the only good day we had was the last one, 21 days out of New Zealand.

Landfall morning was a perfect example of what God can do to fill your cup when He puts His mind to it. The wind blew 12 knots from our port quarter. The swells were gentle. Stern gray warrior clouds had given way to their white fluffy children, contentedly skydrifting. The water soaked up blue from above, drank it deep and gave it back richer, lusher. Nancy's grin restored sallow dispositions. Ed tum-tum-te-tum-tummed as he steered. From the spreaders, Craig eagerly scanned the horizon, then excitedly land-hoed. Laurie appeared topsides wearing a real smile, not a brave imitation, and carrying a carafe of rum punch. We toasted Tubuai as it rose from the ocean like an awakening giant. Relief grew to a great gladness. We swooped in the pass, creamed up the lagoon, and dropped anchor in front of the village.

Ten minutes later we were ashore, earth-kissing grateful, the land rocking gently from inner ear confusion. Strapping, paunchy poppa stood waiting with proud, brown son. Chubby, wise-eyed mother strolled by with lithe, mischief-eyed daughter. Our cheeks ached from responding to welcoming smiles.

"Le magasin? Là-bas? Merci."

We walked slowly along the dusty road, happy to be sweating a little, breathing deeply the *tiare*-scented air, drinking in the green dotted with reds, whites, and yellows; laughing at nothing. There was no hurry. We'd climbed our mountain of easting. We'd earned our downwind day.

TWENTY-FOUR

IT IS CHRISTMAS, 1975. I am sitting in the back of the dinghy, singing "It Came Upon a Midnight Clear" in a hoarse tenor, hacking out the changes on my authentic Marquesan ukulele, strung with monofilament (eight pound test) nylon fishing line. Nancy is in the bow, rowing off her dinner with a strong stroke which suffers only from a little too much right oar. *Sea Foam* is receding slowly astern, placidly at anchor, the only yacht in the flat waters of the lagoon. On my right lies the motu, coconut trees waving their fronds in the afternoon sky, feathery brushes painting brilliant clouds on a canvas of royal blue. On my left is the regal silhouette of the Raivavae mountains.

I polish off Mendelssohn with a flourish and segue smoothly into "Jingle Bells." Nancy giggles.

"What's the matter?" I demand in a hurt tone. "Jingle Bells" is one of my best numbers.

"Oh, I don't know. Snow, and sleighs, and Santa Claus—it all seems so far away. Yet what an incredible Christmas we had."

"Best ever," I say, "but you're using too much right oar." With that I start over at the chorus.

I glance up at Nancy covertly from the sternsheets. Flaming hair, once coiffed weekly in a pompadour, now hangs nearly to her waist in a soft wave. Skin which had been white glows bronze. Blue eyes shine with vitality and enjoyment. She, more than any of us, has pulled the rabbit from the hat, uniting disparate attitudes, and, without the usual shops or hordes of relatives, has led us to create an immensely pleasurable day.

For a while it looked like we would miss out on Christmas altogether. I think back. We just spent nearly a month in neighboring Tubuai enjoying the island, the hospitality of the inhabitants, the limitless, crispy-fresh vegetables. Tubuai surprised us with its roads, many vehicles, an airport, two banks, and two shops with nearly any provisions we might need. The people gave us lifts on the road, invited us to their homes, and gave us gifts of bananas and vegetables.

Raivavae, on the other hand, is more sparsely inhabited. There is a road around the island, but there are very few vehicles. In general the islanders have been difficult to get to know. They don't grow any vegetables. The ubiquitous French imprint is here—baguettes of bread baked daily—but the two shops contain virtually nothing.

The lagoon, navigable all around the main island, is dotted with uninhabited motus—exciting places to dive, to picnic, to explore. We discover a deep cave and explore it. We hear of an old tiki, so we walk there and take a picture. Avocado trees line the road: we ask and are told to take all we want. We decide that Raivavae is unspoiled, whatever that means.

We anchor in front of the village, the only visiting yacht. Good friends arrive in three boats that have come up from New Zealand. Three more boats arrive from Tahiti and we make new friends. There are seven boats in front of the village, more than Raivavae has had visit them during the whole of any previous year. Signs of the times.

The small fleet threads its way through the coral heads to the lee of Motu Haa Amu, and the sailors play musical boats for dinners and drinks. We joke about forming the Raivavae Yacht Club, but we enjoy it, too. Craig and a friend walk on the reef and return with a bagful of lobsters, which they hang over the side. In the morning, all the lobsters have escaped through a hole in the rotting burlap. Undaunted, Craig plans another trip.

One by one the other yachts leave for Papeete until, once again, Sea Foam is alone. Only then do we suddenly realize that Christmas is just a few days away.

"What are we going to do about Christmas?" asks Nancy, hands on hips. She has the air of knowing that if I'm left to my own devices I'll do very little.

"We have to do something on account of Craig," she continues.

"Sure," I answer vaguely, trying to put off facing it as long as possible.

"*I* think," she persists, "we should sail to Papeete and have a big party with all the other yachts—like the one in the park two years ago."

I think back two years and remember 60-plus yachties taking over the little park on the waterfront, barbecuing chickens and swapping potluck pots, yarns, and songs, sharing beer and good cheer till the early hours of the morning.

"Unduplicatable," I say firmly, "and Papeete is expensive."

I expect an argument, but instead she walks away, chewing her lip, knowing that for once I am right. In a few minutes she's back.

"All right, we'll stay. But let's *do* something. Something special."

I think of Craig's earlier shore Christmases—trikes, bikes, and all the other heaps of things—and I figure he's going to have a pretty poor show no matter what we do. But as I've so often done, I underestimate him.

"We can come back to the motu," said Craig, "and get some more lobsters—the moon'll be right Christmas Eve—and we can have a big lobster feast."

Everyone agrees that this is a terrific idea, but there are problems to solve. One of them is Ed's attitude. He's always hated the commercial aspect of Christmas in the States—it taints the whole idea of exchanging presents as far as he is concerned. He isn't against celebrating Christ's birthday, but he isn't going to come all the way out to this remote island to perpetuate the ridiculous custom of gift-giving. Like it or not, that's the way he feels, and we're stuck with it.

Humbugville: score one round for Gloom.

Laurie can go either way. She basically agrees with Ed, deep inside, but I approach her privately and tell her that it's mostly for Craig, so she goes along and, in the end, contributes as much as any of us. Round two goes to the Yulers.

Sea Foam returns to the village for water and for last-minute Christmas shopping (one large can of cashews, all for Craig, the only gift bought). It's good to have fresh bread every day, and we are accumulating bananas, avocados, limes, and peppers. The generous wife of the French gendarme gives us a few fresh vege- tables from her garden, so we stay.

The days pass, overcast, rainy, and oppressive. Nancy, Craig, and Laurie keep the sewing machine humming, fa-la-lahing cheerfully to themselves. Ed is very quiet, always reading. I rack my brain for something to find or make for someone, but I can't come up with anything I like. To combat Gloom I decide to go and get a tree.

I throw some tools in the dinghy—it's still raining, but fresh water is a treat for most boat tools. It's so warm, to hell with the foul weather gear. Trunks'll do. I row out to the motu on the reef in front of the village, a pocket motu, a tiny dot on the "i" of "island." On the motu is a range marker that will be hidden from view in a few months if some kind person doesn't clear out all those young ironwood trees which are growing in front of it. I do it, performing a service both to sailors and to myself. One of the trees is perfect. (Mature ironwood trees are usually gnarly, beautiful in dark needles and twisting branches, but the baby trees are straight and symmetrical, dressed in delicate light-green tracery.) I look at the tree from every angle, absorbing the per- fection of each branch, and I feel the first, faint stirrings of Christmas spirit.

I take the tree back to the dinghy. Then I start walking slowly around the motu looking for a shell, a piece of glass, a bit of drift- wood. I still have nothing particular in mind, but I am more re- ceptive to ideas, less depressed. The rain on my skin is pleasantly cooling. I come upon a battered piece of plywood with "Made in Taiwan" lettered on it and speculate making something out of it as a joke, but I look closer and see that it's delaminated beyond hope, and keep on walking. There are no pieces of drift- wood, no pretty shells, no colored glass. I'm getting discouraged. I come to a place where the beach stops and some strange trees are growing right out of the saltwater. They block my way, and

I curse as I clamber through the maze of roots, slipping more than once, impatient to get back to beachcombing.

Suddenly I notice the roots themselves. The ones growing out of the water are polished to a smooth, rich fawn. Wooden tentacles twist and turn in graceful arcs. The roots are living driftwood, and a second ago I was cursing their existence. Excited now, I rush back to the dinghy for a saw.

The plan takes shape of its own accord. Cut out a short section of one root whose design I like—the tree's gift to Christmas. Find the biggest coconuts I can and husk them. Cut away one-fourth of the sphere. Dig out the meat. Break the shell on the first attempt, but start over without even one bad word. Finally get two good ones. In my mind I see them sanded and varnished, suspended from the driftwood on braid made from marline. It'll be a planter-mobile, and not a bad one if I do say so myself. My spirits improve, and round three goes to the Yulers.

My tree is greeted with "oo" and "ah" from everybody but Ed, who is still standing off. The women go ashore to collect blossoms: yellow-white frangipani and red hibiscus. I stand the little tree in the corner on a low shelf, and the women decorate it with several necklaces made from tiny shells and from beads. Hibiscus flowers, the kind that never open, hang from each branch like fragile, fiery bells. Strings of blossoms hang from every conceivable projection in the cabin, and I decide that their fragrance is one of the reasons Polynesia is called Paradise.

I stand back and look. *Sea Foam*'s cabin has never looked so festive, but Ed is still withdrawn, so we call round four a draw.

Christmas Eve day we somehow get a late start to return to Motu Haa Amu. We always say we'll leave at 8:00 and settle for 10:00, but this time it is noon before we pull up anchor. One of those days.

The lagoon is deep all along the length of the island, but the water becomes shallower between the end of the island and the outer reef where the motu is, a distance of about half a mile, studded with coral heads. With good visibility—the sun overhead or behind, with a slight ripple on the water to break up the glare—and someone aloft, the bottom stands out like a giant road map. We've made the trip before with good visibility. It was tricky, but Craig is excellent at conning and I have confidence in him.

But when we reach the end of the island my heart sinks. A huge cloud has settled around the tops of the Raivavae mountains, completely obscuring the sun. I watch the cloud for a full five minutes. It isn't moving. It looks as though it'll *never* move. Visibility will be terrible.

I work out our choices:

1. Go back to the village—Gloom wins by a KO. (Never.)

2. Anchor somewhere nearby—possible, but that means no lobsters, so Gloom wins a few rounds, maybe even a draw. (Hold in reserve.)

3. Risk damage to *Sea Foam* and go on—almost hopeless. (Give it a look.)

"What can you see, Craig?" I shout.

"Not very much," he says. He is high up the mast, standing on the spreaders.

I believe him. From the deck, I myself can barely make out a coral head when it's *beside* me and no more than ten feet away. I go aloft to see what Craig sees.

It's unbelievable. The water, normally transparent, even in bad light fairly translucent, has by some freak of circumstances turned to an opaque soup. I barely make out a dark shadow in the murk about a boatlength ahead.

"Is that a coral head out there?" I ask incredulously.

"That's what it is," says Craig, laying the problem on the line.

"Good Christ," I breathe, momentarily forgetting it is almost His birthday.

I go back down on deck. Everyone asks what I'm going to do. I tune them out, knowing from experience that no one will make the decision for me, and that whatever I do will be wrong to some extent.

I sort it out this way. There's not a breath of air or a ripple of current. *Sea Foam* will be under perfect control. Craig is experienced, cautious. Anything but going ahead will make Christmas a dead loss.

At this point Nancy arrives from below decks with an old, scratched-up pair of Polaroid sunglasses.

"Where in the world did you find these?" I ask. Without waiting for an answer I fly up the ratlines for another look. The sunglasses make a difference—not much, but a perceptible difference. I can still only spot the coral heads about a boatlength ahead, but they are just a bit easier to see.

"Let's try it, Craig. Shout loud and clear. If you call for a turn, let me know how much rudder you want. We'll take it very slow."

"Do you really think we should?" asks Nancy, wanting to as much as I, but always more prudent.

"I think it's stupid," says Laurie, accustomed to calling a spade a spade.

Ed just stays up in the bow and shakes his head in disapproval. I set my teeth and inch *Sea Foam* slowly forward, feeling halfway between a hero and an idiot with a wish-fulfillment syndrome.

It takes 45 minutes to creep half a mile. It's 45 minutes of sweaty palms; of seeing angry coral heads slide slowly by, sometimes no more than three feet away; of imagining razor-sharp edges mutilating stout fir planks. But Craig not only guides us through the coral, he delivers us to the very same clear, sandy spot where we anchored before. He climbs down from the rigging, grinning like a Cheshire cat. I'm grinning a bit like one myself. The anchor splashes, grabs hold. I put out another anchor astern. Ed and Laurie still think I'm crazy, but they're so happy to have made it without mishap they forgive me. Nancy is bathing the world with a cascade of smiles. Gloom is backpedaling around the ring, elbows covering his face. I arrive topsides with Christmas Eve drinks, and Gloom goes down for the count.

From then on we're home free. Ed catches fire about going

out on the reef with Craig, and they come back with a prodigal supply of lobster and slipper crab, a type of crab with a lobster-like tail whose meat is sweeter and more tender than lobster. Christmas Day comes and Laurie has filled the stockings. Nancy has made clothes for everyone. Craig has made me a hat. Ed gives Nancy an IOU to do her dishes for one day. I give Craig an IOU for a pair of diving gloves. Nancy loves her planter. There's more. Dinner is delicious, and the sun shines.

Nancy turned the dinghy around, tired of all this exercise nonsense. Her musings spilled out in words.

"Wasn't it a great Christmas?" She was getting sentimental and repetitive.

"Great," I said, "but I'm really glad we came up with an IOU for Craig's gloves. I wouldn't feel right without at least one Christmas debt. By the way, you're still using too much right oar." I was trying to get the conversation out of the mush.

Nancy stuck her tongue out at me, then continued, irrepressibly.

"Do you think he'll remember when he's older, if he has to face a Christmas away from family and without any money?"

I thought it over. It was a good question. The reality of Christmas is easily trampled in a busy world, but I was damned if I was going to underestimate Craig again.

"I'm sure he'll remember," I said, and was instantly rewarded with one of Nancy's sunniest smiles.

TWENTY-FIVE

W E LEFT RAIVAVAE and arrived in Papeete after a fast (for *Sea Foam*) but wet trip, close-reaching on the starboard tack, powering the last six hours and steaming in on the range lights just before midnight. We were met with hails from familiar yachts as we eased into a slot in the low-rent district. Shore-dwelling Tahitian, French, and expatriate friends, made on our previous visit, greeted us and entertained us. When the postal clerk who ran *poste restante* (general delivery) welcomed us after 17 months with a warm smile and an umprompted "Ah, *Sea Foam*," I knew we were home.

One afternoon we decided to take a group to a seldom-visited lagoon in Moorea to do some diving. When I informed the official that I was taking some friends out for the day to return their hospitality, I was accused of running a clandestine charter. For an hour I smiled and explained, gave names and addresses, smiled and explained some more. The official finally laughed, said he'd only been kidding, and wished me a good time. *Merci, monsieur, mais tu ne blaguais pas, j'en suis sûr.* And if you were, why the hell didn't I think it was funny?

I hadn't lost the capacity to enjoy the misfortune of others, however. One day I was in a camera store when a French customer came in with two piles of passport pictures. One pile satisfied him, the other did not. His mission: convince the Chinese proprietor-photographer to retake the unsatisfactory photos for nothing.

The Frenchman played the instrument of his anger like a virtuoso. At first he spoke in soft tones using sweet reason and cool logic. Next came the second movement, his voice still well-modulated but rapier-edged, cutting and slashing. A gradual crescendo led to the third movement, his voice rising in pitch and volume with threats of no more friendship, no more commerce between them. The fourth movement climaxed with a total loss of temper, a yelling of imprecations in frantic rhythms, a rending of the offending photos into a blizzard of bits to be stamped upon with flamenco passion. The coda was a whirlwind exit, the final chord a slammed door. It was *formidable*, a perfect illustration of Oriental obduracy versus French flamboyance.

We sailed to Moorea and spent one night tied up to a quay in Cook's Bay. Invaders awakened us early, brown eyes and bubbling giggles stabbing through open portholes, infiltrating a snoring jungle of unconsciousness. (So *that's* why yachts don't make a practice of tying up alongside.) The children had an entertaining hour watching us grope around the cabin retrieving discarded clothes, donning day-things. For an encore we ate eggs and toast and drank coffee. And more coffee. Finally sufficiently revived, we curtailed their childish pleasures by casting off and sailing to Robinson's Cove, where we dropped anchor and backed toward shore, our eyes on a palm tree.

Craig was in the dinghy with the sternline when the motor suddenly stopped. I shifted to neutral, started the motor again, shifted forward. It stopped again.

I dove down for a look. The propeller shaft had become a spindle for some quarter-inch line that was tied to the taffrail. The force of the turning shaft had tightened the line and pulled the strut supporting the shaft away from the hull. The cutlass bearing in the strut had given way completely. I was sick at heart. A stiff yard bill was one thing we could not afford.

I spent two days searching the stores in Papeete for a replacement, then sent for one from the States. We waited. It rained much of the time. Laurie and Ed got dengue fever, a rotten disease much like severe influenza: high fever, accompanying shakes, body aches, headaches, and a lethargy during convalescence like the debilitating aftermath of infectious hepatitis.

During their recovery, Ed's and Laurie's cases of dengue were gradually replaced by acute cabin fever and a disenchantment with Robinson's Cove that bordered on obsession. And still we waited.

When the replacement part finally came, I set about the task of trying to remount the strut. The problem was that the old holes, now stripped, had to be filled with underwater Epoxy and redrilled. It took me several attempts—working underwater with snorkel and mask, as no tank was available—before I succeeded in achieving what I thought was a firm bite for every lag screw. One attempt aborted because the putty was old and set up chalky. Another attempt failed because my template was a tad off, causing misalignment of the strut. We moved *Sea Foam* next to a place where the bottom dropped off in a steep slope, and I was able to stand while using the brace and bit. But it would have been so much simpler in a boatyard.

With Ed and Laurie now completely recovered, we fled the scene of our troubles and set out for Huahine, a night-sail away. In spite of the fact that there were more yachts than ever before, a result of the navigation explosion, the village of Fare remained virtually unchanged. One old store had a new front. A hamburger stand had erupted on the waterfront. Otherwise it was the same sleepy village: a waterfront street lined with gnarled trees under which, around 5:00, yachties would congregate for a cold Sprite or an icy Hinano.

There were plenty of young people around, plenty of places to shell within rowing distance. Memories of the Tahitian wedding here made Nancy and me nostalgic, and we tried to duplicate the ambiance with a giant clambake on the beach. Cruising has at least two dimensions, and we exulted in the social one, before opting for the other dimension: solitude, on the seldom-visited eastern side of Huahine.

We could hardly believe it was the same island. We anchored in front of a village that had not hosted a yacht for over a year. Natives paddled out with gifts of fruit. Of the three who brought instruments, one had exceptional talent and sparkplugged the ensemble to excellence. We stayed two days before moving to a spot behind a motu, close to the reef, where we spent three days snorkeling and shelling, reveling in our complete isolation.

Trouble found us once again as we emerged from our hiding place and made a dash for Papeete. During Craig's night watch, we were hit by a sudden squall with winds of 40 to 50 knots. By the time we were able to react, the mizzen had torn itself along the foot, and a great section of the sailcloth had taken off, airborne, toward Fiji. We power-sailed all night under reduced sail, belted by squall after squall. In the morning the squalls attacked with increasing frequency and venom. One, which we tried to weather with staysail and reefed main, must have brought brief gusts of over 55 knots. When it had passed, both sails were in tatters.

Tahiti was in sight, dead to windward, and we powered slowly, aided by the calms that reigned between squalls. The diesel started to act up, stopping every 20 minutes and requiring that I blow out the fuel lines. We limped into the harbor after dark, engine gasping terminal gasps, Laurie and Ed standing by the running lights and shining flashlights through the lenses, as the circuits had shorted out again. The transmission was making geriatric sounds. By the time we'd anchored and run lines to the quay, *Sea Foam* was a floating basket case, a doddering lady whose Medicare had lapsed.

It is an incontestable, statistically proven fact that whenever Nancy and I want to jolly ourselves out of poverty-actuated blues, we scrape together our last few farthings and go out to dinner. This night was no different and by so doing we escaped, momentarily, *Sea Foam* and reminders of our misery.

Nancy, Craig, and I walked silently along Papeete's waterfront. Eventually we came to our destination, a row of lunch trucks. Beside each was a portable brazier, and the succulent smells of barbecued beef, goat, pork, and chicken filled the balmy night. Each proprietor made or prepared all his wares himself, so it was necessary to walk the whole length of the row of trucks to savor the possibilities. We decided on barbecued chicken livers (two skewers each) and French fries.

The young Tahitian—a plump girl, by no means pretty, but with a slow smile of infinite warmth—took my proffered francs. I counted our remaining few. I had my eye on the coconuts the Tahitian customers were buying—drinking nuts, chilled, full of sweet, cold nectar. It seemed to me I had never thirsted for anything quite so much.

"Combien?" I asked, indicating the nuts.

"Cinquante," said the girl.

"Fifty?" Nancy asked me. She had been in Polynesia long enough to understand basic French perfectly well, but she still asked me everything because she knew it made me feel good.

"Tu veux, toi?" asked the girl, holding out a nut.

A quick calculation dictated my reply.

"Non, merci," I said, trying to be stoic and unwistful.

We finished our meal and stood up to leave.

"M'sieur," said the girl. She had placed three drinking nuts on the counter, straws planted in the holes.

"I said 'no,'" I told her in French, fearful she might have misunderstood me earlier. "I haven't the money."

"Ça va," she said simply, and turned on her languid, thousand-watt smile. It must have started somewhere near her toes, because it warmed me all the way down to mine.

"What an attitude-changer," said Nancy, smiling for the first time that day. One shy young lady had taken our insurmountable problems and shrunk them magically. The trio that returned to *Sea Foam* was stronger and abler than the one that had left her only an hour before.

TWENTY-SIX

BECAUSE SEA FOAM was cruising on what could most kindly be described as a limited budget, we were forced to learn how to be happy with a sailboat almost totally devoid of marine luxuries. By not affording a vane, we learned to sail. By not affording a mechanic, I learned to repair the diesel and the transmission. I learned a great deal about 12-volt electrical systems, boat maintenance, wire splicing, weather, navigation, a smattering of electronics, and a lot about heads. We developed a flair for improvisation. Sometimes we were too confident, sometimes not enough, but as each day went by we gained in our ability to cope with the cruising life.

I considered us lucky to have learned to enjoy life without luxury. Nonetheless, way back in the corner of my Waldenesque mind lurked the wistful remnant of a desire for plenty. In an effort to sublimate these yearnings I compiled a list of wishes entitled "In My Next Life." Along with some personal improvements (self-assurance, excellent lover, better looking), I included a list of accessories for my ideal custom cruising yacht.

For example: I want a composite system of radar and sonar which, when fed through a computer, will print out on a screen in chart form the whole area around me, including soundings, landmarks, and advice. (I'm sure they'll be able to do this by the time I'm reborn.) Then I would like an electronic information center that not only will give me my position, but also, in a soothing, feminine voice, will say such things as: "You are 300 miles from the nearest land. There are no underwater hazards within 200 miles of your course. The weather will remain consistent for the next 12 hours. If any whales, ships, or other floating obstacles turn up, I'll call you in plenty of time."

Of course we will also have a refrigerator, a freezer, worldwide communications, unlimited electrical power, a washer, a drier— in short, all the appliances, tools, entertainment, and comfort we can cram aboard our floating, brave new world.

But I don't want my wishes granted unless it is guaranteed that my toys will never break, that they will always please me, and that I won't fall into their power. And as the interaction of people and machines precludes this, I'm resigned to continue cruising on *Sea Foam*, a paradigm of your basic boat. I decided this after getting to know Roger. I first met Roger in Fatu Hiva—or rather I heard his voice.

"Happy to make your acquaintance. I'll be out, tomorrow or the next day. Got a little problem with the generator." At least that's what I think those engine-room sounds said.

In Hiva Oa our friendship progressed slightly. I got a good close look at his shoes and the legs of his blue jeans to the point that I was sure I could recognize them again. The conversation, however, bore a close resemblance to the one we had in Fatu Hiva.

"Sorry, old man. Just gotta get this hot water heater fixed. Maybe tomorrow we can chat . . ."

It was in Taiohae, Nuku Hiva, that we were invited aboard for cocktails. Both Nancy and I looked forward to meeting Roger. (By this time we'd met his wife, Betty, several times.) Roger, so far, was a faceless myth, a rumor of essence, the only ectoplasmic verification of which was shoes and jeans.

The evening went very well, considering. Betty, Nancy, and I sat around the teak table in the saloon making overlapping rings with our beaded, chilled glasses. At one point I left the party and went forward. There, completely exposed except for his head and neck, lay Roger, curled around the base of his kerosene reefer.

"How ya doing, Rog?"

"Gotta fix this goddamn icemaker," he quipped. The rest of his remarks were swallowed up in the coils of the compressor.

In Ahe we ran into Roger and Betty again. On the night of the feast we rowed by their boat to see if they would like to go ashore with us. Betty accepted our invitation brightly. Roger stuck his head up out of the main hatch. Except for a sunless pallor and a vaguely haunted look, he had a rather pleasant face.

"Wish I could go with you guys," he said, "but I gotta fix the goddamn radar."

"You don't need radar to go to a feast," I told him.

"I know that, but it's broken," he said, and disappeared.

We all ended up, months later, in the lagoon at Punaauia on the island of Tahiti. We aboard *Sea Foam* had grown fond of the delightful pace of life and love in the South Pacific. Roger's boat, however, was a hub of activity. On board were at least two, sometimes three, full-time geniuses whose jobs were to repair or to install a microwave oven, a larger freezer, generator, dishwasher, laundry, autopilot, and what have you. Roger, freed from the actual labor, spent his evenings on the radio calling for parts, his days in Papeete running from store to store, customs to airport, post office to freight depot. He finally bought a motorcycle to save time parts-hunting, and every morning, bright and early, the last thing you would see of Roger was a cloud of dust out of which flapped the tail end of his list. The time he saved by having his own transport he spent maintaining his motorcycle.

Roger was by no means alone. We have met many like him. One skipper spent his whole visa in Papeete trying to get his freezer fixed.

"You've been in this expensive, hectic city for weeks," I said to him one day. "When are you going to visit the other islands?"

"As soon as my freezer's fixed," he replied.

"All your frozen food has long since gone, and your time here is running out."

"Yeah," he said, "but we don't want to leave without our freezer."

Had he been enjoying the sidewalk cafes, the fine restaurants, the conveniences, and the rich social life, all of which are available when one is tied up to the main street of Papeete, I would have understood. The truth was, he spent his whole day, every day, looking for competent help, and keeping the galley and his wife's disposition in constant upheaval.

If I speak as if I had successfully integrated humanism and technology, please excuse me. I have not. My days have been full of absurdities resulting from trying to cope with devices. Take, for example, our depthsounder.

Sea Foam came with it. It was an antique, but I didn't know it. I found it to be extremely accurate in all the slips *Sea Foam* ever occupied. Under power, however, or at speeds of more than two knots, it put on a random display that was endlessly entertaining on nightwatch. I developed a technique which frightened prudent friends. Without warning I would throw *Sea Foam* into hard reverse, shut down the engine, take a quick reading, and with a fool's faith hit the starter button. The few times I did this in tortuous, tide-ripped channels I completely lost the confidence of the whole crew. Left on overnight, this depthsounder could flatten a robust, 200-ampere-hour battery. Compared with modern instruments it was a piece of junk, but knowing no better I loved it.

I finally re-read the owner's manual and learned that the amplifier was powered by a vibrator that hummed when it worked but sometimes might stick. If I would but give it a thump? I thumped. No hum. The manual went on to say that if thumping failed to produce a hum, the owner had best bring the equipment in for service.

My opportunity to do so came three years later back in the States. My call to the factory distributor was memorable.

"Parts department, please."

"This is the parts department, sir." The voice was female, cheerful, and alert.

"I have one of your depthsounders," I said, "and I need a vibrator."

There was a short silence. When she spoke again her tone was guarded.

"Are you sure you have the right number, sir?"

I later discovered that modern depthsounders no longer use vibrators, and that this was a new girl. After I had made it clear that my problem was one and not two, she put me through to her boss. There were no vibrators available. My model had been discontinued for some years. No, the factory didn't have any either. A new depthsounder would be $200 to $600.

I decided we could manage very well with just the leadline. But from time to time I still thumb wistfully through marine-electronics catalogues. A new depthsounder, after all, would be the perfect backup system in tight situations when my leadline lets me down.

For most of us low-budget cruisers, lack of money failed to inhibit our fun or our mobility. What it did do was give us a whole new outlook on security: disparity of funds made the various yachties apportion their worries differently while in port, but when we were at sea we all worried about the same things.

Is Pollyanna speaking? Do I whisper the words of self-delusion? Maybe it really is hell to voyage economy-class and we just don't know any better. Or maybe it's like the man said when his wife, concerning her beauty, bitched about the ravages of time. "You know, my dear, you have a point, but are you ready for the alternative?" Would we do it again on the cheap as opposed to staying home, knowing what it would be like? Yes, was our emphatic reply.

Armed with $43, Nancy, Craig, and I motored a patched-up *Sea Foam* to Moorea and once more dropped anchor in Robinson's Cove. A new boutique had opened, and Nancy had all the sewing she could handle. I jacked up my writing schedule to six hours or ten pages daily. More articles sold, and I began work on my fondest ambition: a book. Craig made coconut planters and sun-visors with MOOREA on them for the boutique; these, plus some choice shells, sold to tourists like hotcakes. Life was simple and productive.

For me, those few weeks were perfect. Never mind that we needed new sails, a new dinghy, and money for another haulout.

I was doing exactly what I wanted to do, where I wanted to do it. I had the serenity necessary for concentration. I knew that if we sailed to California and got jobs, I would never finish the book. We would lose the pace of the cruising life, maybe forever.

Thus it was that when Opportunity arrived in the guise of an all-expense-paid trip to California, I viewed him more as an intruder than as a harbinger of good fortune. Siddhartha would have sent him packing. I, admirer of the East but rooted in the West, invited Opportunity aboard and suffered the total disruption of an ideal existence.

TWENTY-SEVEN

I WAS SITTING ON Mark and Annie's patio in Moorea in the cool of late evening. The couple were former yachties who had settled on the island. Mark was idly blowing cigar smoke into his brandy snifter, contentedly observing the whorls and tendrils. I was tipping my glass to and fro, contemplating the inevitability of the tides as the amber liquid sloshed back and forth, but mostly I was trying not to snore with my eyes open. We were both digesting a Dionysian dinner, thinking our own thoughts while Nancy and Annie sat in the kitchen discussing clothes, cooking, and other women. Mark broke the silence.

"I would like to find someone," he said quietly, "to take *Lissa* back to the States and sell her."

A small contingent of my brain cells perked up.

"Huh?" I commented.

"I said," said Mark, slowly and distinctly, "that I am interested in finding someone to take *Lissa* to the U.S. and sell her."

"You've just found him," I said.

"Do you really mean it?" asked Mark. "I never thought you'd be interested. What would you do with *Sea Foam*?"

"I'd moor her in Robinson's Cove. You could keep an eye on her. She'd be perfectly safe here."

"Sure," said Mark. "I'll watch her for you. But I never dreamed you'd want to do it. I never even thought—"

I got up to go into the kitchen to tell Nancy the good news that we were going to deliver a boat back home. What I didn't see, but what Nancy swears she saw over my shoulder (and in retrospect I believe her), was the genie rising from the smoke in Mark's glass and giving his master a sly wink.

Lissa and *Sea Foam* were completely opposite in concept. *Lissa*, a 41-foot, Laurent Giles, sloop-rigged cutter, had a mere ten-and-a-half-foot beam. Her rig was simple—she could be single-handed with ease. It took two good hands to slab reef *Sea Foam*'s main in a blow, but it took only one to roller reef *Lissa*'s.

Lissa's slenderness created a far different atmosphere below. While living aboard her, I had this strange, end-to-end feeling, much like camping out in a narrow hallway. There was plenty of room, but it was strung out rather than together. There was a galley forward which was rather uncomfortable at sea, particularly when going to weather. For some reason there were two heads. ("Why?" I asked. "Two heads are better than one, dummy," said Mark. "Why is there one in the forepeak?" I asked. "I lived in the forepeak," said Mark. "That's where my head is *at*. That's the space it's *in*." To his credit, he then retreated to another room.)

"She's so simple to sail," said Mark some time later. "You'll come back and sell *Sea Foam* on the spot. If you want to go some-place upwind you don't give it a second thought, you just sail there. And I mean, sail. She really sails, man, but I know you won't know what I'm talking about until you've experienced it. And once you have, you'll never be able to go back to your so-called 'cruising' boat. Maybe you'd better not take *Lissa* after all— I'd hate to make you dissatisfied with your own boat."

It was a big decision, but Nancy, Craig, and I were already hooked. We desperately wanted to see relatives and friends; to buy things for *Sea Foam* that we could only get in the States; to earn money for sails and a new inflatable dinghy; and most of all to go home, if only for a visit. An added dividend would be the chance to revisit the Marquesas on the way. We'd written off our chances of seeing the Marquesas again, because from Tahiti it was generally 800 miles straight upwind. But here was our opportunity: *Lissa* sailed to weather!

"Sure, *she* sails to weather," was a friend's wry comment, "but how do *you* go to weather? That's the question."

His query came back to haunt me in the next few weeks. Beating to weather was different from lazing along with the wind:

upstream versus down; struggling against the elements instead of flowing passively with them. Psychologically it was a completely different bag, and we were about to learn our lesson the hard way.

Lissa slept eight, according to the brochure. There were double-decker single bunks in the salon, two quarter-berths, and a double berth forward in the fo'c's'le. The berth forward was unusable at sea, so she slept eight minus two equals six underway, except that one of the upper berths in the salon was unavailable because the radio was in the way, so that left five—that is, if you insisted on counting the starboard quarter-berth, which was the sump for all the water that came on deck. If not, that left four, and Craig, who inhabited the other quarter-berth, would argue that it was really three, because his bunk became a morass when the weather got rough. This was okay, because three we were.

We left Moorea in June 1976 with smiles on our lips and songs in our hearts. Nancy was singing "California, Here I Come," I was doing a one-part invention based on "We're Off to See the Wizard," and Craig was humming something of his own design. It was a joyful leave-taking accompanied by musical anarchy.

Friends on the shore waved goodbye. We had been given a stalk of bananas to take along with specific instructions to throw the purple flower overboard as we left the pass. ("That means you'll be back.") The flower bobbed on the wavelets of Opunohu Bay and was quickly out of sight behind us. The image was to intrude in my dreams constantly during the next three months, a reminder of the tranquility we had left.

Lissa soared. She flew. We were just a little tighter than a beam reach, flying jib and main in 20 knots of wind. Light drops of spray licked tenderly at our tanned, happy faces. We were players in a symphony of wind, water, and sail. *Lissa* cut relentlessly through the waves like a knife in soft butter. Her lee rail never dipped. We were doing seven knots—eight off the crests.

"Wow," I wowed. "This is really sailing. She does it so *easily*. *Sea Foam* would be bobbing along, making a great fuss over it all. I can't believe it."

"We'd better check the bilge," said Craig. "It's been two hours since we left."

Mark had warned us that "she takes a drop or two going to weather—hull works a bit, you know." But even so, I wasn't prepared for what I saw when I looked in the bilge.

"Good Lord," I breathed. "Didn't we pump when we left?"

"We sure did," said Nancy.

I reached for the switch, turned on the electric pump. The bilge was dry in 15 minutes. Then I started pulling up floorboards. It wasn't long before I found the major cause of our problem.

"It's in the galley," I pointed out, "just above the garboard. The seam actually spurts when the boat heels over."

Nancy and Craig gathered round to have a look. Their faces were glum.

"I think we should go back," I said. But even though I said it, I didn't really want to. None of us did.

Once you've weighed anchor for a long passage, it's disheartening to have to turn back. You've taken fresh bread and vegetables aboard; your water tanks are topped off. But above all, somehow you have accumulated enough resolution to leave shelter, to foresake the calm lagoon for the sometimes wild and threatening unknown. All this has to be redone, not the least difficult of which is regrouping the forces of courage, adventure, and optimism. Nope. Once away, it is decidedly wasteful to dissipate that psychic momentum.

"Couldn't we stop in Rangiroa?" asked Nancy. "We could patch it there."

"Or Ahe," I said, "or the Marquesas. But the prudent thing to do would be to turn back."

"I know," said Nancy. "But we're already a month later than we want to be, and we've said goodbye to everyone so many times we're all sick of each other. I think we should go on and try to stop someplace along the way."

"Craig?"

"I'm for going on," he said.

"I am, too, I guess," I said decisively. So we continued.

With the electric pump it was easy to keep up with the leaks. Ten to twelve minutes of pumping per hour was all it took, and flipping a switch was certainly no hardship. It was only the next day when I toted up our mileage for 24 hours that I thought we might wisely reduce sail.

"Incredible," I said. "Look, Hon—an honest 164 miles. No help from current or anything." Our best day ever on *Sea Foam* was 150 miles, and an estimated 25 miles of that had been help from the current. Her best honest mileage was 140 miles for 24 hours, banging along in the troughs on a broad reach. At that time we knew we'd been pushing *Sea Foam* hard; but with *Lissa* there had been no sensation of strain whatsoever. Only the fact that the Walker and Sumlogs agreed made me believe it. But it seemed reasonable that there *was* strain, noticeable or not, as she was leaking like an orange crate and getting worse.

We were now past the Tuamotus, and Rangiroa was an impractical goal with the wind the strength and direction it was. Ahe was still a possibility, but it looked like the Marquesas would be our best bet. Hard on the wind, main roller-reefed down to the top spreaders, we were making four to five knots through relentlessly building seas. And day by day the force of the wind increased, finally leveling off at 30 to 35 knots. So day by day we reduced sail until we were jogging along under storm jib, main reefed down to the second spreaders, still making four knots only 55 degrees off the wind.

The motion, though far gentler than *Sea Foam*'s windward pounding, was still far from the relaxed motion of a boat off the wind. Occasionally *Lissa*'s bow would come down on a wave with a slam that sent a shudder through the whole length of the hull. The fluttering of the leech of the ill-fitting mainsail caused the mast to transmit a constant vibration, visible below in the form of an ague-ridden salon table. Water, both white spray and raw green, swept aft over the decks, or crashed into and over the cabin trunk, finding its way below everywhere; as a result, on the third day the alternator went out.

"There's the problem," I said to Nancy, crawling from cramped quarters and nursing bruises from the bashings of persistent, sadistic waves. I showed her where the water had run down the wires into the open ends of two connectors and had festered there electrically until the whole assembly was a cyst of acidic green pus. I tugged gently at one of the wires and it came apart in my hand, the metal completely dissolved. I redid all the connectors, administered shotgun first aid of baking soda followed by WD 40 on everything I could see that was greenish, cursed all saltwater everywhere, and started the engine. The alternator worked. After only a couple of hours of hand-pumping we were happy to return to switch-flipping, letting electricity do the work.

The engine, a 25-horsepower Bukh, could be started by hand. Mark had shown me several times how easy it was. His six-foot, 195-pound frame spun the flywheel to a certain rpm, at which point he would engage the compression, and the putt-putt of success would give rise to a grin of triumph. The starter had gone out along with the alternator, so I had the opportunity to try my own strength.

Twenty minutes and a dangerously rapid heartbeat later, I admitted defeat. The engine, nearly new, was too stiff for me to spin to the required speed. In addition, on my final attempt I'd hit my forehead on a protruding bolt, and blood from a small severed artery soaked my beard and covered my chest. When I turned around to face Nancy, my appearance made her day.

Cleaned up, the wound revealed itself to be minor, and I determined to try again. Final success was a team effort. Craig held a cushion over the offending bolt, Nancy worked the compression release on command, and I spun myself blue. Even this would have failed had we not turned *Lissa* downwind and engaged the transmission in forward, after which the force of the water turning the propeller made the difference.

My success with the alternator was short-lived. Two days later, a talented wave that had developed the ability to make 120-degree turns hung a right around the doghouse and cascaded down the companionway. The ladder resembled Niagara Falls. With leaden heart I took a look at the disaster underneath. Starter: soaked. Alternator: ditto. Two little wisps of blue smoke. Pervading aura of electrical death and disaster. I replaced the ladder and turned to face the others.

"Well, team, that's it. From now on we pump by hand."

Nancy stared at me gloomily. She had more than her share of courage. She also suffered from encroaching arthritis. She insisted on doing her share. For her it would be more difficult than for either Craig or myself, but she still wouldn't consider turning back.

"If we must, we must," she said simply.

By this time we were sailing under storm jib alone. Even so, *Lissa*'s leaks continued to grow worse. We were already pumping 300 strokes—60 gallons—every hour. We were exhausted, as much from anxiety as from pumping. (It is a fact that an anxious, inexperienced scuba diver will use up air twice as fast as a relaxed, experienced one, and a tense skier will run out of energy long before a confident one.) This common fear was as big a threat as *Lissa*'s tired hull. The only thing that sustained us was the knowledge that each day brought us 100 miles closer to respite.

As the leaks and pumping increased, little problems loomed larger. Sailing on the edge of luffing, as we were, meant that the sails were constantly fluttering a little. I must have lashed each hank on all three jibs at least three times. Finally relaxing after a run of chores, I would have to get up out of my soggy bunk and go up to the bucking, spray-lashed foredeck to seize on two or three hanks. Some of the hanks wore completely through the metal and had to be replaced, and my supply of spares was diminishing at an alarming rate.

One morning the wind lessened, and we were able to raise the reefed main. By early afternoon it was blowing 30 knots again, and the main had to come down. It took Craig and me half an hour to manhandle that flogging, 12-ounce demon, as all the cars were sticking on the track about halfway up the mast. We later discovered that one of the screws holding the track to the mast had come partly out of its hole, thereby obstructing the track.

At the time, however, it just seemed as if everything was turning against us.

We seriously discussed falling off downwind and sailing for Hawaii. It was midday, the sun was shining, and all three of us were in the cockpit.

"If we go to Hawaii," I said, "we'll be able to haul out, but God knows what kind of delay that'll involve. And expense. And if we have to do that, then we'll definitely be into fall weather. Besides, even though it's off the wind, it's five times farther away than the Marquesas. At the rate things are going . . ."

But the lure of falling off and having the leaks slow down was, in light of our ebbing strength, almost irresistible.

"My God," cried Nancy, looking down the companionway into the saloon. "We're sinking! Didn't you just pump, Craig?"

He had. I dashed below, pulled up floorboards. Although the area where the bilge pump pumped was dry, the whole forward part of the cabin was awash. The carpet looked like the lawn when I forgot to turn the sprinklers off. Inaccessible limbers, the drains that allow bilgewater to flow throughout the length of the hull, were plugged.

For two hours I laid on my belly, stabbing blindly with a stiff length of cable at the area where the limbers should be. Finally I was successful. Water could now drain back as it was supposed to, to be removed by pumping. And pumping. But the damage had been done: the fresh water in our only tank, located in the bilge, had somehow been contaminated. One full jerry-can was all the sweet water we had. Although we could have survived on the now-brackish main supply, we no longer felt like exchanging a 350-mile passage for an 1800-mile one.

The leaking continued to increase, but the winds stayed constant, varying from 25 to 35 knots depending on the time of day. We were being headed from our destination, Taiohae Bay on the island of Nuku Hiva. Fifty miles from Taiohae's longitude we tacked south overnight, hoping to be able to get a line on Taiohae the following day. However, my early morning sun line showed that in 15 hours we had lost nearly 35 miles of easting. (When the stiff trades blow constantly for days, one can expect the east-to-west equatorial current to reach its maximum speed.) At this rate, Nuku Hiva would be two, even three days away, whereas if we changed our destination to Eiao, one of two uninhabited islands which lay 80 miles north of Nuku Hiva, we could make landfall that afternoon. We all needed rest so badly that the choice was never in question.

The psychological high of landfall is in the category of miracles. When Eiao and Hatutu appeared on the horizon, easily reachable by late afternoon, our spirits soared. Although the pumping had by now doubled to a terrifying 60 gallons every *half* hour, we sang as we worked, yo-o-heave-ho-ing like drunken sailors. When we reached the lee, still three miles offshore, we started the engine and putt-putted along through a diamond-studded, azure flatness, land-breeze ripples flashing in the late afternoon sun. We were a portrait of contentment. Nancy was sipping a vodka collins, describing in titillating detail the succulent dinner she planned to cook. Craig was slurping a limeade, drawing up a campaign to rape and pillage Eiao's virgin shelldom. I was happily nursing a martini, steering for a sheltered cove that we'd chosen from the chart. The tireless windvane was relieved after 12 brutal days and nights at sea. Our minds were giddy with the wonder of being alive.

We had been motoring for an hour. The revs of the diesel dipped, momentarily, then returned to normal.

"Look! The alternator's working again," said Nancy, pointing to the valiantly flickering ammeter.

"Sure seems like it's trying to," I said, wondering why it would suddenly decide to resurrect after seven days of death by immersion. "Maybe it'll be okay, now that it's dried out."

But I should have known. One of the axioms of cruising is that whenever you're satisfied with the way things are going, something fails. To prove it, the motor suddenly slowed, then stopped completely.

"No oil," I said flatly, looking with disbelief at the dipstick. I had been checking the crankcase level every three hours of running time. Since leaving Papeete we had run the engine a total of 20 hours, and I had managed to add only a single, overly cautious teacupful.

"All the oil's in the bilge." I inserted the crank and tried to spin the flywheel. "Frozen solid," I concluded.

"Can you fix it?" asked Nancy hopefully, partly through ignorance of seized rings and melted bearings, and partly because, in spite of my track record, she firmly believes I can fix anything.

"Sure I can—in Los Angeles, with a machine shop, nine dozen special tools, an infinite supply of parts, a consultant, and a small fortune."

We stared at each other in bleak silence. I felt as though the referee had raised my gloved hand and then kicked me in the groin. Nancy was close to tears.

"What'll we do?" she asked.

"Who knows," I said, climbing back up to the cockpit. The three of us sat together silently, each ruminating his own bellyful of gloom. Eiao now loomed sinister, menacing, and unreachable under sail in the remaining light. Beyond the lee we could see the heavy swell, the steep chop—imprint of the stiff trade winds we had so recently escaped.

"There's no point in heaving-to here. We might as well continue down to Taiohae where there are communications, a machine shop, probably other yachts. I don't know—what do you think?"

"I suppose you're right," said Nancy. "Oh damn—it was going to be such a good dinner."

"Another day of pumping," Craig sighed.

"Maybe two days," I said. "It's nearly 80 miles, right straight into the wind."

"Your optimism blows my mind," said Nancy. "Why can't you just lie, for once?"

The night seemed endless. The wind dropped, the seas calmed, and relief from tension soon turned me into a zombie. Groggily,

I tried to be concerned about passing upwind and upcurrent of a little island called Motu Iti, Marquesan for "little island." I finally spotted it in the waning moonlight a good ten miles to starboard. I'd worried about it, as I worried about every problem at sea, but it was with only one-tenth of my capacity for worry. Nine-tenths had already collapsed into unconsciousness, where I followed it upon handing over the watch to Craig.

Dawn was doldrummy. In the lee of Nuku Hiva, a 3800-foot barrier against the now-gentle trades, we learned yet another aspect of motorless sailing: when the wind ain't, you don't. At first we hopefully left all the sails up, trying to catch each tentative breath. Then, tiring of the main boom's slatting, a Brobdignagian billy club in the rolling swells, we took everything down. Next, in a spurt of anti-defeatism, we raised a very light genoa which sagged and filled with the rocking of the boat, every so often filling with an explosive crack that threatened to rip seams and tear nerves.

As we ghosted along at a knot or a knot and a half, a school of sperm whales lazed along with us. There must have been 30 of them. They spumed and blew all around us, sometimes only 100 feet from the boat. I relaxed in the cockpit, and my imagination floated. I wondered idly if one of the monsters beside us had our taffrail log rotor in his stomach—we had lost it the night before. If so, I hoped he had indigestion.

At dawn the following day we sailed into Taiohae Bay, having spent the night hove-to outside, viewing the beckoning lights with longing. Having been there before in *Sea Foam*, we knew the bay, and with a motor I would have gone in despite the darkness. But under sail alone I wanted daylight to illuminate the ripples of shifting land breezes, the rocks along the shore. The wind came in wispy little puffs, whimsically changing direction, causing enough sail-handling drill to force me across my threshold of irritability. No clumsiness on the part of the crew escaped my acid comment. I was the embodiment of blighted cool.

Finally, we dropped anchor, I apologized to Craig, kissed my fed-up wife; we had arrived.

"Is it okay to anchor here?" I asked a bikini-clad blonde who was busy scrubbing the waterline of a sleek, modern 60-footer.

"They'll ask you to move—the officials, I mean. You'd be better off over there," she answered, pointing.

"I guess I'll take my chances here—we have no motor."

"You shouldn't have told me," she said, scales falling from her violet eyes. "I thought you were a purist."

A purist used to be someone who chose not to have an engine aboard. A purist nowadays is someone who sails with a perfectly functioning engine—but never uses it. Either way, a purist I'm not, and I lusted, impurely, for the use of an engine.

Later, having checked in with the gendarme, having walked the length of the waterfront, stopping at each little store for ice cream or a cold beer, having marveled at the rocking terrain underfoot, and having swapped lies with other yachties, my sense of humor seemed to return. But it was bravado, a thin laminate over discouragement. How in hell were we going to sail *Lissa* another 4000 miles to windward, leaking as much as she was? Going back would be disaster—we had already spent a large portion of our delivery money. Hawaii was a possibility, but with the extra time needed to get there and then to be hauled before proceeding to the mainland, we would be facing weather that would make the last leg a real battle.

We were between a rock and a hard place, and the rock was moving in.

TWENTY-EIGHT

"WELL," I SAID CHEERFULLY, "the first leg was a piece of cake. We've gone a little less than a quarter of the way. Who's for throwing in the sponge and going back to Papeete?"

"Not me," said Craig.

"Of course not," said Nancy.

"That's what I figured," I said, wishing, not for the first time, that I had married into a family of cowards.

"One step at a time," said Nancy. "First we fix the leaks."

"What do you mean, 'we'?" snarled Craig.

With Nancy standing shark watch for the resident hammerhead, Craig and I spent three hours in mask and snorkel covering eight feet of seam and filling two leaking plug holes with underwater Epoxy. Later, for good measure, I tacked battens bedded in Epoxy on the inside. *Lissa*, band-aided and TLCed, leaked mere drops. Flushed with success, we blew a small fortune at the local restaurant: poisson cru, lobster mayonnaise (white wine), steak in butter sauce (red wine), green salad, mousse, and a brandy. We were due for a splurge.

"Your rigging," said a neighboring yachtie who had rowed over for a visit the next morning. "Isn't it a little loose?"

Used to the sloppy rigging on our own dead-eyed gaff rig, I shrugged my shoulders.

"The owner prefers it this way," I said.

"This way?" asked my visitor in disbelief. He grasped a lower shroud and swung it in a circle a foot in diameter.

"Well, maybe it is a little loose."

He nosed around some more, saying "hmm," making me nervous.

"Is your mast wedged?" he asked.

"No," I replied, "just a rubber gasket at the partners."

"It should be wedged. The mast has virtually no support. No wonder you're leaking, with the mast working the way it must be. How in hell you ever made it here I'll never know."

I walked around and shook all the shrouds. They were all slack and sloppy. I turned to agree with my new friend, but he was preoccupied, sighting up the mast.

"Tightening up the shrouds might take some of the bends out," he said authoritatively.

I sighted up the mast. It was straight as an arrow to the lower spreaders; but then it took a slow, graceful curve to starboard up to the top spreaders, and a jaunty little kink to port along the top six feet. The mainsail track looked like a slot-car Le Mans. My heart and my confidence drained down to about knee level, dipstick reading "add."

"I'm a sort of let-well-enough-alone person," I muttered vaguely. "After all, we did get here."

"You don't dare set out like this," said my friend. "It's suicidal."

Because of the leaks, I'd already come to that conclusion myself; but if doing something about the shrouds would improve our overall chances, I supposed I must. I grabbed one of the plastic tubes which covered the turnbuckles and yanked it up, revealing the rustiest, most frozen-looking turnbuckle I had ever seen. I pulled up the rest of the covers. All the turnbuckles were the same. Unturnable.

"Get out the old penetrating oil," he said cheerfully, rowing back to his own boat. You've made my day, I thought bleakly as I stumped below to gladden Nancy's heart with our new problem.

"Well," she said, having heard me out, "I guess we'll just have to fix them."

" 'We'?" I snarled. But she was already back in the galley, cooing and purring over a salad she was making from a half-bushel of fresh green things she'd found in the village. "And I won't leave without another bilge pump," I snapped at her busy back.

"Pump? Why? We've got a pump."

"Yeah—one!" I said. "What if it wears out? At the rate we're using it, that time can't be far off. What then?"

What I was hoping for was that she'd see what a fix we were in and decide we ought to go back to Tahiti. Then, after she'd pleaded with me a little, I would finally agree to go back for her and Craig's sake, conceding that such dangers as lay ahead should not be undergone by mere women and children.

"Okay," she said, turning to me with hands on hips, chin up and out. "We write to Papeete for another pump, or we barter or buy one from another boat. Someone's bound to have a spare," she concluded. She turned back to her salad, another problem solved.

Shaking my head in disbelief, I set to work. The unwieldy, 225-ampere-hour battery was horsed ashore to be recharged. The turnbuckles finally capitulated to penetrating oil—all but one, which gave up only after being barbecued over the galley stove. One of the other boats had a spare bilge pump (does Nancy *always* have to be right?), and I spent three days inventing and making a new check valve for it, and another two days installing it, cannibalizing our sadly unneeded, flexible exhaust pipe for hose.

It was time to tune the rigging—time to call in the experts.

Expert #1: "Well, I'd just snug up the shrouds. If the mast is happy with a bend in it, let her stay that way. Just support it. But I'd wedge it at the partners."

Expert #2: "The modern way is to let laminated hollow masts float at the partners. Leave it. But I'd sure tighten the forestay and get that rake out of the top."

We did. The rake was gone, all right, but we had a new reverse curve from the top spreaders to the deck. I wasn't happy, so I yelled to another friend to come on over. After we had fussed with the shrouds for half an hour, it was plain to see that every bend we eliminated produced a new one.

Expert #3: "I don't know how you're going to get rid of all those bends. Why don't you just take the boat back to Papeete and return it to the owner?" He then sat down on the cabin top and got into a long, involved discussion with Expert #2 about visas.

Expert #4 (calling from his boat): "Hey! I've got a whole file of articles on tuning rigging—you're welcome to read them if you want to."

I rowed over to glean microfacts from the proffered trove. Never have I seen such diversified opinion, with each author maintaining that only his method was correct. Start at the top and work down; the bottom and work up; uppers loose, lowers tight; contrariwise. By the time I finished reading my head was in a turmoil.

"To hell with it," I told Nancy. "I'll go with Expert #1, minus the wedges. Nobody seems to know what to do about masts that won't straighten, so I'll just take the slack out of the standing rigging and hope God and habit will keep the mast upright."

The time had come to leave. We had bought kerosene lamps and extra kerosene. We had reprovisioned, patched leaks, and tuned the rigging. We had scrubbed the bottom and topped off the water tanks. Some last-minute shopping in the morning and we would sail out of the bay on the afternoon land breeze. The only trouble was that some people dropped by for coffee, and some others invited us ashore for a last beer, so that by the time we were ready to weigh anchor we were running around the boat in a desperate rush that guaranteed clumsiness, foul-ups, and, eventually, yelling at each other like maniacs.

"Hang on," I said, "this is ridiculous. We're tired. There's barely enough light and almost no wind. Let's stay and leave tomorrow."

"But tomorrow's Friday," said Nancy.

Friday. Incredible that in the twentieth century, full-grown, rational-minded sailors could be so influenced by superstition, but there it was. In Los Angeles we wouldn't have given it a second thought. In the Marquesas, where voodoo and telepathy are tangible forces, one feels differently.

"I know tomorrow's Friday," I said, "but we're exhausted, we're at each other's throats. It's no way to leave."

"We could wait till Saturday," suggested Craig, always ready to spend another day looking for shells.

"No," said Nancy, "we've waited long enough. But I agree with you—let's get a good night's sleep."

So we left on a Friday, for the first and, we have since agreed, the last time. Three hours out and *Lissa* was leaking badly. Instead of putting back, we decided to continue on to Eiao and patch the leaks there. But at Eiao, even after patching the leaks we could see, *Lissa* was still taking water aboard at an alarming rate from somewhere amidships, under the fresh-water tank. We would have to put back. Our decision was seconded by the wind-vane, which, we discovered, had rusted through at a weld and would have to be repaired.

Back in Taiohae, Craig and I took the vane to the Bureau of Public Works, where we found a welder who agreed to fix it. We pumped all the water out of the fresh-water tank, removed it, and located the leaks underneath. One seam had no cotton left in it for a distance of three feet. We patched about 15 feet of seam on the outside with underwater Epoxy. With the leaks stopped, we were able to cover all the seams on the inside with battens bedded in Epoxy. We then replaced the tank, carted out 90 gallons of water in jerry-cans, and the job was done.

As a reward for all our hard work, we headed for Anahoe Bay on the northeastern shore of Nuku Hiva, where we knew that a species of rare murex could be found. The bay is shaped like a backwards "L," the lower-left tip being completely sheltered from the ocean. For three days we shelled and picnicked on the ledges, dove for murex in the coral, and did last-minute things on *Lissa* at a relaxed, non-pressured pace.

One afternoon, while scrubbing the bottom, Craig and I noticed a broken gudgeon strap on the rudder. I didn't remember seeing it before, and Craig was positive that it was a new break.

"One gudgeon out of four," I told Nancy, "leaves three. The rudder will probably stay on if we don't treat it too rough, or get in any gales. It's just another little message to keep us from feeling too sure of ourselves."

The day we chose to leave was the first day in four that an afternoon land breeze hadn't come up around 3:00. We all sat on the foredeck, the anchor rode heaved short, sticking wet fingers into the air and looking for cat's paws. Amphibious bugs were practicing takeoffs and landings on the glassy surface. We waited, halyards in hand, for meteorological history to repeat itself, as I confidently assured everyone it would.

It didn't. With an hour and a half of light remaining, we played out sufficient rode for the night and went below to bolster our flagging spirits with refreshment. With all our delays thus far, I can't explain why one more day made any difference, but as Nancy fiddled with tea things and I got out the rum, the silence in the cabin was charged with frustration.

"Hey!" said Craig, suddenly. "We've got wind!"

We dashed topsides. A beautiful, light breeze was coming from the saddle in the hills on the opposite shore, tickling the water till its skin erupted in a rash of goosebumps. In less than five minutes the anchor was up, the sails raised, and we were cutting through the fragile ripples at three knots. In ten minutes we were halfway out the bay, and suddenly there was no wind at all. None.

We sat, helpless, in the fast-fading light. Once in a while one of us would whisper "there," softly, as a teaser of a breath would kiss *Lissa*'s jib, sliding her along perhaps another 50 feet before dancing away, flighty and fickle, seeking other pleasures, leaving us to drift with the current toward the rocky western shore. I watched the distance between us and the rocks get shorter and shorter, my nerves humming with tension. The surge, which was gentle enough in the center of the bay, rolled giant curlers along the cliffs. I was a mere eyelash from crying "Sailors, man the oars!" (Craig) when a hint of ocean breeze drifted around the eastern promontory and, gently at first, but gradually stronger, pulled us out into open water and safety.

I came on watch seven hours later to a brilliant sky, the half-

moon laying out a soft yellow carpet of promise across the eastern sea. I took one look and went to get the sextant.

I took two shots and went below to work them out. I hadn't
used the moon much for navigation, and there are a couple of
extra steps in the solution. I worked slowly, checked each operation against the examples to see that I was doing it right, and
came up with an impossibility: we were already 15 miles west of
where we should have been.

Panic flew into the approach pattern, but I told it to circle the
field. I considered. Maybe the compass was off—maybe one of us
had banged it, accidentally. Perhaps it was reacting to magnetic
anomalies, but those were usually indicated on the chart. Perhaps
the current—but 15 miles in seven hours? A 50-mile-a-day current? Possible, but it was more likely I screwed up the moon shot.
I tried it again.

Careful, now. *Zap*, the moon; *zap*, to make sure; and *zap, zap*
on Jupiter, just as a check. I went below and worked it out carefully in the lamplight. Same result!

Unbelievable. We had gone one one-hundredth of a 3500-mile
journey and already I didn't know where I was. Distrust of compass, log, sextant, mathematics, and even the chart fogged my
brain. Our course led us between two submerged reefs roughly
40 miles apart. They were still ahead of us, and I didn't want
to go one step further until I knew where we were. I heaved *Lissa*
to and went to sleep.

As soon as the sun was ten degrees above the horizon I took
a shot. Same result. The evidence failed to convince me, yet I
distrusted my dead-reckoning position also. Wasteful as it seemed,
there was only one answer: give up 40 miles of precious easting,
miles we'd fought for against wind and current, and sail west-
northwest until we could see Eiao and know where we were.

It was late afternoon when we picked up Eiao's neighbor, Hatutu.
Using it as a guide, I was able to uncover the reason for my
navigational confusion: a combination of sextant error and unexpected current. I was able to keep Hatutu's silhouette in view as

we slipped past in the darkness. Eiao, just beyond to the west, was a mere smudge of gray against the darker gray horizon.

"Hey gang," I shouted below. "We're really away, this time. All due to your intrepid captain's nerves of steel."

Bubbles of laughter foamed up the companionway.

"Nerves of steel—would you believe spaghetti?" giggled Craig.

"Cooked spaghetti," gasped Nancy.

"*Over*cooked spaghetti," said Craig, hugging himself and laughing so hard he rolled off his bunk and onto the floor.

At that point I couldn't have cared less about my tarnished image. *Lissa* was leaping ahead, reaching north on the starboard tack. Her leaks were minimal. George, *Lissa*'s self-steerer, was working like a charm. As we pulled away from the dark shadows of Eiao and Hatutu, I was convinced that the odds for our making it safely to Los Angeles had finally tipped in our favor.

TWENTY-NINE

2030 HOURS, 17 AUGUST, 1976. We are heading for the equator, 450 miles distant, making five knots on the starboard tack. We have finally passed Eiao and Hatutu, and with each mile we put between them and us, I can feel us slipping farther away from the influence of Polynesian taboos, of ancient pagan curses. I maintain that I'm not superstitious. I'm not even traditionally religious. No, I am a product of the Age of Reason: pragmatist, empiricist, what you see is what you get. Which is why I find it hard to understand my feeling that we are leaving bad luck behind us.

"Omens, Lord," I say quietly into the soft folds of darkness. "To renew the slums of my courage, I need omens."

"What?" says Nancy from below. She can hear me muttering three rooms away. The only time she doesn't hear is when Craig or I ask her to hurry.

"I was talking to the Lord," I say defensively. (I often wonder, however, about the supremacy of the Being I converse with at sea; I suspect that, if I am getting through at all, it is to some Cosmic Flunky.)

"And what were you *saying* to the Lord?" she asks sweetly. She will not be put off.

"I was asking for omens—signs—portents."

"*Lissa*'s hardly leaking at all," she says. "We're sailing the way we want to. Except for the doldrums, some hurricanes, and a few freighters, there's nothing between us and Los Angeles. How come you need omens?"

"Because I worry," I say crossly. "I'm the only one aboard who does. I'll probably have to worry us all the way to L.A. by myself. If I didn't worry, we'd never get any goddamn where."

"Don't get huffy," says Nancy, going back to her book.

"*She* may not need omens, Lord," I think to myself, being careful not to speak aloud, although sometimes Nancy can hear me anyway, "but I do. Just throw a few shopworn seconds my way."

1015 hours, 21 August. For the last two days we've been making five knots under yankee alone, and for two days prior to that we were making five knots under working jib alone. We are close-reaching in 25-knot easterly trades. The seas are turbulent, confused. *Lissa*'s leaks, still well within bounds, are nonetheless increasing steadily. It is worrisome.

We've just now crossed the equator. We know because we've all been watching the log like hawks. Now we get to open the package.

About the package: it was given to us in Tahiti with specific instructions not to open it until we'd reached the equator. I have been advocating "let's cheat." Craig and Nancy have been adamant about waiting. Because of our unplanned layover in the Marquesas, we are over a month later than planned. We're hoping the contents aren't biodegrading.

With great ceremony and suppressed excitement, we cut the strings. The first thing we see is a photograph of Mark and Annie, *Lissa*'s owners. Then comes a note: "We invite you to share a candlelight dinner with us at the equator." Next: a tie-dyed shirt for me, one for Craig, and a pareu for Nancy. Then, in order: a tablecloth, a candle, canned chicken couscous, candy, nuts, six jiggers of fruit-sweetened brandy, and a box of small cigars.

We follow the instructions to the letter: dress in our new cloths, spread the tablecloth, light the candle, eat the couscous, eat the nuts and candy, and toast our friends with a brandy and an after-dinner cigar. It's a feast, a party, a moment of gaiety in a bleak, lonely ocean.

"It's an omen," I say to Nancy.

"Omen, shmomen—it's a thoughtful, generous gift," says Nancy. "We'll never be able to tell them how much it pleased us."

"It's still an omen," I insist, opening another thoughtful, generous brandy.

26 August. We are in the doldrums. For the past two days, at least half the time we've lowered all sail and sat around waiting for something to happen. *Lissa*'s leaks have slowed down, so it's an ill calm that brings no good.

There are mahi-mahi all around the boat. Sometimes, when we're sailing, they strike at the lure, but they won't take it. Craig is unhappy. He is the sheriff of fishing. He has failed to buy either enough or the right kind of gear. I try to encourage him.

"When your brother Chris was on the boat, we always had plenty of fish. What the hell are you doing wrong?" Then I go below.

Twenty minutes later we hear the desperate flopping of a captured fish. We rush topsides. There is a 20-pound mahi-mahi in the cockpit, but the fish line is still trailing behind the boat.

"How did you do it?" I ask.

"I gaffed him," says Craig, about to burst.

"Gaffed him? What do you mean, you gaffed him?"

"I took the gaff and held it over my head, and when he swam near the boat close to the surface I hit him—wham!—and hooked him in the head and pulled him aboard. I gaffed him," he finishes. He is having trouble talking clearly through his face-splitting grin.

I can't believe it. There's no other way it could have come aboard, but I still can't believe it.

"Must be another omen," I conclude.

Nancy fixes poisson cru. We have huge fish steaks for lunch and dinner, fishcakes for breakfast. We slice what we can't eat and dry it in the sun. We are grateful for the bounty of the sea, for Craig's skill and luck, and for all good omens everywhere.

27 August. Last night we saw the lights of a ship to the northwest of us. They stayed in view for a long time. We now conclude it must have been a tuna clipper.

It's after lunch. We are sailing in variable winds ranging from 5 to 25 knots from the east. Someone is always keeping watch on deck, as squalls come frequently and with great force. At the moment, the someone is myself.

There's a squall east of us, and just to the south of it is something funny, maybe a waterspout. No, no—it's a *boat*!

"Hey, everybody—a boat's coming!"

Everybody, rudely bumping, bursts topsides.

"They're coming our way—drop the jib!"

The jib falls to the foredeck and *Lissa*, mainsail up and helm down, heaves-to as if we'd tied up to a piling.

Our excitement hangs from the fact that in 16,000 miles of cruising, or since we'd left the coast of Central America, we have seen very few other boats at sea. Now, in the doldrums, which I had figured to be one of the world's emptier sections of ocean, comes an American tuna boat, the *Maria C. J.* She passed astern of us, her whole crew on deck. We wave and smile at each other some ridiculous number of times.

"Okay, raise the jib," I say. *Maria C. J.* is a quarter-mile past us and I figure our mid-ocean intercourse is over. I'm just securing the halyard when Nancy shouts excitedly.

"They're coming over in a small boat!"

"Drop the jib," I shout, promptly obeying my own order.

The two young men who draw alongside in the runabout are smiling and friendly.

"Cap'n wants to know are you all right, and is there anything we can do for you—anything you need?"

"If you have enough, could we buy a bottle of whiskey and a couple of packs of cigarettes? And we'd like to know our exact position." Sometimes I surprise myself with my ability to think on my feet.

They are back in five minutes with a fifth of Canadian whiskey, three cartons of cigarettes, and our position. They refuse my money.

"Thank your captain," I say gratefully, "and tell him he's a prince among men." They depart, and once more we raise the jib.

"Sometimes I wonder about your priorities," says Nancy. "Didn't you remember that we're soon going to run out of yeast, flour, sugar, coffee, and tea?"

"Details. You always get hung up on details." (One could hardly call me a viewer-of-the-big-picture, but she let it slide.) "Just think of it as another omen." So saying, I go below and check our position, which is only three miles different from their electronic one. I decide to quit worrying about my navigation for a day or two.

During the next week we are visited by four more tuna boats. None of them go so far as to lower a boat, but they all alter course to come close enough to see that we're all right. One of them gives us our position over the bull horn, and I stop fretting about my navigation for a couple more days. We feel watched over, protected. Mostly, we no longer feel so totally alone.

30 August. Our position is approximately 11 degrees north, 138 degrees west. We are leaving the doldrums. We have been tracking Hurricane Iva—a real blower with winds of over 130 knots—which is now dying far to the north of us. There are more hurricanes in September than any other month. Lucky us. The Pilot Chart shows that they start near Mexico and move either out to sea or up the coast. When they head out to sea, they travel westward down a corridor between 15 degrees north and 25 degrees north. Most of them die before they reach our longitude, but some don't, and the occasional one will go all the way to Hawaii. Sailing with no engine between 15 degrees north and 25 degrees north will be like crossing the freeway at night while wearing a dark suit.

3 September. We are sailing under storm jib and double-reefed main, and have been for a couple of days. *Lissa*'s leaks have increased with the working to weather. We are walking a fence, as we want to make northing to get out of hurricane alley, but we don't want *Lissa* to open up to where we can't handle the pumping. Our highest rate since the Marquesas has been 35 gallons per

hour. Finally, all this has to be weighed against overstressing *Lissa*'s tired turnbuckles, rusty shackles, and "S"-shaped mast. We would like to handle her like a cracked egg, make good time in 25-knot winds, and not have her leak. Reality will fall somewhat short of this.

Hurricane Iva is dead and gone, but Tropical Storm Joanne is heading out our way, and behind her another disturbance is building. I'm glad we had all those good omens—otherwise I'd be worried (more worried). Station WWVH, Hawaii, broadcasts new weather reports every six hours. At least this gives us a fighting chance.

14 September. We are at 30 degrees north, 138 degrees west. Neither Joanne nor her sister Katie amounted to much as far as we were concerned. Now we're out of reach of the hurricanes and coping with freighters and the North Pacific High.

The freighters have us pretty well bracketed. Three days ago one passed just astern of us around midnight. Yesterday one passed about a mile north of us at 4:00 A.M. At night they look like floating cities. This afternoon Nancy spotted one out the doghouse window, about a quarter-mile distant and heading our way. We rushed on deck. It was a huge Japanese container ship that obviously had altered course to come by and have a look at us. It passed us about 200 yards to leeward. A row of white-uniformed officers lined the bridge, smiling and waving. We smiled and waved back. They turned southwest again once they had passed us, confident that they had our position nailed down and could come back and wipe us out whenever they wished.

The North Pacific High is a large area of high pressure that drifts around the center of the northeastern Pacific, expanding and contracting like a huge jellyfish. Most sailors bound for North America pass the high to the west, then swing east over the top of it, sailing to the westerlies that prevail near 40 degrees north. Because of the equinoctial gales that batter the higher latitudes in September, and because of *Lissa*'s fragility, we have decided to try to sail *under* the high, knowing full well that many a boat, trying this very thing from Hawaii, has been forced to turn back because of lack of wind. We thought we had the boundaries of the high figured out from the Pilot Charts—that we would sneak just under it by tacking toward the coast. We have been sneaking and tacking to light airs for three days now according to my master plan, and we've made good a total of 40 miles.

19 September. For the last five days the sails have lain on deck at least half the time, and *Lissa* has wallowed helplessly in glassy swells. In the calm water it is easy to see that the whole Pacific Ocean will soon be covered with either bits of white plastic or glass balls. It is fortunate that Craig and Nancy are doing two school lessons daily instead of one, and that I have my rusty typewriter to sit and chew my eraser in front of. We have been on this crossing 34 days. We have each read two dozen paperbacks. We have exhausted the distractive possibilities of cribbage, gin, hearts, and solitaire. We've eaten all the munchies and drunk all the liquor. We are trying to recapture the fast-fading allure of long ocean passages. Once again the pumping has dropped to half while we are sitting still.

20 September. We are finally sailing out of the high. Most of our success is due to *Lissa*, who ghosts ahead in almost undiscernible wind. Some of it is due to our own persistence in raising sails for the slightest puff. At the moment we are 600 miles from L.A., reaching to a southerly. The probability of having a south wind this month in this location is represented on the Pilot Chart by a microdot. So much for statistical projection. We are now confident of success—perhaps too much so, as we are eating the munchies out of our survival stores.

1100 hours, 30 September. We are becalmed just outside the entrance to Los Angeles Harbor, one mile from dropping anchor. We have been within sight of Los Angeles for three and a half days. We have exhorted the wind god with creativity and imagination. (I even offered him a couple of Faustian deals which, now that I think about it, I'm glad I don't have to make good on.) *Lissa*, treated with kindness and kid gloves, has come through like the grand old campaigner she is, though not without cost. We have logged 5000 miles, almost all of which have been on the wind, and have pumped 25,000 gallons of water from her bilges by hand—an average of five gallons per mile. We are looking forward to shoreside treats. Bellies bloated with delicious junk food. Drinks with ice. Mexican meals. TV. A double bed. Getting used to living on land won't be easy, but it will be a pleasure to fight the urge to get up for a midnight watch; to prime the kitchen stove; to pump out the toilet every half-hour. And, of course, we are looking forward to the best treat of all—friends, relatives, and a homeland we haven't seen for three and a half years.

1500 hours, the same day. We are in San Pedro Harbor, anchored in a little cove in front of Cabrillo Beach State Park. After 45 days and nights at sea the sails are furled. The gods of sailing and the demons of jeopardy have left and headed back out to sea. *Lissa* is at rest. It feels strange, but it feels good. We are home.

THIRTY

Y OU MIGHT THINK, if you thought about it, that after you'd
cruised around the Pacific for six and a half years and
stuck your nose into this and that lagoon, tropical islands
would attain a tiresome similarity, and the blasé cruiser's line,
"one paradise is like another," would take on a discouraging degree of truth. I have in mind an analogy of a man who enters a
redwood forest for the first time. He walks up to a redwood tree,
appreciates the hell out of it, remarks on its beauty, respects its
age and history, re*lates* to it, and has some sort of fun under it
according to his tastes. He then proceeds to the next tree, appreciates the hell out of it, remarks on its beauty, respects its age and
history, re*lates* to it, and has some sort of fun under it according
to his tastes. I'm certain that somewhere there is at least one phi-
losopher who could spend a lifetime doing this. For me it would
get old about tree three.

Then why was it that tropical isles impressed us with their
differences rather than their similarities? Why was it that Nancy,
Craig, and I still looked forward to each new landfall with a delighted anticipation that was rarely disappointed? "Because you're
stupid," one friend averred. "Lack of imagination," asserted another. "Because you're a bum," opined my stepfather-in-law. And
yet there are others who would agree to the uniqueness and indi-
viduality of each island, each lagoon. In support of the latter, I
offer the following suggestions.

First of all, if you agree with the sociologists who assert that a
great many of the people in the United States hate the way they
live, cruisers are way out front at the first turn. As a group they
have adopted a life-style which is often difficult, uncomfortable,
and frightening, and which contains only a small percentage of

the luxuries of land life, if any. Thus we must conclude, there being an abundance of alternatives to living aboard, that the people who do it either love it or are crazy. Granting to some the privilege of insanity, I would be willing to bet that 90 percent of the people who have cruised for any length of time love the way they live. Right away you can see we're dealing with an unusual group.

Second: each island impressed us in different ways. Sometimes it was the people who lived there, the friends we made. Sometimes it was the topography, the sheer beauty of the surroundings. Sometimes it was the things we did. Often it was the ambiance, the mood that had been created by fact or legend. Usually it was a combination of these.

Third: having arrived at the end of a passage, it's possible you've had a perfect sail and you soar through the pass suffused with a natural high that guarantees a positive attitude. On the other hand, the chances are far better that you have survived one of the tests of voyaging, be it boredom or breakage, squall or storm; and, having survived, arrival equals achievement and shelter equals reward. The goal is already qualified as good, or else why would you have suffered so much and worked so hard to reach it? If our man in the redwoods had had to slog through swamps, chop through brambles, swim rushing rivers, and scale heady heights, all the while paying far more money than he'd planned to pay at each of the various tollgates along the way—then perhaps our analogy would more closely approach the reality of cruising.

Fourth: you have a reason to go there or you'd have gone somewhere else. For example, we each had reasons for wanting to visit Suvarov, an uninhabited atoll in the Cook Islands. Craig had heard it was good shelling and fishing. Nancy had heard there were lobsters and coconut crabs, and that there were always other yachts there, fair game for picnics and parties. I had heard that the newest wreck was loaded with clean, free, accessible diesel. We wanted a carefree spot for rest and relaxation, writing and repairs. We wanted to interrupt our passage in *Sea Foam* from French Polynesia to Samoa—our first passage since delivering *Lissa* one year before—and cut the task in two. The reasons were all for and none against.

Log excerpt: "Dropped anchor behind Anchorage Island about 1515 local time. Three other boats. Tidied up *Sea Foam*. Rowed ashore about sunset to find an all-male, predominantly New Zealand picnic going on. Were immediately invited to have a drink of gin, Nancy being the sole, smiling flower in a swarm of bees. Sat around drinking gin and looking at God's sunset through God's palm trees, and some of the romance of the cruising life struck us all. We discussed loneliness; the absence of movies, night clubs, bright lights."

Since then I've given considerable thought to the "why" of cruising. For us it lies hidden somewhere in the process of search and discovery, the mixture of action and stillness, the yin and yang of adventure and peace. It involves a gut-level response to the idea that there is something more important than comfort and safety. But until someone can say what that something is, in plain language, I am content merely to note its indescribable existence and to continue to live as if the idea were true.

For the next 19 days, we devoured experience the way an express train devours distance. We ate fresh fish. We ate raw fish. We ate lobster. We picnicked on the beach. We drank the sweet milk of countless green coconuts. We hunted coconut crabs at night, blinding them with a bright light and swatting them with a machete. They were delicious cooked, even more delicious cold in a salad the following day. We ate palm heart salad. We ate fresh eggs. We ate lobster again. I fished for elusive sharks with fish heads right off *Sea Foam*'s stern. We ate fresh oysters. Craig found spider conchs and mother-of-pearl shells. Nancy and I made an awning out of our old mainsail. We raided the wreck, liberated 100 gallons of diesel, plus line, swivels, hooks, and wire. We walked everywhere. We nearly lost *Sea Foam* on one of our visits to the wreck. The wind changed suddenly, making our anchorage a lee shore—it blew 35 knots. We were within five feet of going aground, 20 feet of losing the boat. We continued to fish for elusive sharks and finally hooked one. It refused to die,

even with its head off. We chopped open the stomach and mid-
wifed three baby sharks, wondering as they swam out into the
lagoon if they would be able to fend for themselves. Then we
chopped momma into one-inch steaks and ate her. She was delicious. We decided that tern's eggs with their day-glo orange
yolks didn't taste nearly as fishy as we'd been told, but that young
frigate bird, gamy as old goat, was not our favorite dish. I knew
that after leaving Suvarov I would be figuratively looking back
over my shoulder for a long time to come.

There is one good feature to leaving a beautiful place, knowing
that the odds are you'll never go back in your lifetime. The good
feature is that you have fixed it in your mind as it was when you
were there. Fixed it like a photograph, or a painting. Fixed it as
to mood, as to meaning. There is no guarantee that succeeding
visitors will refrain from mistreating, exploiting. We will never
have to see that. We can remember Suvarov as the place where
one is never far from the essential question: what's it all about?
The answer seems to be right at your fingertips; seems to be in
the rustling of palm fronds, tickled by the breeze; in the aroma
of fish cooking over an open fire; seems to speak to you as you
stare meditatively across the serene lagoon; seems to be painted
across the horizon where the sun has just disappeared, falling into
its quilt of gold. It seems, for a moment, that we could be happy
to stay in Suvarov for the rest of our lives.

(Craig, you've got to be kidding. How could anyone in his right
mind want to leave a place like this? You've heard *Star Wars* is
coming to Samoa and you don't want to miss it? Nancy, get a load
of your son. What? *You* think we should be thinking about leaving, too? You're hungry for lettuce? Jesus H. Well, I suppose
we've *done* Suvarov, haven't we? And now that I think about it,
I could do with some cold beer myself. *Star Wars*? Lettuce? Cold
beer? Nobody's ever going to believe it.)